STEVE WILLIAMS

OUT OF THE ROUGH

STEVE WILLIAMS

OUT OF THE ROUGH

**Inside the Ropes
with the World's
Greatest Golfers**

WITH MICHAEL DONALDSON

VIKING

VIKING

an imprint of Penguin Canada, a division of Penguin Random House Canada Limited

Penguin Canada, 320 Front Street West, Suite 1400, Toronto, Ontario M5V 3B6, Canada
Penguin Group (USA) LLC, 375 Hudson Street, New York, New York 10014, U.S.A.
Penguin Books Ltd, 80 Strand, London WC2R 0RL, England
Penguin Ireland, 25 St Stephen's Green, Dublin 2, Ireland (a division of Penguin Books Ltd)
Penguin Books Australia, 707 Collins Street, Melbourne, Victoria 3008, Australia
Penguin Books India, 11 Community Centre, Panchsheel Park, New Delhi – 110 017, India
Penguin Books New Zealand, 67 Apollo Drive, Rosedale, Auckland 0632, New Zealand
Penguin Books South Africa, 24 Sturdee Avenue, Rosebank, Johannesburg 2196, South Africa
Penguin Books Ltd, Registered Offices: 80 Strand, London WC2R 0RL, England

First published in New Zealand by Penguin Random House New Zealand, 2015
Published in Viking hardcover by Penguin Canada, 2016

1 2 3 4 5 6 7 8 9 10 (RRD)

Manufactured in the U.S.A.

Cover and text design by Sam Bunny © Penguin Random House New Zealand

Front cover photograph by Alistair Guthrie

Back cover photographs, clockwise from top left: Steve with Adam Scott (*Simon Bruty/
Sports Illustrated/Getty Images*); with Raymond Floyd (*Augusta National/Getty Images*);
with Greg Norman (*Phil Sheldon/Popperfoto/Getty Images*); and with Tiger Woods (*Jamie
Squire/Getty Images*)

Library and Archives Canada Cataloguing in Publication data available upon request to
the publisher.

Print ISBN 978-0-735-23277-8
eBook ISBN 978-0-735-23278-5

www.penguinrandomhouse.ca

To my mum and dad, for allowing me to pursue my dreams and for instilling in me that with hard work and dedication you can achieve those dreams. Thanks, Mum and Dad.

CONTENTS

CHAPTER 1
STEPPING OUT

I've always been straight-up.

That hasn't changed over 50-odd years but my outspoken nature has stood me in good stead throughout 36 years of caddying, where honesty, directness and the ability to spur a player on with a well-timed word can be the difference between winning and losing.

My readiness to speak my mind cost me a job as the caddy for Greg Norman, who was the world's best player at the time, and brought unwelcome headlines after I was sacked by Tiger Woods.

Sometimes words come out before I've thought about their consequences – such as the day I gave Adam Scott a pep talk on the practice green at Augusta, before the 2011 Masters. I told Adam in no uncertain terms he had to go out there and believe he was the best player, and to keep telling himself: 'I'm Adam Scott and I'm winning this tournament.'

Nothing wrong with that. Except I was still caddying for Tiger at the time.

I don't know why I said what I did – I'd never spoken to a rival player like that. It wasn't entirely professional. If Tiger had found out I was trying to help Adam he would have fired me on the spot, and rightfully so, but I didn't think about the consequences – all I wanted to do was give Adam, as a friend, some encouragement, even though he was someone Tiger and I were trying to beat.

Adam blazed his way around Augusta that afternoon and came within a whisker of winning the tournament – his second-place finish was his best performance in a major championship. Tiger was fourth.

Why did I do it? I didn't have a grand plan to one day caddy for Adam, though that's how it eventually turned out. It was more likely a symptom of how the once brotherly bond between Tiger and me had frayed to the point of breaking. Previously I wouldn't have given a rival any more attention than a cursory 'hello'. Tiger and I operated in our own universe – I was locked in the orbit of his service – with me having dedicated a quarter of my life to helping achieve his goal of winning more major golf championships than anyone else.

But from the day his life descended into a tabloid circus with revelations he had been serially unfaithful to his wife, Elin – a scandal that dragged me in its wake – I increasingly realised the damage to our relationship was beyond repair. I knew our journey together was close to finishing.

————————

From a young age, I expended most of my energy on sport. I was super-competitive in everything I did and whenever I lost I would always examine the reasons for it.

I had dreams of playing for the New Zealand All Blacks – rugby was my first love – and I carry a vivid memory of a winter's day in 1977: I was standing in the tunnel as the players left the field after a test match between the All Blacks and the British and Irish Lions at Athletic Park, Wellington. The Lions represented the pinnacle of rugby – a feared opponent for the All Blacks – yet I had the cheek to blurt out to one of their players as he ran past: 'Can I have your socks?'

'No problem,' he said. I followed him into the locker room to claim my first piece of memorabilia – my only wish later was that I had asked him for his jersey, but then I fully expected one day to be on that same field, swapping jerseys at the end of the game. Having said that, I didn't even keep the socks.

Earlier I'd been out there playing in the curtain-raiser, for the New

Zealand under-15 schoolboys against the Australian under-15s. I was 13 but big for my age. I played prop and scored the only try in the match – an illegal try, I might add: I picked the ball up from an offside position but the referee didn't see me. It was enough to give us a 6–3 victory.

Golf and motor racing were my other passions, thanks to my dad. He would take my brother Phillip and me to Saturday-night speedway at Te Marua, just north of Wellington and a quick trek over Haywards Hill from our place. I was hooked from the start.

Dad had also been a top amateur golfer and was once offered the chance to turn professional with the backing of Wiseman's – a sporting goods retailer that sponsored a major New Zealand golf tournament, which he twice won – but my grandfather said that 'there's no future in golf' and stopped him doing it.

Dad remembers when I started caddying for him, showing a love and desire for the game – he was determined not to stand in my way.

> He was extremely ambitious and had a huge determination for someone his age, and I wasn't going to do to him what my father had done to me. I knew Steve would make the grade no matter what he decided to do. Not that I could have stopped him anyway – right from a very young age he knew where he wanted to go and he couldn't get there quickly enough. He had this overwhelming desire to get on with everything as fast as he could.
>
> Young Steve was a very good golfer – he hit the ball well, putted very well – but his temperament let him down. He was such a perfectionist that when things went wrong he didn't like it. I think that's why he preferred to caddy.

Carrying my dad's golf bag around Paraparaumu Beach Golf Club, one of New Zealand's best links courses, was my first experience of caddying. I viewed it in the same vein as having a newspaper round or mowing the lawns – it was how I earned pocket money. When I wasn't caddying for Dad, I'd work for other members. The going rate was $2 a round.

I didn't just carry the bag, I tried to help these players with their game. I'd work out on my own how far certain players could hit the ball and offer advice accordingly. I didn't know whether the information I gave was right or wrong but I delivered it with a confidence that suggested I knew exactly what I was talking about.

My skill and reputation soon brought bigger paydays. An offer of $3 a round was followed by another of $4, until I found myself at the centre of a bidding war. When I was offered $5 a round I had to say to the player: 'Well so-and-so has already offered me that – you'll have to go higher.'

Allan James, the local butcher, was one of the best employers. He continually raised the stakes until I was getting $10 a round at Paraparaumu on a Sunday and $20 for a day's work on his bag when he played interclub events elsewhere.

I earned it, though. When Allan was playing interclub, there was a lot of travel – followed by a lot of drinking. After the competition he'd be in the clubrooms having a few pints with his teammates and I'd sit in his car listening to the horse races and writing down the results for him and his friends, who would come out every now and then to check on me and see if they'd won any money. I became skilled at filling out their form guides with the details of which horses won and the dividends they paid. In hindsight this was a good thing – I could see how much they were losing on the horses and it put me right off gambling for life.

I also had to drive Allan's car when he'd had one too many, which was frequently. I was a good driver but at 13 didn't have a licence – but someone had to drive the car if we were to get home in one piece. I wasn't taught how to drive a car – I watched how other people did it and picked it up from there. When the time came to get my licence the guy who was taking me for my test got the shock of his life when he learned I'd driven myself to the testing station.

I was a visual learner – it hadn't occurred to me to have a driving lesson or a swimming lesson. I'd watch someone do it, get a picture of it in my head and then repeat it. That ability to visualise physical movement helped me become a good caddy, because I had no trouble picturing golf shots in my mind.

Allan also let me work in his butcher shop – often when I should have been at school.

> Steve had a great work ethic. When we were in the bar after a round – and we were big drinkers back then – he'd be out cleaning my clubs until they were absolutely spotless. He'd clean my shoes and if he still had time he'd go and clean my car, probably because he found money under the seats.
>
> Even when he started working at the butcher shop I didn't have to tell him what to do – he'd find jobs and if he couldn't find jobs he'd create them. One day I found him washing the windows because he had nothing left to do.
>
> Of course he wasn't supposed to be working for me but he hated college – he'd call me and say, 'Allan, I'm not going to school today, can I come to the shop?' And he'd turn up in his school clothes, get changed into his overalls and gumboots, and put himself to work.
>
> The teachers used to say to him: 'You'll never make anything of yourself, Williams – you take too much time off school.'

Allan lived in Waikanae, another 7 kilometres (4.5 miles) up State Highway 1 from Paraparaumu, and it was a base for great Sunday-evening ball-hunting expeditions.

Waikanae Golf Club featured a number of shallow ponds in which you could walk along feeling for balls with your feet – over time I became quite adept at picking them up with my toes.

The only problem was the pro at Waikanae – a tough nut called John Dixon, who lived on a hill overlooking the course. Dixon wanted those balls for himself – selling recycled balls in the pro shop was a handy way to make some extra money – and he was desperate to catch us trespassing. His house had a huge spotlight he could direct onto the ponds if he thought we were in there nicking his balls. Like fugitives on the run we became skilled at avoiding the spotlight – there were a number of hiding places in drains and ditches, and sometimes it was a game of patience. I can remember lying in a drain one night for what seemed like hours waiting for the spotlight to move on. Dixon also had a dog he would send down to chase us and, in those cases, we'd run for our lives with a swag of balls.

If Dixon didn't spot us, we'd have a quick look at our haul by torchlight, leaving the worst ones on the side of the pond so he'd know we'd been there.

We'd take the balls back to Allan's house and dump them in his bathtub to give them a good clean before bagging them up and selling them to the pro shop at Paraparaumu. That had to stop once Allan and his wife started to have kids – she'd want to bath the baby and I'd hear her yelling: 'Steve, get these filthy bloody golf balls out of the bathtub!'

––––––––––

Growing up in Pukerua Bay, a seaside town on the main road north of New Zealand's capital, Wellington, I had to travel 20 kilometres to get to the Paraparaumu Beach Golf Club. I could have taken a train to Paekakariki and then a bus . . . but trains and buses cost money. Hitch-hiking was my preferred mode of transport.

Paraparaumu was a popular club, and members were often driving through Pukerua Bay on their way to golf. Standing on the main road opposite the post office, I rarely had to wait more than 10 minutes for a ride.

Some days I would sell tomatoes or mushrooms on the side of the road before sticking out my thumb. Picked early in the morning and bagged up by my mum, the mushrooms were another way to supplement my caddying income. Of course, I had no idea at that stage you could be a professional caddy – but that changed when I met Australian golf legend Peter Thomson.

Peter was a golfing god in the 1950s and '60s. He won the British Open five times. He won the New Zealand Open nine times and was a frequent visitor to Paraparaumu Beach, which hosted a regular pro-am event that drew the best amateur and professional players from New Zealand and Australia. My dad, as a top amateur golfer, played in these pro-am events and got to know Peter. When the 1976 New Zealand Open was played at Heretaunga Golf Club, now known as Royal Wellington Golf Club, my dad asked Peter if I could caddy for him.

I was only 12 but my age didn't matter to Peter. He was the epitome of an old-fashioned golfer so to him a caddy was, in fact, nothing more than a bag-carrier. He was a totally self-reliant competitor and wouldn't dream of asking his caddy for advice. For him, having a 12-year-old on his bag was no big deal as long as the kid showed up, kept up and shut up. Despite that, Peter was impressed that I knew how to do yardages and understood the rules of golf.

> When Steve's father approached me to ask if his son could caddy for me, my first question was: 'Why isn't he at school?'
>
> 'He was excused from classes,' his dad told me.
>
> I said I'd give him a go. He didn't have to do anything – just carry the bag. When we finished the tournament, I gave him some money, I forget how much. When I said that I supposed he wanted to be a pro golfer, he said, 'No, I want to be a caddy.' Well, that was quite a surprise! But I could tell he had a real passion for it. I watched his career with great interest and he became, I suppose, the perfect caddy. He learned how to get the best out of his player.'

Being on a great golf course with a legendary player in contention to win your national championship was a mind-blowing experience, but it was what happened when Peter finished third that hooked me into caddying: 'some money' turned out to be $150, plus all his practice balls and his golf bag, which I've still got today.

The $150 was almost beyond my comprehension. That was a year's worth of caddying in one go. The practice balls were all balata, the best you could get. When I was hunting for golf balls to sell, a balata was the golden egg – the rarest and most expensive ball. It was like 10 Christmases had come at once. Right then, with $150, a swag of balata balls and an almost-new golf bag, why wouldn't I want to be a fulltime caddy?

I caddied for Peter later that summer at Titirangi, in Auckland, which hosted the Air New Zealand Shell Open. I took the Newmans overnight bus from Wellington to Auckland and got billeted by members of the Titirangi Golf Club. Peter didn't play as well this time around but another $100 was deposited into my bank account.

At Titirangi, I met Nick De Paul, an American caddy, who would go on to become one of the most famous caddies of his era, spending years on the bag of Spanish legend Severiano Ballesteros. I peppered Nick with questions about how to become a professional caddy. Armed with his input, I set my sights on heading overseas as soon as I turned 15 and was legally able to leave school.

———

One of my favourite golf books is *The Greatest Game Ever Played*, the story of how the 1913 US Open was won by Francis Ouimet, an unheralded amateur who learned the game as a caddy and lived across the road from The Country Club – in Brookline, Massachusetts – where the Open was played.

Ouimet was the hero of the story but I was drawn to his caddy, 10-year-old Eddie Lowery, who was barely big enough to carry Ouimet's bag without dragging it along the ground. What I loved about Lowery was his absolute determination to be a caddy. Every day of the Open, Lowery would skip school to be at the course. He would promise his mother he was going to school but would hand his bag to his brother, dodge the truancy officer, and race back to the course to caddy for Ouimet.

When I first read that story it felt like a distant echo of my own childhood. I was forever wagging school to be on the golf course and telling lies to my parents. If I spent a whole day at school it was only because there was rugby practice after class. On other days, I'd sneak out to the golf course or turn up to Allan's butcher shop where work would be waiting for me. Sometimes I showed up to the first class to get my name ticked off the roll, before sneaking out, timing my run to coincide with a passing bus.

When my mother eventually found out I'd missed more school than I attended, it took her a long time to get over the deception and the fact I didn't get a proper education. On an almost daily basis, I'd leave dressed in a school uniform but with a change of clothes in my bag or at Allan's shop. She felt she'd failed as a mother.

Many years after I caddied for Peter Thomson, I bumped into him in a hotel lobby during a golf tournament. I was with my wife Kirsty and son Jett. Peter turned to Jett and said: 'Son, I'm going to give you the same piece of advice I gave your dad, and unlike him I want you to listen to me. Promise me you won't take any time off school. Please, make sure you get an education.'

The problem is that Jett's seen I've made a success of my life without going to school and often asks, 'Why do I have to go to school? Dad didn't go.' And poor Kirsty has to sit him down and explain it's not possible to get away with the kind of behaviour I displayed back then. Peter was right. I made a poor, hard-headed decision not to go to school and wouldn't listen to anyone. But, like Eddie Lowery, my stubborn determination brought me success beyond my wildest dreams.

Peter wanted me to finish my education but at the same time was impressed by what I had taught myself about caddying. His acknowledgment of my skills gave me the confidence to keep going, and I asked Peter if I could caddy for him in Australia over the summer of 1977–78, even though I was only 13.

Peter was happy to let me come over as long as I didn't miss any school. I managed to convince him the New Zealand school year ended slightly earlier than it did in Australia so I could get across the Tasman in time for tournaments in November.

On this, my first trip across the Tasman, I was with another caddy from Paraparaumu, David Wickens, who was a few years older than me. He had family in Sydney who we stayed with while we worked at the Australian Open. We relied a lot on family or friends in those days – there was no way we were staying in expensive motels.

My mother was incredibly resistant to me taking off on this journey, and it turns out she had every cause to be concerned: in my first week in Australia I ended up in hospital!

Walking up the 18th fairway at Sydney's The Australian Club during the pro-am ahead of the Australian Open, I heard a call of 'fore!' but didn't even have time to react as an amateur's snap-hook on the nearby 10th tee smacked me right in the head.

The incident was serious enough for the following day's papers to run articles on the teenage Kiwi caddy who was knocked out for four minutes, stretchered off the course and taken to hospital by ambulance. I needed six stitches and was advised to stay in hospital overnight for observation, in case I had concussion, but after six hours of lying around I discharged myself and went home.

That summer Peter didn't place in any tournaments but the thrill of getting on an airplane and going to another country for a couple of weeks was incredibly exciting and further hooked me into the profession.

I loved caddying for Peter because he liked to talk and would put up with my incessant questions, such as, 'How do you hit that shot?' I learned a lot about the game from just listening to him talk.

When I turned 15, in December 1978, and was legally allowed to leave school – finally – I decided to caddy in Australia and New Zealand for the whole summer. The Australasian circuit started in late October and concluded in early February, with tournaments on both sides of the Tasman. I had saved up about $20,000 from caddying, selling mushrooms, finding golf balls, delivering newspapers and mowing lawns, and could afford to pay my own way. My parents were hesitant but I wasn't going to be stopped. My dad was in my corner, determined not to hold me back the way his father had denied him a chance at being a golf pro. My mother wasn't keen at all but recalls that she eventually had to bow to the pressure.

I was terrified. But John said he wasn't going to stop him living his dream the way his father had stopped him. He said, 'Let him go, let's see how it works. He'll probably be back in a couple of months.'

What kept me happy was that Steve was very good at calling home every week to let us know where he was and what he was doing. And he regularly sent postcards from around the world to let me know he was safe.

I'll be the first to admit I was lucky. Caddying for a respected legend like Peter Thomson gave me a way into the sport but he was just one of the many people who looked out for me.

Another was former pro golfer Jack Windle, who I met completely by chance when I jumped into his taxi at Tullamarine Airport in Melbourne.

Jack had given away the game in despair after struggling to make a living and was now driving taxis. It was pure luck I picked his cab.

'What are you doing in Melbourne?'

'I'm a golf caddy.'

'Where are you staying?'

'I dunno yet. I've just arrived.'

'You're staying with me.'

When I jumped into Jack's cab my life was a blank canvas and a few minutes later it was taking a defined shape. I had somewhere to stay and someone to show me the ropes as I set off on this new chapter in my life.

Jack was only 28 when I met him but seemed a lot older – probably because he'd had a hard life. He played professionally in his early 20s but reckoned he made only $100 from six years as a professional so he applied to be reinstated as an amateur when he was 24. His career wasn't helped by a terrible car accident that left him with numerous shattered bones and a noticeable limp.

Jack described professional golf as 'depressing'. He'd been forced to work at a petrol station, drive a tow truck and then a taxi to make ends meet, yet he was still in love with the game and wanted to help give me a better start in it than he'd had.

His tiny flat was barely big enough for one person let alone two of us, but he was happy for me to camp there. We'd barely got in the door when he said, 'I want to see you hit some golf balls.'

At a nearby practice range, I hit balls while he watched. He didn't say much but when he did it was authoritative – he didn't ask questions, he made statements. After I hit a few balls, he said: 'You're not going to be a caddy, you're going to be a golf pro.'

'Oh, OK, if you think so . . .'

Jack used his contacts to organise a six-month professional traineeship for me at Rossdale Golf Club on Melbourne's famed 'sand-belt stretch'. I started there as the season closed in February and for the whole time I did the course I stayed with Jack in his tiny flat. Even though I had some ability as a player and won a couple of tournaments, I knew being a professional wasn't what I wanted to do – I didn't know if I could make it in the paid ranks and I certainly didn't want to end up as a driving range teaching pro giving lessons to kids and weekend hackers. I wanted to be in the thick of the action, working alongside the best players.

The following summer I was back caddying.

CHAPTER 2
WHAT I DO

When people try to insult me, or have a dig at what they see as my bad behaviour, they resort to cliché: 'He's just a glorified porter.' As if all I do is carry someone else's bags for a few rounds of golf and wait for a tip at the end.

A caddy's job is so much more than what you see on TV. It's eight hours a day, six days a week when a tournament's on, and anywhere from 20 to 40 weeks a year. If it was easy more people would do it – or pros would pick up locals at each event. But the stakes are so high in professional golf. When I started, the prize pools were quite small by today's standards but since Tiger Woods came along and prize money skyrocketed thanks to increased TV ratings, a professional can earn over $1 million for a win, which means the caddy can pick up $100,000 for a week's work, or a 10 per cent cut of a player's earnings. That's a lot to pay a porter.

Being a caddy is one of the most under-appreciated roles in sport. A good caddy can make a huge difference to a player's performance by offering guidance, decision-making and focus.

In a podcast for *Sports Illustrated*, Jim 'Bones' Mackay, the long-time caddy for Phil Mickelson, said he was often asked how much help caddies provide. Bones used my work with Tiger Woods as an example: 'We played the first two rounds with Tiger at the '08 US Open at Torrey

Pines, which he famously went on to win . . . I know for a fact just watching him and Steve Williams work together that day that Steve Williams saved him two to four shots, just in the two rounds we played with him.' Given Tiger barely scraped into a playoff with Rocco Mediate at that event, saving him even one shot would have been enough to justify my role.

At its most basic, caddying is about adding and subtracting, and having a precise, reliable step. My main job is tell the professional how far he is from his target – or, conversely, how far it is to a danger spot. We use distance markers in the fairway – either spray-painted on the grass or tagged to sprinklers along the fairway – and then pace out the distance from that marker to the player's ball, do some maths and provide a yardage. And yes, golf nearly everywhere is still done in imperial measures of yards and feet.

But caddying is about so much more than that. Anyone can learn how to measure a golf course – it's what you do with the information that's important. It's as much about psychology as lugging a bag and giving a player yardages.

There's strategy, which requires understanding a course's design and the type of shots your player is capable of playing in order to get around it in the most efficient fashion.

A good caddy will also understand his player: how he performs in certain situations, how to get the best out of him, how to lift him up when he's down. A caddy is like a jockey on a horse, or a navigator in a rally car. In the same way a good jockey can be the difference in a close race, I've learned how to get my players across the line.

I learned an invaluable lesson in psychology when I caddied for Australian Terry Gale at the Malaysian Open in 1986. Terry and I had a lot of success around Asia and he was the defending champion at the Malaysian Open.

I was struggling to make the cut, and that had never happened before with Steve – we'd always been near the top of the leaderboard.

Normally Steve just loped along beside me – well, suddenly he's five metres behind and not saying anything. He's not giving any advice and just mumbling the yardages. I was getting pretty annoyed with him.

I ended up making a couple of birdies to make the cut on the line. It was as hot as hell and when we were done Steve started walking back to the clubhouse, when I said, 'No, we're going to the practice range.'

There was a shaded area I could have gone to but I chose to go out in the middle and hit balls in the blazing sun for about half an hour, until Steve said, 'What are you doing this for?'

I turned to him and said, 'I'm trying to teach you a lesson. You know what you are, Steve? You're a front-runner. Everyone you've caddied for has won, but when a bloke's down that's when he needs you the most. That's why you're getting paid more money than these local caddies [not that I was paying him a fortune]. You were no help whatsoever today – not only did I have to get myself around this golf course, I had to carry you around as well. It was pathetic.'

Some time after that I was with Steve in Japan. My family had come up as well because it was school holidays, and Steve said to my son: 'You know what – your father gave me the best lesson I've ever had in my life.'

Terry was right in saying I had had a lot of success. From my earliest caddying days for Allan James to my professional debut with Peter Thomson and including my time with Tiger Woods and Adam Scott . . . 36 years of caddying and there's only one player who I caddied for numerous times who I didn't win with: a dapper Japanese fellow named Masahiro Kuramoto, known as Massy. He won 30 times on the Japan Tour but never with me on his bag. Massy was a unique character – he wore new clothes every single day: his shirt, trousers and jumper came straight out of the bag. And he used a new ball on every hole – so in theory I had to carry at least 18 balls, which adds considerable weight to the bag. Usually I carried about 10 balls because I knew if he played a hole with a driver and a 5-iron – clubs that didn't put much of a mark on the ball – I would be able to recycle that ball and he'd be none the wiser. One of the reasons I kept going back to Japan over the years was to try to get that elusive win with Massy, but it never happened – maybe I should have carried all those new balls.

While Massy was the exception to the rule, the first time I caddied for Australian Mike Clayton in 1984 was more typical of the experience I have enjoyed – players would often win soon after hiring me.

Clayton's regular caddy had taken a bet at a tournament in Cornwall that he could leap across a ditch with a golf bag on his back. He lost the bet and broke his arm. Clayton needed a new caddy in France, where he went on to win.

I remembered Steve from the early eighties in Australia. He was one of those caddies you noticed because he was there every week – unlike some – and then he turned up in Europe where the Australian and New Zealand players and their caddies stuck together a lot.

He and some of the other young caddies were in stark contrast to the traditional British caddies – the older guys who would go to the pub every night and sleep in the sponsors' tents in their overcoats. Steve never did that – you could tell he was serious about what he was doing. If you were looking to make a successful career at caddying you had to catch the eye of the better players and to do that you had to take it seriously.

When my caddy broke his arm, Steve caddied for me and we won the tournament – it was no coincidence.

I clearly remember walking to the practice fairway for the first round and Steve said to me, 'You know, I've watched you play and you don't concentrate anywhere near as well as you should so, this week, every shot you play I want you to give it your full attention.' He did a great job.

The going rate for caddies then was £100 a week and a well-paid caddy was getting £120 but I said to my wife, 'He's so good I want him to caddy for me the rest of the year – shall I offer him £200 a week?' He took it, which probably made him the highest-paid caddy on the tour.

He worked for me for the rest of the year, then six or seven weeks the following year in Europe before he sacked me and went to work for Eduardo Romero, which was a step up. I didn't have a problem with that – if someone gets a better offer it's not for the player to hold him back.

I'm a forthright, outspoken, confident person. Those qualities have carried through into the way I caddy.

Nine times out of 10 when you give a professional golfer a yardage they will know exactly what club they need to cover that distance. But sometimes there will be indecision. Wind, elevation changes, and the type of lie they have (whether the ball is on the fairway, in sand, or in the rough) will put a player in two minds about which club to use and what kind of shot to play. Uncertainty can also creep in when a player has to consider the possible dangers: Is there a creek in front of the green that you must avoid? Is there thick rough behind the green? Is it better to miss the green on the left or right? What sort of shape should the shot have?

This is when he relies on his caddy to think clearly and make firm decisions. If a player asks you a question they don't want to hear umming and ahhing – and they most certainly don't want to hear, 'I'm not sure,' or, 'I don't know.' My aim is to give my player absolute certainty – even though it sometimes means lying to them about yardages so they hit the shot I thought was best. I often did this with Tiger. In those cases I was less a confidence-booster than a confidence trickster. The same applied to the advice I gave Australian Terry Gale when caddying for him.

Most players know what club they're going to hit but two or three times in a round of golf there's some doubt – and this can be the difference between winning and not winning.

With Steve, that doubt goes away. I'd be standing there asking myself, 'Is it a five- or six-iron?' I've had so many caddies over the years who would say nothing because they're frightened to back themselves or they just didn't know. But Steve would say firmly, 'Terry, it's not a five, you're hitting the ball well – there's no problem in the front but there's danger over the back – it's a six-iron.' He'd rattle off three or four reasons as to why you should hit the club he recommends.

And when you're standing over the shot and you're convinced it's the right club, you generally hit it well. Most bad shots come from indecision. As a player, with Steve on your bag you were never left in doubt you had the right club – he backed himself and gave confidence to the player that the correct club had been chosen.

I am firmly convinced that because of the way Steve is – with his forthright attitude – you were never left wondering. Tiger Woods wouldn't have won as many major tournaments as he has if Steve hadn't been on his bag. He just had the knack – a gift – for lifting his player.

Historically, a caddy's job wasn't to know all the distances on a golf course. But when yardage books came into vogue during the 1970s it became the caddy's job to consult the book and to not only understand it but add information he gathered from walking the course. A caddy who could compile a good yardage book – a map of the 18 holes with all relevant measurements recorded and dangers highlighted – became an invaluable source of information.

Researching the course and compiling yardages was one of my strengths. With Tiger – because he was liable to spray the ball quite wide of the fairway – I had to know yardages from all over the golf course, but with Adam Scott, who was more accurate, the parameters of the course shrunk.

The hardest places to work out yardages are traditional links courses, such as St Andrews in Scotland. Until the 1995 British Open, there were no sprinklers in the fairways, and not a tree in sight. It was dead flat and wide open. At that course I'd compile yardages off all sorts of objects and natural landmarks – lampposts in nearby streets, corners of buildings, mounds, bunkers. Take the double fairway that makes up the 1st and 18th holes at St Andrews. That fairway is 200 yards wide and as flat as a football field but I'd figured that if I lined up the ninth lamppost with the corner of a certain building, I could use that as a reference point. And I had to keep that sort of information in my head.

A contributing factor in Tiger's two huge wins in the British Open at St Andrews (2000 and 2005) was the way I scouted the course each morning. With sun-up at 4am, I'd head to the course – often passing the famous Jigger Inn, where I'd sometimes see other caddies finishing up an all-night drinking session. I'd walk the course, noting where all the holes were going to be placed, combine that information with the predicted wind direction and set up a plan for how Tiger should play the course. And all the while I had to know where all the bunkers were and how he needed to play to avoid them.

Weather has a huge influence on golf. I monitor weather reports closely and avidly read the *Old Farmer's Almanac*. There are plenty of apps these days too, though you can't use them out on the course as players and caddies are banned from operating mobile phones during a tournament. Over the years I came to be regarded as a barometer for other caddies (those golf bags are heavy enough – if I didn't have to pack an umbrella or wet-weather gear, I wouldn't) and some of the younger guys would know that if Steve Williams wasn't carrying an umbrella, they didn't need one either.

The only time I came badly unstuck was at the British Open at Muirfield in 2002 – Tiger got caught in a freezing, wet blast of bad weather that no one had seen coming. I had no wet-weather gear, no extra layers of warm clothing and we nearly froze to death out there. Tiger shot 81 – which at the time stood as the worst round of his professional career.

At Augusta, a venue for the Masters, it's important to know which direction the wind is blowing, especially down at Amen Corner. The flag on the 12th green can be fluttering one way, the trees bending another, and pollen floating in a different direction altogether. Amen Corner is the lowest part of the course and players get tricked there all the time, which is why the 12th – a tiny par-3 – causes so much havoc. You regularly see players hit balls over the back of the green or into the water at the front because they've been fooled by the wind. It doesn't look that hard a hole but the wind complicates the shot selection.

Judging the strength and direction of the wind is critical. It's an inexact science but one the caddy needs to understand. Yardages are only guidelines, though, and there's a feel that comes with understanding your player and the golf course. A good example in my career was Tiger Woods' penultimate shot on the 72nd hole at the US Open at Torrey Pines in 2008. I convinced Tiger to ignore the yardage book and to hit the club I felt would deliver the best outcome. It was a hell of a discussion but my gut feeling on how he would execute that shot proved correct and allowed him to get into a playoff. If he'd gone with the normal club for that yardage he'd probably have hit the ball too far and given himself a much tougher birdie putt.

If I'd tried that sort of thing with the brilliant German Bernhard Langer, I'd have got nowhere. I caddied a couple of times for Bernhard, who was a stickler for precise yardages. He was also one of the players who would do their own yardages and then compare them with mine.

'I've got 137 yards, what have you got?' he said one day.

'136.'

'Let's measure it again.'

'Why Bernhard, what difference does it make? It's one yard.'

'It makes a lot of difference.'

And off we'd go and measure it again.

When I first started out I met lots of old-fashioned caddies who did everything by feel. The most colourful was known simply as Silly Billy. He was an enigmatic figure who carried a briefcase that was largely empty except for a racing form guide and a yardage book that didn't have anything written in it.

Silly Billy didn't believe in yardages and did everything on gut feel and experience. No one realised Silly Billy was winging it until one day when he was caddying for Jose Rivero at Crans-sur-Sierre in the Swiss Alps. Jose was having difficulty with the yardages in the thin air. Getting increasingly frustrated at Silly Billy, he grabbed the yardage book off him. When he found it empty he looked as if he was going to clobber Silly Billy with a 5-iron. But once he realised there was nothing he could do, he laughed, shrugged his shoulders and pressed on, still asking Silly Billy for yardages.

No caddy would dare take Silly Billy's approach today but it's also a shame that much of the feel for the game has been lost to technological advances. A modern yardage book is compiled using laser and is so accurate it can tell you how many extra yards you should add for an uphill shot or how many to take off for a downhill shot – a lot of the guesswork is taken out of the equation and, with it, a lot of the intuitive understanding a caddy would build up over the years.

———————

At the end of the 1981 Australasian season, I learned a number of players were making the trek up to Asia where a 12-week tour took in the Philippines, Hong Kong, Malaysia, Singapore, Indonesia, India, Taiwan, Korea and Japan. A few of us young caddies decided we'd follow the money and try our luck – it was a good way to see the world, one golf tournament at a time, and bridged the gap until the start of the European tour in May. We didn't see ourselves as professional caddies but we were the first foreign caddies to sweat it out on this exotic tour.

We discovered there was no such thing as tournament yardage books in these developing golf countries and quickly saw a way we could supplement our caddying income. We'd arrive at our destination each Monday and immediately walk the course. I used a measuring wheel to get accurate distances and we marked down the locations of the hazards. On a huge piece of paper we'd draw, by hand, the whole course, with all the hazards and yardages mapped out.

Photocopied 100 times and cut into 18 separate pages, one for each hole, we'd staple the pages together and sell the 'books' for $10 each.

It took hours upon hours of work but it became easier over time as the tour tended to visit the same courses every year. We made decent money on these yardage books – we needed to. Even though there were so few caddies on the Asian Tour, we could pick and choose the best players to work for – we made only enough money to get from one venue to the next.

Accommodation cost next to nothing in many of these Asian countries – but you got what you paid for. We had one regular hotel in Thailand we called Cockroach Manor. The room was essentially a mattress on the floor – no pillow, one sheet – but we were convinced the mattress never made contact with the floor thanks to the multitude of cockroaches underneath it. At $1.50 a night, what could we expect? Besides, it was all we could afford.

At our regular Jakarta digs there was no indoor shower – if you wanted a shower you climbed up to the roof and stood naked under a water-tank tap. After a couple of years of checking into this hotel, we realised there were two Americans actually living there – they had been caught up in the drug world and had their passports stolen so couldn't get out of Indonesia. Not that they seemed to mind – they were happy to waste away their lives in this less than salubrious hotel.

On average I earned about $100–150 a week but most of that was sucked up on the airfare to the next stop. Relative to food and accommodation, air travel was hideously expensive.

The players got paid in cash – US dollars – at the end of the tournament and would peel off a few of the American greenbacks for the caddies. If my player did well the wad of notes could be quite thick so I had to take extra care. Often it was safer to leave the money with the player who could store it in his hotel safe until I needed it.

In the early days it was so much about survival but it was also about the journey. I had no idea where caddying was going to take me and it was only when I got onto bigger tours and started to make a bit of money that I realised how much fun those early days actually were.

We'd do all sorts of crazy stunts. One Sunday night we spent a lot of our pay in the bar of the country club where we'd caddied that day.

A few beers the worse for wear, we missed the last bus and had no idea how to call a taxi, so we hijacked a golf cart, plodding down the motorway and back to our hotel. We could hear the police sirens in the distance and quickly grabbed our gear, climbed out the window and shot down the fire escape.

Another day, the bus to drive us to the course was waiting but the driver had fallen asleep in one of the passenger seats and couldn't be woken. 'Bugger it,' I said. 'I'll drive the bus – I'm sure I can figure it out,' and off we lurched with the driver fast asleep.

The very posh Royal Selangor Golf Club in Kuala Lumpur was another place where I'd buck the system. Every day was stinking hot and I'd caddy wearing just shorts, a singlet and a pair of jandals. When the players walked from the 9th green to the 10th tee, I'd hand my man a driver before taking a diversion through the clubhouse, stripping off my singlet, kicking off my jandals and plunging into the members' pool to cool off, before meeting my player back in the 10th fairway.

In 1985, Terry Gale won the Malaysian Open by seven shots, at Royal Selangor against a strong field, and I was allowed into the clubhouse locker room rather than having to go back to the tin caddyshack.

As Terry recalls the story, I was in the locker room cleaning his clubs and shoes, which were filthy from it having been wet and muddy, when I had a run-in with the establishment.

Steve's in there cleaning my gear when this bloke walks in to the locker room to use the bathroom and tells Steve, 'Hey, you can't clean shoes in here – take them outside.'

After he'd used the bathroom, he came out and Steve was still sitting there cleaning the gear. 'Didn't I tell you to take them outside?' I'm not sure what Steve said to him but it wasn't very polite. That was typical Steve but in this case the bloke he told where to go happened to be the president of Royal Selangor Golf Club.

The next thing I know, I'm being summoned to his office and told, 'Your caddy is rude and won't be allowed to caddy here again.' Steve had to do the right thing so I drafted a letter of apology and shoved it under his nose and when he protested I said, 'Shut up and sign this.'

That kind of aggression – and I don't mean it in a nasty way – defined Steve, and was also why he was such a successful caddy. He wasn't bothered if people thought he was a loud-mouth for telling someone in the crowd to shut up or to stop moving behind his player, which was what he needed to do a lot with guys like Greg Norman and Tiger Woods.

I was never a great player, in the same league as Greg Norman, Tiger Woods or Adam Scott, but I feel lucky to have somehow joined up with Steve. And 30 years later we're still in touch – he sends a Christmas card every year and rings me up from time to time. He's a good bloke and I regard him highly.

As the Asian Tour finished the European Tour started, so it was possible to have a pretty solid run of work: from the Australian summer, then to Asia and on to Europe for the northern hemisphere summer, before returning to Australia and New Zealand at the end of the year to start the circuit all over again.

I was 17 and as nervous as I'd been in my life when I arrived in Europe for the first time in June 1981. Asia had had its difficulties but I had fellow travellers in the form of caddies and golfers who moved in a pack from country to country. Landing in London by myself was daunting. I walked out of Heathrow and was completely overwhelmed. There were so many taxis, cars and buses and a lot more than the one train line I'd been used to back home. That was quite a culture shock but not quite as strange as arriving in Bradford for the Lawrence Batley International tournament at Bingley St Ives and encountering British caddies for the first time.

To put it kindly, most of them were rough diamonds – I look back now and wonder how they made a living. No one seemed to have a proper name – everyone was identified by a nickname, such as the aforementioned Silly Billy, or Mustard and Goat. Then there was

Edinburgh Jimmy, a robust Scotsman who loved nothing more than giving a Glasgow kiss to anyone who had anything bad to say about him or his player; Rick the Rattler, who no matter how he carried the bag always made the clubs rattle; Scotch John, one of my favourite caddies and who, despite never having played the game, was one of the best but also notorious for being late to work if he found a better option in town, normally a female companion; and Yorkshire Bill. Most caddies occasionally picked up a bag while still hung-over, but that never happened with Yorkshire Bill because it seemed to me that he never caddied sober.

These jokers wore overcoats like a uniform, even though it was the middle of summer, and many wouldn't have been out of place on a farm. Heavy drinkers with no fixed abode, many slept rough or snuck into sponsors' tents at night. They were a completely different breed to anything I'd seen before. They were intimidating but welcoming. They didn't care about a few youngsters from down under as there were more players than caddies and in some instances it wasn't unusual to caddy for two players in a day – one loop in the morning, another in the afternoon, on the Thursday and Friday of a tournament.

The caddies personified the laid-back European Tour experience – it was a professional tour but it didn't appear to be that serious. The players were relaxed and the caddies were extremely relaxed, to the extent that many failed to adhere to the first rule of caddying: show up.

Drinking and living rough was not my thing. That side of caddy culture didn't interest me. I wanted to caddy, not party – and players appreciated the fact that I was reliable and keen. Mike Clayton said he first noticed me because I was always there, ready to carry someone's bag at a moment's notice and without the scent of alcohol on my breath or the bloodshot eyes of someone nursing a hangover. If anything, I got a reputation for being the Kiwi kid who ran a lot and did push-ups – and could reliably be found somewhere around the golf course.

The first player I caddied for in Europe was an Australian, Noel Ratcliffe, but I soon got onto Michael King, an ex-Ryder Cup player known as Queenie. A charming, dashing, upper-class English gentleman, he seemed a little out of place in the cut-throat world of professional golf – he had turned to the game after losing his fortune in the stock market crash of 1974. While he was no longer wealthy, he had an air of money about him and was known for paying his caddies above the going rate. But they also earned it because Queenie, while charismatic, was demanding and had a high caddy-turnover rate. He was generous and kind to me – organising accommodation with a relative who had a farm near Sunningdale, his home club. For years that farmhouse was my base in Europe.

———

One of the few times I was lost for words came at the Spanish Open in 1987, caddying for Ian Baker-Finch.

I had a routine with him on the practice range where I would use a folded towel as a makeshift baseball mitt to catch his shots on the fly – it was better than running around picking up golf balls from the ground. On this particular day, as Ian recalls, the routine didn't quite go to plan.

> I was hitting seven-iron. Steve would catch a ball, wipe it, put it in the bag – catch a ball, wipe it, put it in the bag.
>
> For some reason, he looked down for a moment too long for one ball and when he looked up – bang – the ball hit him right in the mouth. It knocked him down, split his lip and broke both his front teeth. We half-carried, half-dragged him to the tournament doctor who had just come from lunch and by the smell of him he'd had a few wines but he stitched him up OK.
>
> I'd known Steve for a while and saw how committed he was. He'd had good mentors in Terry Gale and Mike Clayton and even back then in the mid-eighties it was obvious how good he was. He was no-nonsense, strong-willed, always spoke his mind, always had that brash confidence he's become known for over the years, but that confidence came from having done his homework, having put everything into it.

Over the years people would say, 'He thinks he's good,' but it wasn't like that: it wasn't that he *thought* he was good, he just *was* good. And there's a difference. It was obvious to me that he was the best – always was.

For me to get a travelling companion and a great friend for company in those early years around Europe was fantastic. I'd pick him up on the way to the airport on Tuesdays and we'd fly to whatever tournament we were playing and I'd drop him back on the Sunday. He was a welcome part of the family – you always wanted him around. He was a mate who was always willing to do anything to help you.

Out of that grew a lasting friendship we've maintained over thirty years later. We've always sought each other out for advice and to talk about life – especially at times when things weren't comfortable for him publicly, I was there to reassure him and to tell him what the real view was.

There were times in those early days when I was embarrassed by his abrasive behaviour but at the same time it made me realise he was on my side and doing his best to help me perform at my peak. I always felt I had the best support and the best man on my bag. He gave his player added confidence. He added a couple of inches to your height and strengthened your armour. He was the perfect wingman.

Steve and I had been apart for a couple of years when he came back to work for me on a one-off basis in Japan at the 1990 World Championship of Golf. Australia won the title – I won all five matches and took out the MVP award. Having Steve on my bag for that week made me remember how much better I felt with him beside me – how good he made me feel. It gave me that extra level of self-respect and a jolt of self-belief that I was on the right track.

When he would say, 'C'mon Finchy, why aren't you winning all the time, look how good you're playing . . .' you knew they were not empty words. If you listen to his caddy–player sound bites on TV, you can hear the conviction in his voice: 'No, I'm telling you it's a four-iron not a five-iron – it's a four-iron all day. Trust me, I know.'

Or he'd say to you: 'Right, we're going to the range and we're going to fix this. You're going to stop doing that bullshit . . . we're going to do this instead.' That's how Steve is.

The people who want to bag him will say he's only the number-one caddy because he got lucky - by working with Greg Norman, Ray Floyd and Tiger Woods. But those guys could have chosen anybody and they chose him.

His abrasive behaviour, single-mindedness, pig-headedness – people would like to portray that as his most common trait but those who know him realise that's what he has to do to make his player perform at his best.

His straight-talking has got him into trouble over the years but a lot of people also misunderstand him in that regard. We golfers are all such big heads, we think we're on top of the world and we often need someone who can talk honestly to us because everyone else is just stroking you and worried about keeping their job. Steve was never worried about keeping his job; all he wanted to do was make his guy better.

In the late eighties I had lots of opportunities to win but I don't think I was a strong enough character to turn top fives into victories. I didn't have enough of the killer instinct and I think Steve was a little disappointed in me for that. In my mind, I was never a Greg Norman. I never saw myself as number one in the world – I saw myself as a top-ten or top-twenty guy. Steve was number one in the world at what he did and he naturally wanted to be in with the number-one guy, so when he got a chance to work fulltime with Greg in America I said go: 'He's the best and you should be with the best.'

CHAPTER 3
SWIMMING WITH THE GREAT WHITE SHARK

It was a Wednesday morning, 17 April 1996, and the sun hadn't yet made an appearance beyond the white sands of Florida's famed West Palm Beach. If they'd bothered to look, early morning joggers or swimmers would have seen two men sitting on the beach surrounded by empty beer bottles, one of them with the striking blond hair and piercing blue, sometimes tear-filled, eyes of one of the most famous sportsmen in the world.

And if they were listening closely, over the sound of the waves, they would have heard the distinctive Aussie twang of Greg Norman and the flattened vowels of this Kiwi caddy. Two mates – still mates despite an almighty bust-up in their working relationship seven years earlier – were sitting on an empty beach wondering how an unlikeable Pom had stolen the one golfing crown that Norman so wanted: the iconic green jacket of a Masters champion.

Norman's spirit-crushing defeat in the final round of the 1996

Masters, where he coughed up a six-shot lead to England's Nick Faldo, is one of sport's greatest tragedies – more so because it happened to a player who, despite all his success and massive wealth, seemed to court more than his fair share of failure.

There have been many famous Masters meltdowns and I'd been witness to one of them six years earlier when my then boss, Raymond Floyd, hit a shot into the water on the 11th hole during a playoff with the very same Faldo. Then there was Scott Hoch's so-called 'choke' over a two-foot par putt that would have given him victory over – yes – Nick Faldo in the sudden-death playoff in 1989. If he made that putt he would win, but he inexplicably missed and Faldo got a reprieve and claimed his first green jacket on the next hole. Ed Sneed famously bogeyed the last three holes in 1979 to fall into a playoff, which he then lost to Fuzzy Zoeller. Ben Hogan – the greatest ball-striker in the history of the game, but a terrible putter – three-putted the 18th green to lose by a shot to Herman Keiser in 1946.

But by far the biggest collapse in Masters history was Norman's disintegration at the hands of Faldo in 1996, when he not only frittered away his six-shot advantage but threw in five more axe cuts for an 11-shot swing, as Faldo shot a final round of 67 and Norman carded 78.

Every year when I caddied at Augusta I would share a house with Fanny Sunesson, Nick Faldo's caddy. We had a deal: if your player won the tournament, you paid the rent. On that last morning of the 1996 Masters, I said to Fanny, 'Oh well, second place isn't bad.'

'What do you mean? We're going to win it.'

'You're six shots back. No, my good Aussie mate is going to finally pull on the green jacket.'

I was caddying for Floyd and we finished early in the day. While I don't normally watch golf on television, that year I sprinted back to the house to watch Norman and Faldo. I'm not someone who gets worked up when I watch sport on TV and I'm certainly not one for throwing things at it, but that day I was like a child tossing his toys. I so badly wanted Greg to win because I knew the Masters was the one goal that burned inside him more than anything – he wanted to win that green jacket and join one of the most exclusive clubs in sport. Winning the Masters was the main focus in his life so it was gut-wrenching to watch him tossing it away. It was like an awful nightmare that left me shaking, because I knew it was his time – with a six-shot lead and playing so exceptionally, he couldn't lose.

People say he choked but I don't believe in that word. He lost because he transitioned from playing aggressively for three days to playing conservatively, which is a trap you can easily fall into when you're sitting on a big lead. A few years later I learned one of Tiger Woods' traits was to not settle into playing conservatively with a lead. If he got a six-shot lead he wanted to make it 10. Whenever he had the lead, he wanted to increase it. He didn't slip into playing negative golf.

Greg knew that if he shot 70 he was going to win the tournament, because that would mean Faldo would have to shoot a major-best 63 to win. So Greg walked on to the course with an attitude he was not going to make any mistakes, but by playing conservatively he came up short on a number of holes.

For instance, his wedge approach came up six feet short at the 9th and ran 30 yards back towards him and he couldn't save par. They say the Masters is won and lost on the back nine on Sunday. Even going into the last nine holes, Greg still had a two-shot lead.

But he butchered a chip on the 10th to make a bogey and three-putted the 11th from 10 feet. It was at this time Zimbabwe's Nick Price, who had hung around to watch Greg win, was heard to say, 'I can't stand to watch,' and left the course.

Greg then left it short on the par-3 12th, the ball rolling back into the water. He made a double bogey to go from a two-shot lead to two shots behind in the few holes since I started watching. He laid up on the 13th after his caddy, Tony Navarro, argued against going for the green in two shots, but he still made birdie, matched by Faldo. Any glimmer of hope ended on the 16th, another par-3, when an over-hooked shot drowned in the water.

My phone rang on the Tuesday. It was Greg. I could tell he was devastated by this loss. He knew he had let his greatest opportunity to win the Masters slip through his hands. Suddenly he was begging me to come back to be his caddy. Without knocking Tony Navarro, I truly believe that with a different approach I may have been able to make a difference that day. I could have helped Greg win, but I told him I couldn't go back to work for him. At the time Raymond was playing well and treating me like a son, and after seven years I couldn't turn around and say to the guy, 'I'm going back to Greg.' And Raymond was incredibly easy to work for in comparison to Greg, who had been an exacting master.

More than needing me to come back as his caddy, what Greg actually needed was someone to talk to. He invited me to his place in West Palm Beach and I got there later that day. We grabbed a few beers and sat on the beach together. He was in a terrible state. Even though our working relationship had ended acrimoniously, we were still good mates and shared a lot of common interests. Greg had never been afraid to reveal his goals and ambitions to me, and on that night he badly wanted someone to unburden his disappointment to.

'I can't believe I've just done that,' he said. 'I can't believe I changed the way I played. And of all the guys to lose to, why did it have to be Faldo?' Nick hadn't endeared himself to many players over the years. My brother once caddied for him in Australia, and told me it wasn't until the Sunday of the tournament that Faldo asked his name.

Greg was so distressed that he hadn't played, or thought, the way he usually does. He was so disillusioned with himself. It was sad to see a guy I looked up to crying. He was down and out, like a boxer beaten to a pulp. I thought I knew what winning the Masters meant to him, but I didn't realise quite how much until I saw the state he was in that night.

We spent the night on the beach drinking and talking, and we were still there when the sun came up. Greg had poured out everything – he bared his soul. The Greg Norman who needed me that night was completely different to the man I first worked for more than a decade earlier.

On the European Tour – and especially in Australia – in the early 1980s everyone was aware of Greg Norman. He had more flair and style than anyone else playing, but he wasn't yet a global superstar. I didn't have any plan to try to work for him. I certainly didn't think, 'I have to get on that guy's bag.' But Peter Thomson had drummed into me to do the absolute best I could and everything else would fall into place. So when I was caddying in a group that included the likes of Bernhard Langer, Nick Faldo, Greg Norman, Seve Ballesteros – the big four – I'd definitely be trying to do the best job I could. I wanted to impress them and show those top professionals I was a real professional too.

The times I was paired with Greg we easily found something to talk about – we both loved rugby and motor racing – so there was common ground. And he was impressed enough with my work to seek me out.

The shock of being rung out of the blue in late 1982 by the Great White Shark himself was almost surpassed by the disbelief he was able to track me down in New Zealand. With my feet up at home, I couldn't believe Greg had found my number let alone wanted to hire me.

I was absolutely buzzing. I realised that this caddying lark, which until now had been about travelling the world and having fun, was about to get serious.

I was eagle-eyed for ways to maximise my income and as soon as I knew I was working for Greg I was on the phone looking for a personal sponsor and struck a deal with an Australian hire company, Wreckair, which hired out diggers, chainsaws and the like.

Greg recalls his side of the story.

> I can remember exactly when I first worked with Steve. It was the Australian Masters in 1983 and Steve was this strapping, long-haired kid. I loved his personality and energy, and we just clicked.
>
> I think when you find a personality – whether it's your wife, your best friend or your caddy – it's about chemistry. Steve and I got along right off the bat.

PLAYERS I'VE WON TOURNAMENTS WITH

Bob Charles (NZ) 1
Jerry Anderson (Canada) 1
John Jacobs (US) 1
Andy Bean (US) 1
Mike Clayton (Aus.) 1
Anders Forsbrand (Sweden) 1
Ian Baker-Finch (Aus.) 1
Lu Hsi-Chuen (Taiwan) 1
Terry Gale (Aus.) 2
Adam Scott (Aus.) 8
Greg Norman (Aus.) 22
Raymond Floyd (US) 26
Tiger Woods (US) 84

TOTAL 150

Even at that young age, he was a consummate professional. He didn't go to clubs, he wasn't a drinker. He dealt with his job in a professional fashion. That's where we were similar – I didn't go out and hang around bars and clubs and try to live life to the fullest. I wanted to be the best I could be and so did Steve.

We were both young, determined, like-minded; both very much into fitness. It seemed like when we first met that we'd met before. There was a simple acceptance of each other and he became a very close member of my family. We became like brothers – I'd never had a younger brother and he was like a kid brother to me. My kids nicknamed him the Polar Bear because he would go swimming in the ocean in the middle of winter. They just loved him and grew up with him around.

Steve was definitely hard-nosed – that's what I loved about him. There was no grey about Steve: black was black and white was white. He was determined, protective, but he was also a gentle giant. From spending the best part of a decade working with him and then seeing how he worked with Tiger Woods, I can only imagine he got different marching orders compared with those from other players he worked for. That really disappointed me – I knew what Steve was like but Tiger put him in a box.

––––––––––

From 1982, I caddied for Greg in Australia and Europe but not in America as at that time I didn't have a visa for the United States. When I wasn't with Greg I had a set group of players I worked for, and when they weren't playing I worked for whoever needed me. In 1982, I was with Michael King, the following year it was an American Tom Sieckmann, in 1984 and 1985 I was with Terry Gale in Asia and Mike Clayton in Europe. In 1986, I started working fulltime with Ian Baker-Finch in Europe and was still with Terry Gale in Asia. Those guys understood that if Greg came and played somewhere they were playing, then I caddied for Greg. There wasn't any animosity because they had as much respect for Greg as I did, if not more.

In the back of my mind I thought Greg could one day be my ticket on to the US PGA Tour but in the meantime I had the best of both worlds: caddying for Greg in tournaments outside America and doing what I wanted in between times. And Greg won – a lot. Each year I worked for him in Australia he claimed at least two or three tournaments – he was a money-making machine.

By the time I first caddied for Greg I had an appreciation for good players, but when I took his bag at the Australian Masters at Huntingdale, I got to appreciate what a truly top player was like. I also learnt that it was possible for a player to intimidate his opponents on the golf course. The 1st hole at Huntingdale has an incredibly daunting tee shot. You're either on the fairway or you're out of the hole. Back then there was dense tea-tree on the left (I mean really thick tea-tree), which a lot of the sand-belt courses had. On the right there were extremely tall gum trees, so if you hit it in there you'd be incredibly lucky to have any shot to the green – otherwise you'd have to chip it out sideways.

Most guys used a 3-wood or 1-iron on that tee, with the intention of making sure they kept the ball in play, but Greg would stand there with his driver and pump it 300 yards down the middle. When he did that, I would look at the other players and I could tell they felt beaten then and there. I realised you could intimidate other players – Greg managed to do that from the very first tee.

But it wasn't only other players he intimidated. It's fair to say I was afraid of the guy. When I was working for Greg I was forever on my toes, constantly concerned about making a mistake given he was so incredibly demanding. Looking back, I would say he was definitely the hardest guy I have ever caddied for. Often when I caddied for him someone would ask me what he shot and I'd have no idea, because I'd been so concerned about not making a mistake I wasn't focused on the score. If I made a mistake, he certainly had no hesitation in letting me know what an idiot I was. And if he made a mistake, somehow that would also be my fault.

Off the course, however, he was a wonderful guy. He was considerate and supportive to me and my family, and a true mate. He'd do anything for me. During weeks off in America I'd often go and stay at his home, a large property in Florida that was spread from the inner coastal side to the ocean side of West Palm Beach. He usually stayed at his house on the inner coast while he let me use the beach house. He frequently took me out on his boat and he often included me if he was getting tickets to a concert or to some other event. He'd ring me on my birthday or at Christmas and was genuinely interested in what was going on in my life.

It surprised me, though, how he changed when he drove into a golf course. As soon as he drove through the gates, the hairs on the back of his neck started to stand up and the competitive beast in him came out.

Greg the competitor was never wrong. As a caddy, I give good yardages. I reckon in all my years of caddying I can count on one hand how many yardages I got wrong, but if I gave the correct yardage and Greg picked the wrong club it was my fault. And he wouldn't just tell me I was wrong – he would go absolutely apeshit at me. The first time he ripped me out I was definitely taken aback, thinking, 'Whoa, I didn't see that coming,' but I soon learned to accept that every mistake was my fault regardless. It wasn't personal – it was just the way he was. And you couldn't reason with him.

Let's say he dropped a shot. I'd say to Greg, 'C'mon, let's get more focused,' and he'd yell, 'What do you think I'm doing? I'm fucking focusing. Can't you see I'm fucking focusing?' Every time you caddied for him you had to be so careful about what you said and when you said it. Whatever you said, it was almost invariably the wrong thing. If he was up, you couldn't get him any more confident, and if he was down it was impossible to give him any advice. As a caddy, I believe that when someone isn't playing well you've got to find a way to give them confidence or perk them up and remind them of a time when they were playing well. Or you might suggest something in their set-up or swing that could make a difference. But with Greg it was impossible to say anything. I think that aspect of his game was the one thing that probably worked against him.

Of all the players I have worked for, including Tiger, Greg would be the best in terms of the pure physical side of the game. But his weakness, and it was a huge weakness, was not being able to get over a bad break. A bad break could last a hole, nine holes, a week, a month – he just couldn't shake it off. If he got a bad bounce or hit the wrong club, he couldn't let it go. If he hadn't possessed that particular trait or shortcoming, there was no telling what he could have done in the game. I've been asked if he could have benefited from a sports psychologist or a mental coach, but a guy of his mental make-up wouldn't let someone else tell him what to do or think. He wouldn't listen to anyone else – his ego was too big for that.

The beginning of the end with Greg came at the 1989 Masters. I caddied for him part-time from 1982 to 1987, in Australia and Europe, and he'd had a lot of success. Greg encouraged me to join him on a fulltime basis and worked behind the scenes to get me the right visa to work in America. I had never planned to caddy in the US but in 1988 I took the leap.

In the previous three Masters, he'd been in contention. In 1986, he'd birdied four holes in a row from 14 to 17 and was tied with Jack Nicklaus playing the last. A par would have been enough for a playoff, but Greg wanted a birdie and a win, and pushed too hard, flaring his approach to the right of the green and making bogey. In 1987, he was in a playoff with Seve Ballesteros and Larry Mize when Mize holed a miracle chip to stun Greg and the world. In 1988, my first Masters with Greg, he flew home in the final round with 64, which was good enough for fifth place.

In 1989, we were in contention once again. We came to the last hole needing par to get into a playoff. It was cold and raining and Greg was driving the ball great. He said to me, 'What do you think?'

'Absolutely driver,' I said. 'You can't reach that bunker today in these conditions and you need to be as far up as possible, otherwise it's a really long shot in and you'll be hitting off a steep slope.'

But he disagreed and stuck with the 1-iron he'd chosen. He hit it well but as predicted it left him a longer second shot than was desirable. I gave him the yardage for the second shot and in my view it was a 4-iron all day, but he wanted to hit with a 5-iron. I spent a couple of minutes trying to convince him otherwise: 'With a five-iron, there's no way it can get there, and if it does get there, you'll have to hit it your absolute maximum,' I argued. 'It will spin off the front of the green because it's wet. Take the four-iron and take some spin off it, put it on the bank and let it trickle down.'

The hardest thing with Greg was that when he was adamant about his club choice, and I was equally insistent it *wasn't* the right club, I couldn't find an easy way to make a convincing argument. He wasn't going to budge and he stayed with the 5-iron.

The worst feeling in golf is, having lost the argument over club selection, to stand there powerlessly while my player takes the wrong club and I know he cannot reach the green. Greg hit it as well as he could have, but it came up short and spun off the front of the green. He was using a Tour Edition golf ball, which spun more than any other ball, and Greg could put more spin on the ball than any other golfer, so it spun way off the green and ran 12–15 yards down the hill. He needed to get up-and-down – a chip and a putt – for his par but missed his putt and the playoff by one shot.

Mark O'Meara, his playing partner, had been listening to our discussion in the 18th fairway and later said to me, 'Steve, you did your best. You tried to persuade him every way you could and he wouldn't listen.' It was some comfort. That incident may also have played a part in me getting a job with Tiger Woods a decade later, because O'Meara became one of Tiger's most trusted friends on tour and Tiger definitely sought his advice when looking to hire a new caddy.

Greg knew I was right. He knew he should have listened to me and acknowledged as much. Though I should have let it rest there, foolishly I brought it up again a week later but Greg hadn't yet come to terms with it. It was still a sore point. He sacked me a month later.

We were in Japan for The Crowns tournament at Nagoya, which is a tight, narrow golf course. My job was to get there before he did and scout the course, which I did. We were playing in the first two rounds with Masashi 'Jumbo' Ozaki, a legend in Japan, and we got to a hole on the back nine that I didn't realise was a driveable par-4. Actually, it shouldn't have been a driveable par-4, as it was a dogleg with some significant pine trees on the corner that looked too high to hit over. When I measured the course, there was no way I considered the option of driving the ball onto the green. But what does Jumbo do? He takes a driver, knocks the ball over the trees and close to the green, and makes the hole look easy.

After the round, Greg asked why I didn't have the information to know that it was possible to drive the green by taking the route over the trees. We had a massive argument over this, which carried on for two or three days and didn't end even when Greg won the tournament. To me it wasn't a percentage play. Even though Greg hit the ball a long way, Jumbo hit further and higher. I also had to remind Greg that it wasn't uncommon for Japanese fans to throw Jumbo's ball back into the fairway if he was in trouble. I swear, one day Jumbo hit his ball out of bounds but when we got there it was in play. But Greg wouldn't hear any of it and was furious I didn't give him that option.

I figured he'd cool down once we got back to the US. He headed home straight after the tournament, while I stayed on in Japan to caddy for Jeff Sluman, an American who was in the same IMG management stable as Greg. It was about 2am when the phone rang in my hotel room. It was Greg and down the phone he gave me the news that my services were no longer required. He fired me in the middle of the night from thousands of miles away! It was one of those times when you wake up the next morning and wonder if it really happened. But it did, and I was suddenly out of a job.

Off the course, he was great to me, but I didn't know when to be a friend and when not to be a friend. When he was giving me a mouthful, I would give him a gobful back because that's what you do with your mates. He had had enough of that. Even though I'd been caddying for more than 10 years, I was still only in my 20s, and in many ways I didn't know any better, but Greg gave me a wake-up call.

Steve is right to say we probably became too close off the course. But I made a mistake to let him go in 1989.

I don't remember exactly the debate over club selection on a driveable par-4, but he was probably right and I was probably being stubborn-headed. Steve was just trying to get me into a place to win the golf tournament.

What Steve taught me was to communicate better and not to be so stubborn. In that situation we didn't communicate very well and on reflection the problem was at my end. And from my perspective, I made a big mistake. I regret letting him go. But at the end of the day he probably ended up in a better place with the bag – it was one of those moments in time where it just happened.

We've stayed friends and we'll remain friends because the infancy of a relationship is the core of it all – we had our ups and downs as a public team but I will always regard Steve as my kid brother. I love that he's become successful but I hated the way he was stuck in the corner by Tiger.

While my working relationship with Greg had been tough, I had also learned the greatest lesson you can learn as a caddy – on the golf course, the player's the boss and you're working for him. Friendships go out the window. He was the first guy I caddied for who was 100 per cent professional about everything he did. For him, the only thing that mattered was winning. He wasn't playing for a cheque, he was playing to win.

———

You don't expect to get fired after you win a tournament.

The argument with Greg was pretty big – there was major friction over that driveable par-4 at Nagoya – but it was still surprising to be sacked. Looking back over the previous few months, the fight over the driver in Japan was probably the last in a series of clashes that eventually wore thin for Greg.

The disagreement over how he played the final hole at the 1989

Masters had been preceded by an incident at Port Douglas, in the far north of Queensland. The Port Douglas Golf Test in 1988 was dreamed up as golf's answer to the fierce cricket rivalry between Australia and England. Greg was the captain of the Australian team and I was designated caddy captain.

A TV crew dragged us down to a small jetty for interviews and while I was talking, Greg got under the jetty and started splashing me with water. It was a bit of fun at first but quickly started to irritate me. Naturally, when it was Greg's turn to speak to the media I pulled the same prank and Greg got annoyed with me. What followed can only be called a dust-up. There were no punches thrown but a bit of push and a shove ended up with Greg in the water.

Looking back, by the time the Japan incident played out Greg was tired of me telling him what I thought. It reminded me what the great Jack Nicklaus said after he sacked his afro-haired Greek caddy Angelo Argea after 20 years of service: 'Every little thing he would do was beginning to upset me.'

As a caddy I knew nothing was permanent and while I thought Greg was hard to work with, I also realised I'd probably become a difficult caddy to put up with. But it still came to an end sooner than I expected.

For the first time in my life, I was unemployed. I knew there would be someone else to work for – I just didn't know who. IMG, Greg's management company, knew there had been a split and organised for me to work with American Andy Bean, who had won 11 times on the PGA Tour but not for three years. There was no break – I had one bag taken away from me and picked up the next straight away.

While it seems I jumped on the first player available, one thing I don't like doing is sitting around. And I didn't want to be one of those caddies who hang out in the car park looking for work. There's always action going on in the car park at tournaments – caddies looking for work or looking to change players, to go up the food chain, and there's predictable chatter about who's not getting on, who's leaving who, who wants to get off a bag. I've not been involved in that and didn't want to start now.

Andy had been a good player – twice runner-up in major champ-ionships – and while he wasn't in great form I saw it as a challenge to help him get his game back on track. But I'd only been with him for a handful of tournaments when Raymond Floyd made an unusual approach.

CHAPTER 4
THE GOOD LIFE

Raymond Floyd was a legend of golf in the twilight of his career. He was a four-time major winner often cited in the same company as the 'big four' – Jack Nicklaus, Arnold Palmer, Gary Player and Lee Trevino. When Raymond approached me he hadn't won in three years, but he had a proposal for me – a first for me – which mapped out his goals and how he hoped to reach them and what he expected of me. With anyone else I'd worked for previously, I picked up the bag and started walking. None of them said these are my goals and this is what I want to happen. But Raymond was committed to staying at the top for as long as possible.

I first got to know Steve when he was caddying for Greg Norman. He was the most professional caddy I'd ever seen – he was all business and I liked that on the golf course. I admired his professionalism and I knew he and Greg had done well together.

What I liked about Steve was that he understood golf was a serious business and as a result he was serious about his work. You never saw him bantering away or chatting idly on the practice range. When he was with me he knew that practice was for a purpose and if people came over to have a chat he'd tell them politely, 'Sorry, we're working here.' He protected me. He got a lot of flak in later years for incidents with cameramen when he was working with Tiger. But when a cameraman interferes with a player's backswing, it's the caddy's job to protect his man. Steve did that, but it didn't make him a bully – he was doing his job.

Raymond was a few years away from joining the Seniors Tour for players aged 50-plus but his priority was to play as well as he could on the PGA Tour for as long as he could before he rode off into the sunset of the Seniors Tour.

He had won four major championships over a 17-year period, from 1969 to 1986, and was considered one of the better payers on tour. It was too good a package to turn down.

When I joined him, Raymond was in a minor form slump but that soon changed.

At the 1990 Masters, I was sharing a house with Fanny Sunesson, Nick Faldo's caddy. The banter in the lead-up was that one day we'd be in a playoff against each other. On the Wednesday before the Masters, there is a traditional par-3 competition, which is a bit of fun but comes with the reputation of being a curse for whoever wins it – nobody has won the par-3 contest and gone on to don the green jacket.

When I arrived back at the house on the Wednesday afternoon, Fanny asked, 'How did you go?'

'We won.'

'Well, you can't do that – you can't win the Masters now.'

'Well, I'm not sure we're going to win anyway.'

Raymond was 47 years old and playing for 'fun'. While he'd won the Masters in 1976 by eight shots and remained a consistent performer at Augusta, it didn't make much sense to think he could win it again.

Even when he took a two-shot lead after the second round, he told media: 'I'm putting no pressure on myself now. I decided I've got nothing more to prove. I used to be so tough on myself. Now, I'm just having fun.'

That two-shot lead became four late on Sunday but as Faldo made a charge with birdies at 13, 15 and 16, Raymond made a succession of pars and was robbed of a chip-in birdie on the 14th when his ball was headed to the hole, only to hit John Huston's ball-marker and jump off line.

He was one ahead of Faldo with two holes to play and what happened on that penultimate hole is one of the moments in my career that still keep me awake at nights.

I don't have many regrets – there are only a handful of incidents in almost 40 years of caddying where I wish I could have my time over – but there are two that still bother me: the 1989 Masters with Greg, when I couldn't convince him to go with a 4-iron into the 18th green in the final round; and my choice to say nothing to Raymond on the 17th hole at the 1990 Masters.

The rule with Raymond was not to say anything unless I was specifically asked. He was an old-fashioned player who didn't want or need as much input from a caddy as other players did.

And I'd learned my lesson from my time with Greg about keeping my views to myself.

All the same, I had to bite my tongue as we surveyed the approach to the 17th green, where the pin was located in the front-right. A ridge to the left and a severe downslope from left to right meant the percentage shot for a miss was to the right – if you drifted too far off that line it was still a simple chip and putt. The last place you wanted to be was left of the hole.

Raymond told me he was going to aim a little left of the hole and work it back toward the flag. My immediate thought was, 'What if you aim left and pull it even further left?' I wanted to tell him to fire straight at it, but he hadn't asked my opinion so I said nothing.

> When I knew what I wanted to do I didn't need a caddy. I didn't need his input. I'd ask him for the yardage; he would give me the yardage. If I didn't say, 'What do you think?' he wouldn't say anything.
>
> I made a mental mistake on that hole. I should have been playing to win the tournament but I elected to play a little safe. Steve said to me later, 'I wanted to say go right at it.' He blames

himself for not saying anything – but I was the one who made a mental mistake.

Raymond pulled it left. His difficult downhill putt slid six feet past and he missed the return for a three-putt bogey.

Now level with Faldo, Raymond had to draw on all his fighting character to make par on the 18th after hitting into two bunkers. The banter Fanny and I shared about one day being in a playoff had become a reality, as she recalls.

> The only sad thing was that if we won it, it meant Steve was going to lose. If Nick and I lost, the only positive would be that if there's anyone I was happy to lose to it was Steve.

Raymond had a birdie chance on the first playoff hole to win but came up short. In fading light on the second playoff hole, he had one of those moments that leaves a golfer devastated.

Raymond's eyesight wasn't as sharp as it used to be. He wore light-enhancing glasses but as the twilight deepened they were of no use. He asked a rules official if they were going to keep playing because he was having trouble seeing his ball. It wasn't impossible to see, but Raymond was entitled to ask the question. He was told play would continue. Good sportsman that he is, he accepted that.

A good drive on the second playoff hole, the 11th, left him on the fairway, but as soon as the second shot left his 7-iron, I could tell it had started left and was heading further left – into Rae's Creek – but Raymond couldn't see it. He turned to me and asked, 'Steve, where's that gone?'

I could barely speak – it was like telling someone a relative had died.

This is one of the reasons I believe the Masters shouldn't be a sudden-death playoff. All the other majors have multi-hole playoffs. The US Open is decided over an 18-hole playoff, the British Open over four holes, the PGA Championship over three holes. But the Masters is sudden death. Even though sudden death has worked in favour of Tiger

Woods and Adam Scott at Augusta, my belief is that it should be played over three or four holes. When you've battled over 72 holes it doesn't seem right that you can lose it with one bad stroke on one hole.

In the end I blamed myself, not Raymond, for that loss. I should have said something on the 17th – I wish I'd said something.

It might have changed his thinking – he had to finish 4-4 to win and the only way to make a five on 17 by three-putting was to be way left. If he'd aimed further right, the worst he would have made was four. Even if he missed the green to the right, he was such a good chipper it wouldn't have been a big deal.

Years later we were able to joke about it – when he was building a new house and I was looking at the plans for the bedroom I said, 'If only I'd said something in 1990 you'd be building a bigger wardrobe for that extra green jacket.'

At the time, though, he was devastated to miss out on being the oldest player to win a major championship.

'To be the oldest, to win another major . . . nothing has ever affected me like this,' he said at his press conference. 'At this stage of my life, how many chances are you gonna have? If you're twenty-five and you lose one, you still believe in yourself, you still believe you're going to get a lot more chances.'

Remarkably he did get another chance.

In 1992, he was 49 and weeks away from joining the Seniors Tour but his game was in tremendous shape. And were it not for one of the most inexplicable incidents in Masters history, he might have won: Fred Couples' tee shot on the 12th hole came up short and started rolling towards the water. It was doomed. Yet six inches from disappearing underwater, the ball stopped on a steep bank, allowing Fred to save par.

Raymond had his own miracle moment when he made what is still considered to be an impossible chip-in on the 14th.

Raymond was the most masterful chipper of the ball I've ever seen. He could chip the ball from anywhere, using any club, and he had great vision for how the ball would land and roll once it was on the green. From the years I spent with him I got an incredible understanding of chipping and I passed a lot of that information on to Tiger, who was fascinated by Raymond's ability around the greens.

When I first came to work with Tiger, he would chip with only one club. I shared some of Raymond's tricks with him – the key being to pick the right club. Raymond could chip with a 3-iron, a 5-iron, a 7-iron . . . you name it. He would treat every chip as if it was a long putt and believed he could put it in the hole every time. After I'd been with Tiger for a while his chipping improved, and he'd often say to me when he wanted to hole a chip, 'OK Stevie, time for a Raymondo here.'

The greens at Augusta are famed for their contours, slopes, ridges and plateaus, and the 14th green is probably the most severe. Tiger once said, 'A good shot can turn into a disastrous shot, just by being a yard or two off line or the wrong distance.' When the pin is placed on the front-right of the green, room for error is infinitesimal, especially if you come up short, which Raymond did in the final round in 1992. By my reckoning, his chip had only two possible fates – roll back to his feet or go some ways past the hole. The other option – hitting it close – would have been like winning a lottery, such were the odds.

My old mate Allan James, the butcher, was there watching. Now Allan is a big man – six foot two and weighs at least 120 kilograms – and I don't think I've ever seen him jump off the ground. But when Raymond hit his chip shot hard into the bank so it popped delicately over the ridge and rolled gently into the cup, all I saw was Allan leaping into the air – all I heard over the roar of the crowd was Allan screaming at the top of his lungs.

That lifted Raymond to within two shots of Couples but that's as close as it would get. This time Raymond was OK with his fate: Fred was one of his best friends on tour and it was Fred's first major win.

Raymond Floyd was famous for 'the look' – the moments when his focus was so intense his eyes would drill right through you as he applied his mind to executing his next shot. His wife Maria said there had been times on the golf course when he'd be looking right at her in the gallery but not see her, so intense was his concentration.

He was in stark contrast to Greg Norman in that nothing distracted him, nothing derailed his attention and he never got down on himself or blamed anyone or anything that conspired against him.

He had an unorthodox, self-taught swing and unusual physique: he was a big man but had slender wrists and hands that seemed out of proportion to his powerful body. And his mental tenacity was unlike anything I'd ever seen.

He was a big believer in making the world conform to his way of thinking – that you could will the ball into the hole. Standing over a putt, he often said to me, 'Come here, Stevie. Stand beside me and will this ball into the hole.'

That mental strength and will to win was unflagging. He played every single stroke as if it was the difference between winning and losing. What I loved was when he walked off the golf course, whatever score he'd shot it was the best he could have done. Giving in was not an option, frustration was kept at arm's length, each round was unhurried.

His absolute will to win was no more evident than the week his house burned down.

We were in California, playing at Torrey Pines, when Raymond got a call in the middle of the night from Maria telling him their family home in Miami had been destroyed by fire.

The Floyds lived in an exclusive neighbourhood on Indian Creek Island, Florida. I often stayed with them and loved being there as it was an area full of rich and famous people. I'd go running around the streets to see who I might bump into. I'd often take off my shirt because it was so hot, and Raymond was forever telling me off: 'Steve, you have to keep your shirt on when you run around here – it's not a good look.' He didn't want me embarrassing him in front of Julio Iglesias or Miami Dolphins coach Don Shula.

As soon as Raymond got the call that the house had been gutted – but that his wife and children were safe – he was on the first plane back to Miami.

The family had lost everything: 30 years of golf memorabilia, 18 years of family memories. Raymond was devastated. He moved the family into a rented house five doors down the street while they made plans to rebuild their home. It was February when he flew back to Miami, and almost as devastating for Raymond was the realisation that he couldn't host his annual lavish party ahead of the Doral-Ryder Open, his hometown tournament.

Maria understood her husband's ability to go deep into the well of determination. She told Raymond she would look after the problems associated with the fire if he did his part by focusing on golf to distract them from the nightmare. 'Raymond has a wonderful ability to reach down and do what he has to do,' she once told the *New York Times*.

Raymond launched himself on a mission: he was going to win the Doral-Ryder Open no matter what. The fact that he was 49 years old, hadn't won for six years, and was almost ready for semi-retirement on the Seniors Tour was irrelevant. He took all the negative emotion from the loss of his house and his family memories and created a fire of his own. He practised incessantly for two weeks and thought of nothing but winning.

He shot 17 under par that week to become the oldest player to win a PGA Tour event since Art Wall won the 1975 Milwaukee Open, aged 51. And it made him only the second player, alongside the legendary Sam Snead, to win a separate tour event in four different decades.

That win was followed by his near miss at the Masters and he later lost a playoff at the Byron Nelson Classic – he was playing some of the best golf of his career in the wake of that fire. He turned 50 in September, near the end of the season, yet he managed to win three times on the Seniors Tour before the season was done. Multiple wins came in 1993, '94 and '95.

When anyone quizzed Raymond about life on the Seniors Tour, he'd say, 'It's great – you just have to make sure you keep your back loose.'

'Why's that?' they'd ask.

'Because the money's just lying there on the ground and as long as your back's loose and you can touch your toes you just have to bend down and pick it up. It's easy money.'

That's not to say life on the Seniors Tour was completely idyllic. It did tend to get stale. It was the same players turning up every week, and complaining every week about the same problems.

There were three distinct groups on the tour:

- those making up the numbers;
- those who thought it should be a retirement tour with short holes and accessible pins and who bitched and moaned all the time about the length of the course and the pin placements; and
- the competitive ones like Raymond who wanted the courses set up hard – it was professional golf after all, not a carnival.

––––––––––

Offsetting the boredom was the fact I was earning good money and got to watch a lot of speedway.

The Seniors Tour set up shop in places where the PGA Tour didn't and as a result events had a small-town, relaxed feel to them. The fields – outside of the majors – were limited to only 78 players, which meant the days were compact. We'd tee off late morning and be done by 4pm. This allowed me to indulge my passion for dirt-track motor racing. Almost every Friday and Saturday I could find a dirt track close to where a tournament was being played and spend the evening breathing in the heady mix of petrol and dirt.

It was a dream life for me, in a way, and the only thing that put a ruffle in my plan for an easy few years before retirement was the slow-burning feeling I was missing out on something. My career had an obvious void: a major championship.

Both Greg and Raymond had twice been runner-up in the Masters and those disappointments had stayed with me. The question was whether to go back to the regular tour and try to find another player who was capable of winning a major or stay with Raymond and enjoy the lifestyle. I chose to stay with Raymond.

Even when Greg begged me to come back in 1996 – a year Raymond won only once – I stayed on the path I'd chosen with Raymond, despite knowing that his performance in the 1992 Masters was his last chance at a major. I accepted I would be one of the many caddies who would forever crave that moment where they get to take the flag from the 18th green as a memento for being part of a major-winning team.

———————

Through my career, I've prided myself on being able to identify talented players as amateurs.

I saw Ernie Els as an amateur at the 1989 British Open and thought, 'This guy is going to be a great player.' At Carnoustie in 2007, there was a lot of talk about Rory McIlroy, a teenage amateur who was mixing it with the pros. One day at the range I stood behind him to see what the fuss was about, and instantly knew he was going to make it. He had that look – the way he walked, the way he practised, even the way he was watching his ball. He had the look of a champion.

Sergio Garcia and Adam Scott are other amateurs I predicted would have great careers. Probably the only one I thought would be a great player and who hasn't yet achieved that status was Aaron Baddeley. For a while the jury was still out on Jason Day – I wondered a lot who would be the better player out of him and Adam Scott, and believed they could both win majors. Jason seemed to have the game and the desire to win a major but took a long time to break through until his brilliant and emotional win in the 2015 US PGA Championship at Whistling Straits.

When I first saw Tiger Woods up close I had no doubt I was watching someone special – yet also completely out of my reference sphere.

On a cold, damp, foggy morning at Augusta in 1996, this skinny little kid who was touted to hit it prodigious distances joined Raymond Floyd, Greg Norman and Fred Couples for a practice round. An amateur, he was playing the Masters for the first time.

On the first hole we could see he could give it a real rip but he sliced the ball so far right it was hard to judge exactly how far he'd hit it because it soared over the trees and we didn't see it again.

On the second hole there's a bunker on the right-hand side that none of the experienced players worried about – no one could reach that bunker on such a chilly morning where the air was heavy with moisture. The ball was going nowhere.

So the kid turns to his caddy and asks, 'Can I fly that bunker?' and we're all looking at each other with little smirks on our faces and sharing a look that says, 'He's got a lot to learn.'

When he knocked it over the bunker, a deathly silence descended on the group. I was lost for words but in my head a voice was screaming, 'Wow.'

These legends of the game were dumbstruck and the silence was broken only when Tiger cracked a joke as we all walked off the tee with our tails between our legs.

I've only asked for an autograph once in my life – after we walked off the 18th green that day. This was a special moment – playing with my former boss, Greg, my current boss, Raymond, and my future boss (not that I knew that at the time). I had a gut feeling I needed something to mark a memorable day and asked all four to sign a copy of the scorecard: three major champions and a kid called Tiger Woods who I thought could be quite good.

———

Raymond and I were chatting on the practice green on the Monday before the 1999 Doral-Ryder Open, which he still played religiously.

I'd landed that day from New Zealand for Raymond's first event for the season. We talked about the fact this was the start of the end for us – his career was winding down and I'd previously decided 2000 was going to be my last year. There was something nice about caddying through to the end of the century. We were both happy about it and accepted it.

The next day the buzz around the range was that Tiger Woods had fired his caddy Mike 'Fluff' Cowan. Fluff, with his aging hippy looks and droopy moustache, had developed a profile by working for Tiger over his first three years on tour – he was now appearing in his own TV commercials and apparently Tiger wasn't happy his caddy was building a celebrity status on the back of Tiger's achievements.

DITCH THE CART

I HATE MOTORISED CARTS. On the Seniors Tour a player–caddy combination is allowed to use a cart. Either the player or the caddy can use the cart, but not both. I told Raymond Floyd there's no way on earth I'm taking a cart anywhere. They go against my belief system. There are some courses in America where golf carts are mandatory. If that's the case, I won't play that course. A big part of the game is walking, not only for the physical exercise but for the social connection – talking to your fellow competitors as you walk to your ball. Golf carts are anti-social. The few times I've played in a golf cart it's left me with an empty feeling. There's not the same banter. And as you walk towards your ball you get a sense of distance and a feel for what the next shot is going to be. When you're in a cart it's as if you hit your shot and the next thing you know you're there, bang, ready to play again without having thought about it. The game seems to rush past you – there doesn't seem to be time to take it all in. You also lose perspective. When you hit a shot off line you keep an eye on where it goes and walk on a line to a landmark you've identified. In a cart you lose that reference point and end up driving around and around trying to find the ball. I understand why golf clubs have carts – they are a great revenue stream – but the best courses in the world don't allow them. You can't take one around Augusta or St Andrews and for good reason.

On Wednesday the phone rang in my hotel room. 'It's Tiger Woods here.'

I had a mate who could imitate Tiger to a tee, and I thought he was pulling my leg so I put the phone down. It rang again and this time I was a bit irritable because it was late. I was still jetlagged after the flight from New Zealand and I wanted to get some sleep. I hung up again. Third time around Tiger is pleading, 'No, it really is Tiger. I've just parted ways with my caddy and I want to know if you'd like to come caddy for me.'

I wasn't jumping out of my skin about this as I'd made up my mind about how my career was going to wind down. I said I'd think about it.

I said nothing to Raymond but it turned out he already knew an offer was coming as Tiger and his coach Butch Harmon had done the right thing and called Raymond to ask if they could approach me. But he kept that to himself.

On Sunday, at the end of the tournament, Raymond was the one who brought it up.

> When Butch and Tiger approached me, I told them Steve was like a son to me. He stayed at my house and played golf with my two boys. I told them he absolutely had my good wishes. And then I told Steve, 'You'd be a fool not to take this position.'
>
> I think it was the best thing that ever happened for Tiger, because of Steve's professionalism and work ethic.

It wasn't an open-and-shut decision. Tiger, at 23, was a lot younger than me. I was 35 and until now had caddied only for older players. He was a budding superstar and I'd been caddying on the Seniors Tour for seven years with a guy who was now 56. It would be a real culture shock. We agreed to meet to suss each other out.

On Monday I drove up to Orlando from Miami to meet him. He greeted me at the door but hurriedly left me, saying, 'Come in, but can you wait a minute? I've just got something I need to finish.'

What he needed to finish was a video game – something completely foreign to me. I had no concept of what he was trying to achieve in this game or even how to play the thing but I could see how competitive he was. He was so focused on what was in front of him he was almost in a trance. I'd seen Raymond's 'look' so I knew what intense focus was but I'd yet to see anything quite like this – and this was over a video game. I knew right then that he was different.

One of the deal-makers was that in the off weeks I wanted to go back to New Zealand rather than hang around in the United States. He was fine with that but I still didn't say yes straight away.

'I'll give you a call tomorrow,' I said.

I rang Allan James and Fanny Sunesson and a couple of other people to discuss it. I knew from the way he was playing this video game it was going to be a whole new kettle of fish. Tiger, even then, with one major to his name, was a world figure – not exclusively a golfing figure – and I knew I was going to have to give up my nice, easy lifestyle.

CHAPTER 5
EARNING MY STRIPES

I couldn't believe my eyes. The so-called best player in the world was hitting some of the worst shots I'd seen in my life.

On the 13th hole at Bay Hill, the venue for the Arnold Palmer Invitational, Tiger Woods had 115 yards to the green and a sand wedge in his hand. From that position, with that club, most pros would stick the ball pretty close to the flag – and most amateurs would knock it on the green – but Tiger hit it 30 yards long and 30 yards left.

As I took the club off him, I said: 'Mate, I don't know what all the fuss is about – you're overrated. That's probably the worst shot I've seen from a golf professional from that sort of a distance.'

It was our first competitive round together and he'd been playing terribly all day. I'd not yet seen him up close in competition – only in practice – and was looking forward to this day. All I saw were incredible misses, awful shots.

Tiger had a swing fault that plagued him throughout his career. As he described it, he got 'stuck'. The club was too far behind his body as he rotated and he had to flip his hands at the bottom of the swing to get the club head in the right position. If he was too slow with his hands he'd block the ball out to the right, and if he was too fast he would pull it left and long.

This was evident in our first outing together and all I could think was, 'We've got a lot of work to do.'

Then came that shot on the 13th – the worst of the worst – and I figured it was time to break the ice and have a bit of banter. Before I knew it, I was telling Tiger Woods he was overrated. Luckily, he understood my sense of humour or it could have been the shortest caddying gig of my career. Every time we came to that hole over the next 10 years we'd laugh at the memory of that moment.

What surprised me about my first tournament with Tiger was how hard he kept trying and how, despite the fact he was playing badly, he believed he wasn't out of contention until such a point that it was actually impossible to win.

I've seen a lot of players on the PGA Tour give up much more easily than that – and I can understand why. The prize money in golf is so top-heavy that when you get down to thirtieth, fortieth, fiftieth there's not a lot of a difference in the purse so three or four shots wasted through lack of care or cruising might cost you only $5000, which is not a lot of money to these professionals. A lot of them, when they fall down the leaderboard, go through the motions over the closing holes.

Tiger was different. Like Greg Norman, all that mattered to him was winning. Money wasn't the primary focus. After that first week at Bay Hill I realised we had to quickly get a win otherwise it could turn into a tough job.

I didn't have to wait long – eight weeks and five tournaments after my debut on his bag he won the European Players Championship in Germany. I immediately found out there was no such thing as a celebration with Tiger Woods. We simply jumped on his private plane and flew home.

It was the same when he won the following week at the Memorial Tournament on the PGA Tour. He wasn't one to revel in a win the way you'd think he'd be entitled to – in fact, when he was winning regularly, celebrations were non-existent. He expected to win – that was his baseline. At a run-of-the-mill PGA Tour event, where a win for other players might be a once-in-a-season or once-in-a-lifetime event that warranted an all-night party to match the $1 million payday, Tiger would barely acknowledge his triumph before turning his focus to the next tournament.

I soon learned Tiger's focus intensified significantly when it came to major championships. His lifetime ambition was to beat Jack Nicklaus's record of 18 major championships and he put more energy into those events than regular tour stops. Like a swimmer aiming for the Olympics or a cyclist bidding for the Tour de France, he had, more often than not, the ability to peak for these four events each year, lifting his form and focus to a higher level.

But at the 1999 US Open at Pinehurst No. 2, I worried he wasn't taking his national championship seriously enough.

Normally regimented in his routine and to-the-minute punctual, if Tiger set a time and place to meet he would be there on the dot, which suited me perfectly as I'd made a career habit of being early. As Ian Baker-Finch once said about me, 'You never have to ask: where's Steve? He's always there.'

On the Sunday ahead of the final round of the US Open, I was 'there' – in this case the car park of the golf club an hour before Tiger's designated tee time.

Starting the day two shots behind Payne Stewart, this was a tournament he had a chance to win. I figured all his energy would be directed towards the best possible preparation. When he didn't show up at the appointed time I started to worry. I didn't own a cell phone, much to the amusement of many people, so he had no way of contacting me once I'd left my accommodation. It was unusual if Tiger was even one or two minutes late, so I was starting to worry after 10 minutes without any sign of him.

'Sorry I was a bit late,' he said with a smile as he pulled up, 'but I was watching this cartoon and it was a really good one that I hadn't seen before.'

Forget for a moment that a 23-year-old was watching cartoons on a

Sunday morning, but this Sunday was the final round of the US Open and he's telling me he couldn't drag himself away from a cartoon. He was definitely wired differently to anyone else I'd met.

I don't know whether that extra 10 minutes had any effect on the outcome – Tiger started with a birdie and played well but had trouble controlling his wedge shots and three times he hit it over the back of Pinehurst's notoriously difficult greens.

He and Stewart were level with two holes to play but Tiger made bogey on 17, where Stewart made a brilliant birdie. That was the difference at the end of a day that finished the way it started, with Stewart one shot clear of Phil Mickelson, and Tiger one more back in third after all three had shot even-par 70s.

Like anyone involved in golf, I'll never forget 25 October 1999, the day of the 'ghost flight', when Payne Stewart and four others on board his private plane died following a sudden loss of cabin pressure.

I liked Payne Stewart a lot – he'd cut his teeth on the Asian Tour in the early '80s when I was working the circuit and it was there he met his wife Tracey, the sister of an Australian professional Mike Ferguson. In many ways Payne acted more like an Australian than a typical American – he had a down-under manner about him and we always got on well.

Only days before his death, I had been talking to Payne after Tiger and I had been paired with him at the Disney tournament in Orlando. He had a huge interest in motorsport and we used to talk about racing quite a bit. Outside the scoring trailer at the Disney event, he told me he was close to inking a deal to become a part-owner in a motor-racing team that competed at the level below NASCAR. This had been a dream of his and I was excited to hear how it would pan out.

The following Monday I was walking the course alone in Houston, the venue for the Tour Championship, when a rules official approached me in a cart. The course was practically empty bar a few caddies like me who were out measuring the course. The official asked, 'Have you seen Mike Hicks?' referring to Payne Stewart's caddy.

Word of the crash quickly spread and we all gathered in the clubhouse to watch the story unfold. It's impossible now to even describe how awful it felt to be in that room – it was eerie and chilling. All of us had been in private planes like that one as so many professional golfers used them. We all realised it could have been any one of us lying dead on that plane as it continued flying on autopilot.

––––––––––

Major championship venues are supposed to be tough but the 1999 British Open at Carnoustie in Scotland was almost nonsensically tough. It was fitting that the tournament ended in farcical circumstances.

To illustrate just how difficult it was, Tiger played pretty well, shot 10 over par and finished seventh.

On a links course such as Carnoustie, the natural defence is the wind, with substantial bunkering adding another layer of trouble. That should be enough to protect the course but in 1999 the greenkeeper went overboard and grew the rough to excessive length. In my view, the Royal & Ancient Golf Club of St Andrews (R&A), which administers the game in Britain, didn't have enough control of the golf course set-up and the greenkeeper was allowed to get away with creating an open-air torture chamber. It was one of the least enjoyable major championships I've been to. If a ball travelled a couple of feet off the fairway it was in rough so deep it was in danger of being lost. Recovery shots were next to impossible.

People charged with setting up major championship courses have to realise the game has a fun element – for both players and the spectators – and this tournament would have been relegated to the bin of bad events had it not been for French player Jean van de Velde, who created more drama than a Hollywood scriptwriter. His complete disintegration on the last hole, where he made a tragicomic triple bogey, made sure the tournament lived long in the memory of golf fans around the world.

Tiger had finished his round and I was back at my hotel room watching the conclusion on TV. I'd grown friendly with Jean and wanted him to win – he was a mad rugby fan and we often shared some banter when the All Blacks played France.

He came to the 18th tee with a three-shot lead – a double bogey would be good enough for a win. I reckon if you'd taken any half-decent golfer out of the gallery that day and told them they could win the Claret Jug if they could make a double-bogey six on the last hole, most of them would have been able to do it. A professional golfer and his caddy, between them, should have been able to make the right decisions and correct plays required to make a five without any trouble.

I don't blame Jean for the mistakes he made on that hole – it was the caddy's fault. Every time I measure a golf course I ask myself, 'What if we are coming down the last with a one- or two-shot lead – how are we going to play it?' The caddy should have had a plan for that circumstance – though perhaps Jean was such an outside chance the caddy hadn't considered the possibility of winning.

Jean had made par at the brutal 17th – if he was going to lose the tournament it would have been there. As he walked to the 18th tee, he knew the win was his – or should have been. He was leading by three. It was all but over. He was probably thinking, 'I've just won the British Open. What's my wife thinking? What are my friends thinking? What about the people who have helped me through my career – what are they thinking? What are the people of France thinking? I'm going to be the first French major champion.' That's the stuff that goes through a player's mind. His emotions would have been all over the place.

He stepped up to the tee and took out his driver. That's when I believe his caddy, Christophe Angiolini, should have brought him back to reality and told him the best way to ensure a win was to play conservatively. He should have said, 'Let's play for a bogey five here. Take a five-iron and keep the tee shot short of those bunkers on the right. Keep it short of the Barry Burn with the second, wedge it on, two-putt and win the championship.'

A driver was the worst possible club he could take – it brought all the possible dangers into play but, even then, he hit it so far right he avoided the worst of the trouble. At that point there was still time for a calm head to prevail. They'd made one mistake, there was no need to compound it. But no, from 200 yards out, he decided to go for the green – his whole thought process was in disarray. The caddy should have said: 'No, let's take a seven-iron and leave it short of the water, wedge it on and make five.'

Christophe either wasn't experienced enough or not confident enough – and it was no surprise he got fired within a month of this debacle.

No one who saw what happened next will ever forget it. The second shot bounced off the grandstand and into the rough. Jean then slashed through the long grass and dunked the ball in the shallow water of the Barry Burn, a creek that snakes all the way down the 18th hole. When he took off his shoes and socks and seriously thought about playing it out of the water, it was horrendous to see how muddled his thinking had become. Eventually common sense prevailed and he took a penalty drop, chipped on and made a fine putt for a seven to settle for a playoff, which Paul Lawrie won.

It was so sad to watch – for Jean to have played the best golf of his life on the most difficult course set-up imaginable would have been a hell of a story had he won. Instead, he's relegated to a comic act in golf history all because his caddy didn't slow him down and point him in the right direction.

Unlike Jean van de Velde that day at Carnoustie, Tiger Woods played his major championship golf as cautiously and meticulously as possible. His attitude was to minimise mistakes and make the fewest possible bad shots.

As a result, I put a lot of time and effort into scouting major championship courses so I could navigate him away from potential disaster and towards the safest options – what we call the best miss.

I'd be looking for the widest area off the tee: to avoid the trouble areas that could lead to a big score. I spent more time working out the golf course for Tiger than any other player I caddied for because he had the ability to hit it a lot further – and a lot further off line – than anyone else I had worked for.

With Tiger I had to have a wide-open mind. In contrast, when I later worked for Adam Scott – one of the best modern-day drivers of the golf ball who seldom hit it far off line – the parameters of the golf course shrank.

With Tiger, I had to constantly ask myself the question, 'Where could he possibly hit this golf ball?' I would get yardages from the strangest places. I'd take measurements in adjacent fairways, in the middle of the trees. When he got into trouble he wanted to know exact yardages because he could often see a shot possibility no one else could.

He has played some miracle shots in his time – often because he got into tight spots demanding miracle shots. But he was better than anyone I've seen at hitting through small gaps, under branches, over tall trees or manoeuvring the ball around objects. And when he pulled off these shots you'd hear people say, 'Gee, that was lucky.' But as Gary Player famously said, 'The harder I practise, the luckier I get.'

Tiger would often dump a few balls in awkward spots during practise and hit a variety of shots – off side-hill lies, downhill lies, big curving shots, high shots, low skidding shots. He practised them all and it was fascinating to see what he could conjure up. In practice rounds it's not uncommon for players to pick up their ball when they hit into trouble but if Tiger hit it in the shit, he played it out of the shit because he knew that if he put it there in practice he could put it there during the tournament.

When I scouted Medinah, the venue for the 1999 PGA Championship, I felt it was going to be good for him because it was such a long course, which made it so much harder for short and even average-length hitters to be in contention.

In the end, they all fell away until only one player was able to handle the pressure of going head-to-head with Tiger down the stretch.

Sergio Garcia was only 19 and everyone expected him to one day be a great player but that day at Medinah he set up a rivalry with Tiger Woods, then 23, that I think has plagued him ever since and stopped him playing to his absolute potential.

Anyone who watched Sergio that day would shake their heads in disbelief if you'd told them that 15 years later he still wouldn't have won a major. Yet if he'd won that tournament and Tiger had folded, they would have owned one major each and who knows what Sergio could have gone on to do or how many more majors he could have won. It was a critical juncture for both their careers and it was also the start of a feud that threatened to consume Sergio.

It started on the par-3 13th hole in the final round. Tiger began the day two shots clear of Sergio and after 11 holes was five clear but Sergio was on the charge and Tiger was wobbling. He'd made bogey on the 12th and, standing on the par-3 13th tee, we watched as Sergio sank a bold birdie putt to further reduce the deficit and put the pressure back on Tiger. What Sergio did next was a rookie mistake. He spun back to Tiger on the tee with his hand aloft and gave him a look that said, 'I know you're struggling. This is a hard hole to even hit green let alone make two and I've just done that – I'm coming for you.'

Tiger turned to me and said, 'Did you see that?'

'Yes, I did.'

Initially it seemed to affect him because he played that hole awfully, duffing a chip into the water and making a double-bogey five that slashed his lead to one shot. But it also galvanised his competitive resolve.

Waiting on the 16th tee with a two-shot lead after Sergio had bogeyed the 15th, we knew something was going on ahead of us but not exactly what. Suddenly, Sergio appeared from the treeline, ran up the middle fairway, skipped and leapt in the air. I'd not seen anything like it on a golf course – professionals don't run anywhere, let alone leap in the air. The roar from the crowd suggested he had done something miraculous. His curling recovery shot from the base of a tree – closing his eyes and hitting in hope and praying his club didn't break – landed the ball on the green to give him a straightforward par. It was a great escape.

Again Tiger faltered in the wake of a dramatic shot by Sergio and bogeyed the same hole to lead by one again.

Another mistake at the par-3 17th put Tiger's lead in jeopardy. Missing the green to the left, he needed the hands of a surgeon to play an extremely delicate chip shot and leave himself a slippery putt of about six or seven feet to save par.

In our few months together, Tiger hadn't often used me to read his putts but he sought my opinion on this one. His view was that he needed to aim fractionally to the left of the hole but he wanted a second opinion.

I knew exactly how that putt would behave having seen it during practice. When players practise, their caddies put down tees where they think the holes might be placed later in the tournament so we can look at putts to these imaginary spots. I distinctly remembered Tiger putting on that side of the green and seeing the ball not breaking as much I'd expected.

'The line is just inside the hole,' I said with complete authority.

Despite my definitive response, I swear my heart skipped a beat as I walked to the edge of the green. With an awful sinking feeling in my stomach, I thought, 'Shit, what if I'm wrong here?'

When he knocked that putt in he looked up and gave me a wink. He later told the media, 'Stevie said "inside left" and I said "perfect", trusted the read and made a good stroke.'

Two good swings down the last and two putts later, he won the tournament by a stroke.

Tiger's first reaction was one of absolute relief – he was mentally exhausted. It had taken him more than two years to add a second major to his dominant maiden triumph at Augusta in 1997, and he'd had to fight for every single shot.

Later he got a photo of himself holding the Wanamaker Trophy, which he gave to me. On the photo he wrote, 'Great read on 17, Stevie. Thanks for your help, Tiger.'

That putt was vital. Victory was falling away from him and he was starting to unravel under the pressure from Sergio. For the sake of his own self-belief, to win that tough battle and make the step forward towards his goal of 18 majors was massive.

If he hadn't won that tournament you don't know where he might have gone – he had a huge lead at one stage but made errors and uncharacteristically bad shots. A loss could have been a real blow to his self-confidence.

After taking the job in March, I was rapt, five months later, to tick off a major championship in the first year. To have input into the win also strengthened the bond between us and built the trust we needed on the course and the belief that we were both trying to achieve the same thing. That putt was a turning point for us, and cemented our relationship. If I'd been wrong and he'd not made that putt and perhaps bogeyed the last and not won the tournament, the whole thing could have been over by the end of the year.

Sergio waited for Tiger as he came off the 18th green and the two exchanged a quick embrace. Tiger said, 'Well played, Sergio – great play,' but that was the last time those two shared a greeting of that nature. Sergio had made a mistake on the 13th by trying to play mind games with Tiger. As others would learn over time, you couldn't play mind games with Tiger because he was the best at it. He was an extraordinary competitor with a deep well of mental fortitude, but when someone irritated him he could dig deeper than I thought possible in order to crush anyone who'd crossed him.

———

Sergio Garcia is an exciting player who wears his heart on his sleeve and, in some ways, it's a shame for him that he didn't win that 1999 PGA Championship, as his career could have taken a completely different tack.

Since then he's had many chances and I think each near miss has got the better of him. Now, I don't think he's ever going to win a major because all the failures have affected his attitude. He doesn't have the mental toughness required to overcome adversity – he's had some heartbreaks and they've become a weight he struggles to carry.

If he had won that one there's no telling how good he might have been. He probably felt he played well enough to win that day. The birdie on 13 and the miracle on 16, coupled with his youthful exuberance, would have created a beautiful storyline for the media and it would have given his fledgling career a rocket-fuelled kick-start.

Instead, that event is now the starting point for a timeline of his many run-ins with Tiger.

Over the years, Sergio got it into his head that rules officials favoured Tiger and treated him differently to other players; that Tiger intimidated rules officials. There might be some truth to this – Tiger had a thorough understanding of the rules and there were definitely times when rules officials were nervous in his presence. Under the pressure of the spotlight constantly trained on Tiger, they would make the odd mistake.

Sergio has also complained that officials conspired to give Tiger favourable treatment – by making sure he was given the best opportunity to win. This started at the 2002 US Open at Bethpage Black in New York. The weather that week was biblically wet. In the second round, Sergio was caught in the worst of the Friday-afternoon deluge and argued play should have been abandoned, adding that if Tiger had been on the course officials would have called off proceedings.

He let incidents – which others would treat like a stone in their shoe – dig under his skin.

The worst incident between the two of them came after I had been sacked by Tiger, and typified how bitter their relationship had become. Sergio and Tiger were paired together at The Players Championship in 2013. Sergio hit a bad shot and subsequently complained he was distracted by Tiger pulling a club out of his bag. The argument escalated over the following days and Tiger called Sergio a whiner. 'He called me a whiner. He's probably right,' Sergio told media later. 'But that's also probably the first thing he's told you guys that's true in 15 years. I know what he's like. You guys are finding out.'

Soon after, at a dinner, Sergio responded to a question about his relationship with Tiger by saying he would have Woods over every night during the US Open and serve him fried chicken, an insulting slight against African Americans, prompting Tiger to slam him on Twitter.

I'd already lost patience with Sergio's bad behaviour by then. My respect for him disappeared completely at the 2012 PGA Championship at Kiawah Island.

I was caddying for Adam Scott and we were paired with Sergio and Hunter Mahan. In the second round, Sergio carried on like an absolute pork chop. His behaviour was unacceptable for a professional golfer – it put both Adam and Hunter off their games.

He was loud, abusive, bad-tempered, threw his clubs, kicked his bag, hit out of turn . . . and hit one shot on the run, which is inexcusable. He gave no consideration to the other players or even his own caddy, who told him to shove the job after Sergio missed the cut.

Hunter Mahan shot 80 in the second round to miss the cut and was visibly upset. It was a difficult day, with a stiff breeze, but there was no way a good ball-striker like Hunter Mahan would shoot 80 in those circumstances. Mahan's caddy, John Wood, is as professional as you get – he was furious at Sergio for costing his player a chance to play at the weekend.

To lose your temper on one or two holes is one thing but this was an 18-hole display of poor sportsmanship and child-like petulance. Adam is the most laid-back professional you could hope to meet and to see him as frustrated as he was that day was a first for me. It was so bad he gave Sergio a blast that night, telling him he was out of order and to grow up.

From the caddy's point of view, what made it even worse was that Sergio, after missing the cut, made a last-minute decision to enter the following week's tournament, picked up a local caddy and won.

———————

At the end of my first season with Tiger, I witnessed one of the most infamous incidents in modern golf at Brookline, Massachusetts. I was there beside the 17th green of the Ryder Cup match between Jose Maria

Olazabal and Justin Leonard. I had been carrying Tiger Woods' bag for a few months and it was my first Ryder Cup with him.

When Leonard made a remarkable putt to all but ensure the Americans' victory in the Cup – though the deal was not yet sealed – the players, wives, girlfriends, supporters and media stormed onto the green to celebrate.

It was one of the most despicable acts of bad sportsmanship I've seen and typified why I don't like the Ryder Cup. The sad thing was that Jose Maria still had a putt that could have kept the match alive – and the overall contest. After that disgraceful dancing on the green there was no way he was going to make his putt. Jose Maria is one of golf's true gentlemen and I'll never forget how awful it was for him.

I can, however, see why the Americans were so jubilant. The night before – when it looked like they didn't have a sniff of victory – the captain, Ben Crenshaw, delivered a heart-thumping, morale-lifting speech in the team room. One of the few treats for caddies at the Ryder Cup is that they're allowed in the team room and I was privileged to hear Ben's speech. It wasn't so much what he said as the way he said it. With that firm but gentle Texan inflection, he took a group of unconvinced players and turned them into believers – every player and caddy left that room knowing it was possible to win if they each played their part, and walked out full of hope and faith.

In the singles on Sunday, Tiger played against Andrew Coltart, who was one of three Europeans who hadn't been picked in any of the four-ball or foursome matches on the first two days. Those players are allowed to practise and to play the course after the last match of the day has gone through. They are familiar with the golf course – they just haven't been involved in any matches. On the first tee, Tiger turned to Andrew and said, 'In case you don't know, this is a slight dogleg left.' Talk about putting him in his place.

On a later hole, they both hit great approach shots to within three feet. As they went to mark their balls, Andrew said, 'Good, good,' which means both players agree to halving the hole as they both were unlikely to miss such short putts. Tiger said, 'No, Andrew. I'll make mine and then stand here and watch to see if you can make yours.'

That kind of amusement aside, as a neutral I've never enjoyed the Ryder Cup. I used to joke to Raymond and Tiger that when it came to the Ryder Cup, I'd happily take a week off, thanks. The other thing I don't like about the tournament is that the compensation paid to the caddies is not equal to the work required for that week, which is more than a normal week on tour, usually involving two loops of 36 holes on the first two days of foursomes and four-balls and a fifth round in the singles. The caddies' pay is about the same as you'd get if your player finished fortieth in a PGA Tour event – but these are the best players in the world playing in a huge event, which creates massive revenue. Some of the money the organisers spend on trivial things like spas for the wives and girlfriends could be better spent on those who are actually working.

The lack of compensation for the players is offset by the fact they have the thrill of representing their country – or in the case of the Europeans, their continent – and to play for national pride one week every couple of years shouldn't be too much to ask. But for a Kiwi caddy, a bad payday and no sense of national pride makes it feel like there's no reason to be there.

Caddies also get dealt a raw deal in other ways. The last Cup I caddied in was at Celtic Manor in Wales in 2010. One of the ways the PGA of America makes money out of the event is to charter a plane for players and caddies and they sell the leftover seats to people who are prepared to pay vast sums for an exclusive package: fly with the players, stay at the same hotel, attend the tournament, get all the access. This year they sold too many tickets so what did they do? Offload the caddies. They had to ditch two of us and they decided to base the selection on reverse alphabetical order, which meant myself and Frank Williams, Stewart Cink's caddy, were jettisoned. If that didn't tip me over the edge in terms of respect for the Ryder Cup, the shambles of a week that followed certainly did.

The 2010 Cup was a complete disaster, not helped by the atrocious weather. I've seen plenty of golf courses cut up by bad weather but nothing as bad as this. It was green grass in the fairways surrounded by trails of mud where the galleries walked in their gumboots. If a player hit off the fairway he was in mud or water. The only place to get relief was to drop it back in the fairway.

It was raining from the get-go and in the first practice round we donned our wet-weather gear and trudged out, only to discover the so-called waterproofs weren't waterproof at all. It was a catastrophic mistake. The supplied golf bags also leaked.

The embarrassing solution was to buy £4000 of waterproof gear from the merchandising tent as well as getting new bags. When the players came back into the team room after getting drenched in practice, there were boxes of rain-suits lying all over the floor and everyone had to dig through them looking for something their size.

I didn't know it at the time, but this would be my last Ryder Cup and, in retrospect, the wet and miserable week was a fitting sign-off for an event that didn't exactly fill me with joy.

CHAPTER 6
TRUST

The 1999 PGA Championship win changed something in Tiger, lifted a weight of expectation. Gaining that elusive second major freed something in him and he accelerated his game to go on a peerless winning run, matched in modern times only by his own eight-win streak a few years later.

He won five tournaments on the trot, including two World Golf Championship events, at Akron, Ohio, and Valderrama, Spain, as well as joining his good mate Mark O'Meara for a win at the World Cup of Golf team event in Malaysia.

He started 2000 in similar fashion with three wins and three seconds. Such was his dominance that world number three Colin Montgomerie said, with an air of resignation, that whenever Tiger teed it up he felt he was playing for second place.

A second Masters victory and a third major title looked like a distinct possibility. But he started badly at Augusta National in 2000, with a drive that crashed into a tree and a first round tally of 75, his worst score of the year.

In the worst weather of the tournament he shot a third-round 68 to get back into contention but the damage had been done and, despite a closing 69, he had to settle for fifth behind Fiji's Vijay Singh.

To not win the Masters after being in such exceptional form was a huge letdown – and that disappointment was not helped by seeing Vijay Singh claim the green jacket. In my view, Vijay should never have been allowed to tee it up in such a prestigious tournament – in fact, I think he should have been banned from golf completely.

There's no doubt Vijay's a great player – he's won three major titles and has been number one in the world, but I have absolutely no respect for him. None.

Vijay and I shared similarly humble beginnings on the golf circuit, earning our stripes in Australia and Asia, before moving on to Europe and America.

Our paths crossed frequently and I was aware of his reputation in Australia in the early 1980s when his nickname was 'Telecom', thanks to his frequent requests to use the telephone at pro shops and clubhouses around Australia and New Zealand, asking to make a local call and then dialling Fiji. The club wouldn't find out until it got the bill and by then it was too late to chase him up. He left a trail of unpaid bills behind him and was banned from the Australasian PGA Tour over unpaid debts.

You can almost forgive that kind of thing – he was a young professional who possibly didn't know any better – but I cannot forgive him for his dishonesty at the Indonesia Open in 1985.

To this day, Vijay denies he altered his scorecard to make the cut at that tournament. I was caddying for Terry Gale and was rooming with my mate Irish, who was on the bag of Canadian Jim Rutledge, who played the first two rounds with Vijay.

On the bus heading to the course on Saturday morning, we were looking at the draw sheet for the day ahead when Jim turned to Irish and said, 'Didn't Vijay shoot 149?'

'Yeah, that's right.'

'Well, he's first off today on a score of 148.'

'No, he shot 149. He was five over.'

We marched up to the officials and Jim asked to see Vijay's scorecard. Back then there was no electronic scoring and he was handed the hard copy of the card. I could see clearly on the last hole where he'd made five to miss the cut by one shot that it had been changed to a four. Vijay's defence has always been that he took the fall for the son of an Indonesian VIP who made the change.

An investigation was launched but not before Irish had a chance to play a memorable prank on Vijay when his birthday fell during the Malaysian Open. Irish handed Vijay what looked like a nicely gift-wrapped jewellery box, only for Vijay to open it and find a box of erasers. Vijay was humiliated but I thought it was one of the cleverest pranks I'd seen.

Vijay was eventually suspended by the South East Asian Golf Federation (the Asian Tour as we know it now didn't exist back then) for two years but I believe he should have been disqualified from all golf. During his suspension, he famously honed his game while working as a club professional in Borneo.

He reappeared on the Safari Tour in Africa, worked his way onto the European Tour and eventually made it to the world stage.

Do I think he paid the penalty for cheating? No, not really. Getting suspended from playing in Asia was no big deal. Did he own up to his cheating? No. I think you have to man up and admit your mistakes. Vijay has vehemently denied he did anything wrong and I'm still angry to this day he hasn't admitted his error. If he'd said, 'I was young and desperate and made a mistake,' I could forgive him but he's constantly denied it. And now it's so far in the past it's almost impossible to tell the truth.

To make matters worse, at The Presidents Cup in 2000, between the International team and the United States, Vijay's caddy Paul Tesori turned up wearing a cap that had the words 'Tiger Who?' written on the back.

It was totally disrespectful, not in the spirit of the game and a ridiculous thing to do anyway – while Vijay had won the Masters that year, Tiger had won the other three majors on offer. Tiger was furious and from then on any time we came up against Vijay it was a grudge match – we both had something against him now. To Paul's credit he eventually apologised and said it was a joke that backfired, and

Tiger was OK with that, but Vijay Singh remains the least impressive character I've ever come across in golf.

———————

It's still hard for me to fathom how Tiger won the 2000 US Open at Pebble Beach by 15 shots. And I still have nightmares about the Sunday morning of that tournament, when I thought there was a possibility I was going to get him disqualified.

Going into the tournament, Tiger had the ball on a string. He was hitting it brilliantly and was highly motivated because he loved Pebble Beach – it was one of his favourite golf courses.

While he was hitting the ball well, there are plenty of other tournaments where I've seen him play better from tee to green. The supreme scoring was down to putting: he made every putt he looked at inside six feet. If you had asked me at the start of the week about his chances of not missing a single six-foot putt, I would have said 'impossible'. To do that on Pebble Beach's notoriously bumpy greens, where I expected he would get at least one bad bounce – impossible. And he could have won by more if you take out a triple bogey on the 3rd hole in the third round, which came completely out of the blue on Saturday afternoon.

To think, one of the greatest golf performances in modern times could have been ruined because of me.

We'd completed the 12th hole on Friday when we had to pack it in because of fog. We had to finish the second round on Saturday morning.

In this situation, most players would stash their gear in the locker room and come back the next day. But Tiger avoided the locker room – something he was often criticised for by other pros. He was concerned that if he left his gear in a storage room, someone would tamper with it or steal his precious putter, which was his prized possession.

Instead, he loved to call himself the car-park pro. He would quite happily play out of the back of his car – a nostalgic reminder of how he played growing up and when he was in college. He would have everything in his car – spare clubs, gloves, balls, rain gear. It was a self-deprecating game he played with himself as a way of remembering his humble beginnings.

At Pebble Beach, he was staying at the lodge on the golf course and didn't have a car so kept his clubs in his room. At the end of the Friday's play, I took his bag to his room. When I came back the next morning it was exactly where I left it so I picked it up and set off for the driving range, which was at the polo fields, some distance away. Because of the early restart, we didn't have time to go through the usual pre-round routine – to go to the driving range, back to the putting green and then out to the 13th tee, where our round would resume, would take too long so we skipped the putting green.

On the 13th tee, I put my hand in the bag to get a ball and was shocked to find only three in there. I knew there were six balls in there when we finished the previous night and as far as I knew the bag hadn't left Tiger's room.

I consoled myself with the fact we had to play only six holes to complete the second round and three balls should have been enough.

But when Tiger nonchalantly tossed one to a young child on the side of the 14th green, my heart was in my mouth. He threw it away because it had a scuff mark on it but, scuffed or not, I thought we might yet need it. Of course, the kid was over the moon he'd got Tiger Woods' golf ball, whereas I was thinking, 'How can I convince him to give it back to me?' I thought about promising to meet him with a box of balls behind the 18th green in exchange for the one in his hand but I figured it wouldn't be a good look if Tiger Woods' caddy took a ball off a happy kid. There'd be tears for sure.

I looked around the meagre gallery for someone from Tiger's entourage who could go back to his hotel room and get some more balls but it was so early that no one was out there, and I wasn't about to hand his room key to a member of the public.

Nervous as hell, I watched him play 15, 16 and 17, with the second-to-last ball, consoling myself that he was playing so well – his lead was out to seven or eight shots – he couldn't possibly lose a ball now.

On the par-5 18th, he asked, 'Do you like driver?'

He had no reason to think he shouldn't hit driver and was simply asking for confirmation, but I was nervous as hell because if he pulled it left the ball would end up in the ocean and there's an out of bounds down the right. The fairway is generous, though, and driver was the right choice. I had to say 'yes' but right through the shot I was thinking, 'Don't hook it – please don't hook it.' What does he do? Hooks it left onto the rocks down by the beach. A burst of swearing that got picked up by the TV microphones created a small scandal in its own right but nothing compared with the potential disgrace now facing his caddy.

'Give me another fucking ball,' he barked.

I was in a panic as I handed over the last ball.

I'd already put Tiger's driver back in the bag and had my hand on the head cover as a way of saying 'it's staying here', and suggested perhaps he'd like to take a 2-iron, play for safety, cop a double-bogey seven and still take a big lead into the third round.

'Take your fucking hand off that,' he said, referring to the driver.

I wasn't about to tell him that we'd run out of balls and that if he hooked this one into the water we were done. I made another brief, pitiful argument for the 2-iron, but he was hitting driver again, no matter what.

As he prepared to tee up his second ball, I started working out whether I'd have time to run the length of the 18th fairway, which is over 500 yards long, get up to the hotel room and back to the 18th tee in the five minutes you're allowed to look for a lost ball. Probably not.

I was thinking, if he hits it right and it goes out of bounds – which is possible if he overcompensates for the hooked first shot – at least I'll only have to run about 300 yards to retrieve the ball, but I knew that would look like amateur hour.

Finally, I thought if he doesn't keep this next ball in the golf course and gets disqualified because I failed to check how many balls were in the golf bag, my job is over. I was almost shaking as I waited for him to hit that final ball.

Safe. But even when he hit it onto the fairway the tension didn't recede because the second shot is not easy – there's still a chance it could end up in the ocean. My heart rate didn't return to normal until he'd reached the green and made a bogey to take a six-shot lead into the third round.

It was only much later I learned he wouldn't have been disqualified if we'd run out of balls. If I'd had to run back to the room for some spares he would have incurred a two-stroke penalty and if that had happened I'm sure he still would have won the tournament. But I'm also sure I would not have lived down the humiliation and would probably have been looking for a new job.

I couldn't bring myself to tell Tiger about the ball drought straight away – he was pretty hot at how he finished the round and we had to go back out later that day for the third round. I eventually told him after he'd won the tournament. By then he was relaxed enough to have a good laugh about it.

Where did those three balls go? Tiger often practised his putting in his hotel room and on this occasion he had taken out three balls to practise with and hadn't put them away. For whatever reason – perhaps the early wake-up call – I didn't notice them on the floor.

Another thing I'll remember about that tournament is what happened at the little par-3 7th during the final round. Miguel Angel Jimenez and Padraig Harrington were playing in front of us. It's the normal etiquette that players on the 7th green mark their balls and wait for the players on the 8th to tee off. There must have been some kind of delay because as Tiger was getting ready to putt, Miguel and Padraig were getting ready to hit.

I asked Tiger, 'Are you going to wait for them?'

'No,' he said. 'I'm going to make them stand there and watch me bury this putt.'

It was his way of making sure they knew who was going to win this tournament.

Tiger and I were standing on the fairway of the par-5 14th hole at St Andrews in 2000. The hole is famous for the huge bunker in front of the green, known as Hell Bunker. It's a difficult hole, with out of bounds on the right and a massive trap short of the green, which lives up to its name. You can't see the green from the fairway so if you're going to attack it with your second shot, you have to pick an object in the distance to aim at. I'd scouted the course and knew the line he wanted was the spire of a cathedral in the distance. There are a number of churches and castles in the town that stand out against the skyline and I was pointing at the one I wanted him to aim for, but it took some explanation. When Tiger hit his shot, the ball was like a missile aimed straight at the spire. He twirled his club and, without missing a beat, said, 'Is that the one you're talking about?'

That was typical of the way he played en route to winning his first British Open.

There are three golden rules to winning at St Andrews. Avoid the bunkers; perfect your lag putting because you have so many long putts on those big double greens; don't miss a green long because that's where all the trouble is – if you're going to make a mistake, make it short.

Our plan that week was focused around rule number one – avoid going into any of the incredibly difficult bunkers. Given the contours of the fairways, the number of blind shots, and the wind, the chances of avoiding the bunkers at St Andrews were pretty slim but that week he played up there with the best I've seen him play – it was a stellar performance of almost perfect shot execution. He didn't find a single bunker all week.

I love St Andrews because the way the course is played depends on how the wind blows. At face value it doesn't look like a difficult golf course but it has super-wide fairways and huge greens. Where the hole is placed on the green determines the best angle of approach but to put your drive in the optimal position can be determined by the wind direction.

A good caddy has to understand all the possible angles and then figure out a way to utilise them without landing in any of the bunkers, which the player cannot see from the tee. It becomes like a game of

THE LONG PUTT

AT THE 2000 BRITISH OPEN AT ST ANDREWS, the fairways were rock hard and rolling faster than the greens and one day, on the 9th hole, Tiger stunned the gallery by using his putter from about 85 yards and rolling the ball the whole distance to the green. He loved that aspect of links golf, where the game was designed to be played as much on the ground as in the air. Many people were stunned to see him putt it from such a distance but he'd practised that shot. The idea was to run the ball along the contours of the fairway as it was more controlled to do that than to hit a pitch shot. If you hit in the air it can land on an upslope and stop dead or it could catch a downslope and spring forward so putting – while it demanded a remarkably deft touch – was the best option.

chess or a boxing match, where you're looking for weaknesses in your opponent you can exploit. In this case, the opponent is the course and to beat it you need a wealth of information.

Every morning at the Open, I'm up at 4am to walk the course before play starts. When I'm out doing that I get an idea of who is going to play well based on which other caddies I see out there. A player whose caddy scouts the course has a much better chance of being in contention. It's the one golf course where a good caddy can make a tangible difference.

———

Outside of my own career, one of my greatest memories in golf is when Nick Faldo won the British Open in 1990 with my good friend Fanny Sunesson as his caddy. Fanny and I have been close friends since she started on the tour in 1987. I have so much respect for her – I thought I worked hard but she outworked me and had the harder job of being a woman in a male-dominated environment. Life was difficult for her in the early days as the caddy facilities were pretty poor to start with and set up for men. At Augusta back then, the toilets didn't even have doors on them and she had to share with the men – it wasn't a pretty scene.

Watching Fanny come up the last hole at St Andrews in 1990 was one of the coolest experiences I'd had in my life. It's the greatest amphitheatre in golf and seeing her cross the Swilcan Bridge and look up to the clubhouse – I thought, 'That's something I want to do one day.'

Ten years later, I was doing just that as Tiger won the Open by eight shots to claim a career grand slam. I'm not a spiritual or religious person but there was an almost mystical feeling to that walk. The day had been overcast and dull but as we approached the 18th green late in the day, the sun burst through and created an eerie light. It was surreal and emotional. This was the absolute pinnacle of my career. To win at St Andrews, which really is a caddy's course, was a dream come true.

———

Tiger's aim in life was to better Jack Nicklaus's record of 18 major titles. The stories are well-documented – the way he'd have pictures of Jack on his wall as inspiration. But there was another golfer who had a place on Tiger's childhood wall: Bob May.

When Bob found himself in a toe-to-toe battle with Tiger at the 2000 PGA Championship at Valhalla, it was painted as if a fairytale: the unheralded journeyman against an unbeatable giant of the game. Most fans and many in the media knew nothing about Bob May but Tiger was well aware of his abilities and when we were matched with him in the final round, the one thing he said to me was, 'This guy won't back down.'

Both grew up in southern California, with Bob a few years older. In the mid-1980s, Bob was the best junior golfer in the area and Tiger had his achievements pinned to his wall as motivation – he wanted to overtake Bob May as the most successful junior golfer in southern California.

I was familiar with Bob May because one of my mates, Max Cunningham, another Kiwi, was his regular caddy. But Max suffered from blood-pressure problems and was advised to stand down from caddying at the PGA as there was risk attached to being out in the heat and humidity of a Kentucky summer. For most other people, Bob May wasn't a household name.

The hype around this tournament was already turned up a notch because Tiger had won two majors in a row and if he could win here the media were already building the narrative that he could go to the Masters next year with a chance to hold all four major trophies at the same time.

But it was August, stinking hot, the end of a long season, and Valhalla wasn't a course Tiger had any advantage on. It wasn't a great golf course back then. It has improved over the years but in 2000 it wasn't a championship venue by any stretch of the imagination, and that factor brought a wider range of players into the mix.

Tiger played well but not great by the standards he'd set at St Andrews and Pebble Beach. He was fractionally out of sorts but had this knack for getting himself into contention on the back nine on Sunday. When he did that the intimidation factor would usually kick in.

Except this time, Bob wasn't buying into the fear factor. It was one of the few times during Tiger's dominant years when he met a rival who not only stood up to him but played better than him for most of the day. That final afternoon Bob matched everything Tiger could throw at him and more, shooting 66 to Tiger's 67. Late in the round, he led by two strokes and was still one up with two to go. It was punch for punch and the fans were starting to root for the underdog.

There were many times in my career when I knew what Tiger would do in certain situations. Standing on the 17th fairway in the final round of that tournament, with Tiger trailing by one shot, was one of those moments.

'What have we got, Stevie?' Tiger asked.

I'd measured it – 95 yards – and I knew if I told Tiger 95 yards he'd want a sand wedge but I wanted him to opt for his lob wedge as my gut told me that's the club he should hit.

'90 yards,' I said.

'Lob wedge.'

He hit it to two feet and made the birdie putt to draw level. My gut instinct on that hole had proven correct but if I'd given him the correct yardage we would have ended up in a debate over the club. It was easier to lie.

On the 18th, they both had birdie putts, with May going first and making a double-breaking downhiller to put all the pressure on Tiger, who had one of the most difficult putts in golf – eight feet, downhill and breaking considerably left to right – to force a playoff.

As Tiger lined up his putt, Bob motioned to shake my hand as if it was all over. I could tell he was expecting Tiger would miss. I could read the look on his face – it was full of anticipation that said, 'I'm going to win the PGA.'

I moved away from him and watched Tiger drain his putt to force the playoff. As we were headed to the 16th tee to start the three-hole playoff, I said to Tiger, 'What were you thinking when you made that putt?'

'Stevie,' he said, 'my mum could've made that putt. I'm Tiger Woods – I'm supposed to make that putt. It ain't no big deal, Stevie.'

In the playoff, Tiger made a birdie bomb on the first playoff hole and ran across the green waving his finger at the hole in one of the stranger celebrations I'd seen him do – but it was the putt that proved the difference and after matching pars with Bob on the final two holes, he became the first player since the great Ben Hogan in 1953 to win three major championships in the same year.

CHAPTER 7
THE GRAND SLAM

I f St Andrews is a caddy's course in terms of scouting, preparation
and vision, Augusta is the ultimate test of the teamwork between
player and caddy. Accuracy in club selection and decision-making
is paramount. Missing any of those convoluted greens leaves often
impossible chips.

I didn't think about the result around Augusta – it was all about
the process. On every hole I was completely focused on choosing the
right club off the tee, the right club into the green. I found it the most
mentally draining of all the tournaments – I could not afford to be
wrong on any yardages or any decisions.

The difficulty of Augusta's fast, undulating and unforgiving greens
is compounded by the fickle wind, especially around Amen Corner,
the lowest part of the course, where the wind swirls in all directions.
It's a hard, undulating walk, often made in the heat, and caddies have
to wear those ridiculous jumpsuits. At the end of Masters week, I'm
usually exhausted.

After the 2001 tournament, I wearily made my way back to my hotel
room but I don't know why I bothered – I was more exhausted than I'd
ever been but there was no possible way I was getting any sleep. I was
buzzing like a roomful of bees.

After Tiger had won the last three majors of 2000, all the talk in the golf world was whether he could win the Masters and be the first person to hold all four major trophies at the same time.

Golf's grand slam is a weird concept. It started in 1930 when Bobby Jones won the US and British amateur titles as well as the US Open and British Open against professionals. No one had achieved this feat let alone tried to describe it until one writer borrowed a bridge term – grand slam – to mark what Jones had achieved.

When the Masters came into existence in 1934, amateur events lost their prestige and the PGA Championship grew in status. The concept of a professional grand slam was non-existent, mainly because it was impossible to achieve it. Ben Hogan came closest in 1953 when he took out the Masters, US Open and British Open but he couldn't even line up in the PGA Championship as in those days it was on at the same time as the British Open!

Arnold Palmer was the first player to dream up a modern grand slam after he had won the 1960 Masters and US Open. As he headed to the British Open, he convinced the media to buy into the concept of a grand slam, albeit one he failed to deliver.

Tiger was the first person to hold the US Open, British Open and PGA Championship trophies at the same time and the main discussion was what to call it if he won the Masters as well. Was it a grand slam? Some called it a 'consecutive grand slam' but the phrase they landed on was 'Tiger Slam'.

Regardless of what it was called, Tiger was aiming for something I don't think anyone will replicate. In the golf world from August 2000 to April 2001, it was all anyone could talk about. It was constantly in the papers, on the news, in the golf magazines. Everyone was talking about it . . . everyone except Tiger.

Normally a chatterbox about what lay ahead of him at majors, Tiger fell surprisingly quiet on the subject of a fourth straight major win.

I knew his mind must have been whirling with information and he was probably bursting to talk about it, but shutting down and drawing a curtain around his thoughts was his way of dealing with the unrelenting media speculation and the fact that every press conference from August to April featured questions about this supposedly impossible goal.

His physical preparation remained the same. At the start of each year, his sole focus was on the Masters. He didn't care that much about results in the lead-in tournaments – it was all about that second week in April. It was about getting the right ball flight, being able to draw the ball at will and honing the shots he would need for Augusta. On the range, I'd often stop him and say I wanted to see a particular shot for a particular hole at Augusta and he was expected to execute it on cue.

One shot he practised more than any other was a big sweeping draw for the tee shot on the par-5 13th. If he could pull that shot off, he would have a short iron in his hand for his second and a good chance for an eagle. The irony was while he practised that shot over and over, he hardly ever used it because he found it hard to take that option under pressure. His conservative mentality at the majors would overrule the risk associated with it: too much draw and he would be in the hazard on the left and out of the hole. In contrast, if he pushed it right and ended up in the pine straw under the trees he could still make birdie. That comfort meant he found it difficult to commit to playing the very shot he'd been practising more than any other through the weeks prior.

In the final round at Augusta in 2001, he finally put that shot into play. His lead was two shots over Phil Mickelson and David Duval – two of his greatest rivals in that era – with another great competitor, Ernie Els, also in the mix. Tiger needed that kick. On the tee, he aimed 15 yards further right than normal and executed that much-practised swing to perfection, giving himself a short iron into the green and a relatively easy two-putt birdie that kept him two in front of his playing partner Mickelson, who also made birdie.

Duval briefly got level with Tiger but both he and Mickelson faltered at the 16th, each missing par putts of around six or seven feet.

We came down the 18th needing a par to win and Tiger absolutely ripped his drive – hitting it 330 yards and leaving himself a simple sand wedge from 75 yards, icing the cake with a 15-footer for birdie.

As great as Jack Nicklaus and Arnold Palmer and others had been, nobody had got close to winning four major championships in a row and to come up the 18th fairway knowing he was going to achieve the impossible and move into his own echelon was one of the most memorable experiences of my life.

The exhaustion and relief were there for everyone to see: Tiger pulling his cap down over his face to hide the raw emotion. I was as empty as he was. Those 72 holes were more mentally draining than usual. I was so aware of what winning meant. It was impossible not to think about the potential outcome and the history it would change – I couldn't turn that off and it made the fear of a wrong call all the more intense.

To me, that's one of the most mindboggling sporting achievements of all time – simply because there was so much pressure on him to do it. He knew it was a once-in-a-lifetime opportunity and he prepared for it without letting anything else influence him. He dealt with that pressure for months. And in the weeks leading up to the Masters, he'd won at Bay Hill and The Players Championship, which further intensified the burning focus on him. Tiger was persistently and intensely scrutinised but there was no other week in his golfing career where the spotlight was as zoned-in as it was that week at Augusta.

For me, it's the grand slam, not the Tiger Slam. Everyone has their own opinion and the purists will say the grand slam is holding all four in one year, but if you've got all four on your mantelpiece that's the grand slam in my eyes.

I was heading back to New Zealand the next day and that night I drove from Augusta to Atlanta, where my hotel room was little use to me – I was so wound up on the thrill of this win, I couldn't sleep a wink. Once I got home, I slept for a week.

————

The presentation ceremony for the Masters requires last year's winner to put the green jacket on the new champion. In this case, Vijay Singh had to help Tiger into his jacket. There were so many cameras searching for the perfect shot that Vijay and Tiger had to repeat the move a number of times. Jacket on, jacket off, jacket on, jacket off . . . the media and the Masters Committee understood the symbolism. They thought Tiger was going to be pulling that jacket on many more times. The course suited him so well and the talk was that if he ever passed Jack Nicklaus's record of 18 majors, he could win half of them at the Masters.

After all the talk of the Tiger Slam, the next topic of conversation was Tiger-proofing Augusta. No sooner had the 2001 Masters finished than they started changing the course. The fact Tiger had a ridiculously short shot of 75 yards into the 18th green typified the concerns – players, and not only Tiger, were hitting it so far they were in danger of overpowering the course.

Strategically, Augusta was laid out as well as any other course in the world, but a lot of fairway bunkers had become obsolete. Holes 1, 2, 5, 8 and 18 in particular had bunkers in great positions. But once players started hitting it 300 yards those holes became far simpler, far shorter.

In general, I agree with the changes they made. If today's players were navigating it as it was set up in 2000, they'd murder it. Lengthening needed to be done but there are some daunting holes out there now – the 11th is incredibly difficult unless you're one of the longer hitters in the game. On the 1st, because you can't carry the bunker on the right any more, it becomes a lot narrower off the tee. It's the same with 18 – for a period there Tiger stood on the tee knowing he could hit it straight over the bunker out towards the TV tower. He would aim for an area that's not even part of the golf course – a huge swathe of grass that's bounded by the 18th, 9th and 8th holes. It's an area where a lot of people walk and the grass was well trampled down so he aimed out that way, trying to cut it back into the fairway and knowing that if he mishit he still had an easy shot. Lengthening that hole brought the bunker back into play and it's now a much narrower drive – when people first go to that back tee and look up to the fairway, they let out an audible 'whoa!' because the chute they have to aim down is the width of a small country lane in New Zealand.

The only hole that changed for the worse was the 7th. It was one of the greatest little par-4s because you had so many options. The changes failed to improve it and it lost its character. The other thing I disliked was the addition of rough. Originally the course was designed without rough and the fairway would roll into pine straw and under trees. The addition of rough stops mishits rolling into the pine straw and makes the course easier – the rough is not long enough to cause the players problems but is just long enough to stop the ball rolling into tree trouble.

———————

Tiger had expended so much energy, devoted so much time, and practised so much for Augusta that it took its toll on him at the subsequent majors that year.

The US Open at Southern Hills brought a lot of focus on him because here it could be five majors in a row, but his effort wasn't the same as at Augusta, on a course that didn't suit his eye and presented several holes he didn't feel comfortable on.

Southern Hills finishes with an unusual 18th hole. A long par-4 plays uphill to a green that's the most severely sloped on the course. It's so steep officials leave the grass a little longer than on other greens to compensate. While it's a long hole, big hitters cannot use a driver off the tee because a creek runs across the middle of the fairway, forcing a lay-up and a long second shot into a difficult green. It's not a great finishing hole for a major championship, and due to its difficulty there was regularly a wait in the fairway.

I caddied there with Raymond Floyd at the 1994 PGA Championship. We were standing in the fairway waiting for Bob Estes, who was as slow as a turtle in those days. He's got better since but at the time he was incredibly slow. Raymond got so frustrated waiting he whistled at Bob to get a move on. I'd seen a few funny things in my day but nothing like this. There are plenty of professionals who play slowly but it's rare for a fellow pro to publicly point it out. I had told Tiger the story of Raymond's hurry-up whistle. So every time we came to that hole and had to wait, Tiger would threaten to whistle at the group ahead.

The difficulty of that 18th green was there for all to see when Stewart Cink three-putted from 15 feet at the 2001 US Open and missed a playoff by one shot, allowing Retief Goosen to beat Mark Brooks in an 18-hole playoff.

———————

There were not many rivals Tiger Woods had strong relationships with. He had close mates, such as Mark O'Meara and John Cook, but they were older and coming to the end of their careers and certainly weren't foes in the way Phil Mickelson, Vijay Singh and Ernie Els were.

But there was one player Tiger was fond of and had the utmost respect for: David Duval.

Some of the most enjoyable team events I've been involved in came when Tiger joined David in the two-man United States team at the World Cup of Golf, or when he was paired with him at the Ryder Cup. He loved playing with David. They were contrasting players in that David showed almost no emotion on the golf course and Tiger tended to let his passion overflow with bursts of temper that weren't to everyone's taste. But Tiger could see something of his own steely determination in David, who had a huge desire and killer instinct hidden behind a poker face.

Tiger was also intrigued by the way David transformed his body. When he first came on the scene, David was a weird shape: short, stocky, strong – quite an unusual physique for a golfer – and he managed to transform himself into a lean machine. The shame was he couldn't play quite as well with his new body shape. He had some other issues in his personal life and quickly fell out of the upper echelon after being right there as Tiger's main rival. He even held the world-number-one ranking for a period.

As his career climbed and dipped like a rollercoaster ride, his body followed suit, changing shape again back towards what he was originally like. But through all that I continued to admire David because he kept trying and didn't doubt he was going to come back. Incredibly, he had a fleeting moment back in the spotlight when he came from nowhere to contend at the 2008 US Open at Bethpage Black. Suddenly, he was right there on the back nine . . . and just as quickly his challenge faded and he was gone again.

In the early part of the twenty-first century, David and Phil Mickelson vied for the tag as the 'best player never to win a major'. If that bugged David he didn't let it show and answered questions about competing against Tiger by saying it would make any major victory more special. The shame is that he had that special feeling only once, at the 2001 British Open.

Tiger was motivated solely by majors and his greatest rivalry was with Mickelson. When Phil started winning majors, it spurred Tiger to win another one, but when David won the British Open in 2001 Tiger was genuinely thrilled for him. He felt David was a deserved winner and there was no better event for him to win because he had all the shots, loved links golf and prepared himself well, which few Americans do when they go to Britain. It takes some time to get accustomed to the wind, hitting off the hard ground, hitting the low shots – David did all that and Tiger was rapt for him.

———————

The year following Tiger's historic Masters win, I was proud to welcome him to my home course in New Zealand – where I'd started out earning $2 a round caddying for my dad's friends. It was quite a homecoming.

Tiger and I stood on the 10th tee at Paraparaumu Beach golf course on a sunny Tuesday in January. The fairway before us was lined with people from tee to green.

I felt an incredible sense of accomplishment. All I could picture was how many times I'd walked down that fairway caddying for members; how many hours I'd spent in that drain on the left, squelching through the mud looking for golf balls, and here I was on the tee next to the world's best player on a perfect afternoon. That practice day ahead of the 2002 New Zealand Open is forever etched in my memory. It was the

MY TOP 10 COURSES

1. **ST ANDREWS, SCOTLAND:** No course offers you the variety of options that St Andrews does — all dependent on the wind direction. Architecturally brilliant.

2. **AUGUSTA, US:** No other course puts as much pressure on a caddy in terms of club selection.

3. **KINGSTON HEATH, AUSTRALIA:** Considerably shorter than many championship venues, it makes up for a lack of length with superb greens where hole locations can be difficult to get close to.

4. **ROYAL MELBOURNE, AUSTRALIA:** A sand-belt gem with one of the world's best par-3s — the 5th hole on the composite course.

5. **PINEHURST NO. 2, US:** Following the renovation ahead of the 2014 US Open, this masterpiece requires pinpoint accuracy from tee to green.

6. **ROYAL COUNTY DOWN, IRELAND:** Fantastic blind shots and superb bunkering.

7. **OAKMONT, US:** Perhaps the hardest course I've seen. It challenges you on every hole — there is no let-up.

8. **SHINNECOCK HILLS, US:** Best links-style course in North America — you must have your A-game to do well here.

9. **NEW SOUTH WALES, AUSTRALIA:** You haven't played in the wind until you've played at NSW.

10. **PARAPARAUMU BEACH, NEW ZEALAND:** Has the best collection of par-3s you'll find. If it was my last day of golf, this would be the venue.

pinnacle of the week and it slowly slid downhill from there.

Every time I started working for a player I would say to them, 'If you win a major championship when I'm caddying for you, I'd love for you to come and play in the New Zealand Open.'

As a caddy, that was the one tournament I'd wanted to win all my life but never did. The closest I came was with Terry Gale, who was runner-up to Corey Pavin in 1984.

The ball got rolling on a plan to play in the New Zealand Open after Tiger won the PGA Championship in 1999.

I'd shared my dream with Allan James, my butcher friend – he'd met Tiger at the US Open in 2000 at Pebble Beach – so he and Alan McKay, the resident professional at Paraparaumu, started thinking about a way to get Tiger down to New Zealand. At the same time John Freer, who was a manager at the Hillary Commission (now known as Sport New Zealand), and Wellington golf manager Owen Williams were plotting a way to get the New Zealand Open sanctioned as a European Tour event. When all four came together they formed a syndicate called Plus Fore, which attempted to raise the multi-million-dollar appearance fee for Tiger to play overseas plus other costs, such as increased prize money for the Open.

They did all the work in New Zealand, but the project also consumed a lot of my time in 2001. The main thing was to find a suitable date that took into account the Australasian and PGA tour schedules.

We aimed for February 2002 – the New Zealand summer weather is more settled then – but had to settle for January. Tiger could fly from Hawaii where he was scheduled to play the season-opening tournament reserved for players who had won an event the year before. With his own plane, it was a pretty easy jump down to New Zealand.

Nothing in my life had offered as much anticipation as this. It was the realisation of a dream I'd wanted to achieve with Greg Norman and Raymond Floyd but neither had been able to win a major when I was caddying for them.

For a number of reasons, however, one of the most anticipated weeks in my life had turned into a damp squib.

In the background a lot of tinkering happened that I had no control over. The Plus Fore group struggled to get the money needed and at one stage the whole thing was destined to collapse. Mark Steinberg, Tiger's manager, was steadfast with his deadline for the money to be paid and the contract drawn up. The exchange rate at the time meant the syndicate had to raise more money than they first expected and they were still considerably short as D-Day approached.

A mad scramble resulted in some extra backers coming in but the price was a loss of control for Plus Fore. In many ways, it had become too big for Plus Fore to manage anyway and they needed financial experts involved. The fact people I knew and trusted had lost control of the event took the gloss off it for me – especially when they were criticised for ticket prices being too high and security being over the top.

The other thing I couldn't control was the weather – we'd wanted to hold the tournament the following month when the weather would be at its best – but circumstances dictated it had to be held in January and the rain was unrelenting.

The entire summer had been bad, leaving the greens in poor condition. The one thing Tiger hated above all else was playing on bumpy greens. At Paraparaumu, they were spongy and soft, and after that sunny Tuesday the weather was ratshit and the condition of the greens worsened by the day.

Tiger loved the course. He thought the collection of par-3s were among the best he'd seen. My main wish was that the greens had been better, the weather had been kinder and money hadn't assumed so much importance – this should have been a celebration of golf because it was probably the one and only time this guy was going to be in New Zealand to play. It was a chance to promote golf, to give people a chance to see this global star at the peak of his career and grow the game of golf, but everything became about money and to me that was sad. So when I look back, it wasn't quite the highlight I was anticipating.

One of the many qualities I admired about Tiger was that when he was getting paid to play he gave it 100 per cent no matter how important the tournament was. He prided himself on putting on a good show for people who had paid for him to be there and I cannot think of a tournament where he got an appearance fee and didn't finish inside the top 10.

But no matter how hard he tried, I could see how he hated putting on those Paraparaumu greens – he did his absolute best. He had a four-putt on one hole and throughout the tournament I could read his mind – he knew it was my home club and I was incredibly proud of it so there's no way he was going to say anything bad, but I could feel his frustration as he battled into seventh place.

Despite the negatives, this was still a celebratory homecoming for me after I'd left as a 15-year-old more than 20 years earlier. I'd quit school against the wishes of my parents and set off to forge a career as a caddy without the slightest idea that it was even possible. And here I was, returning with the world's best player to a kind of hero's welcome I'd never imagined.

CHAPTER 8
THE BIG WET

The year of the big wet started at Paraparaumu in January 2002 and continued through the major tournaments.

Weather is a persistent problem for golf but what happened at the 2002 Masters at Augusta was a disgrace in terms of how inept the officials were. The rain was so bad on the Friday that play was suspended and we had to come back on Saturday morning to complete our second round.

Sometimes you get a break and we had one that wet Friday. Tiger had hit his tee shot on the 10th when play was called off. As he approached his ball to mark it, he found a huge clump of mud on it. Being able to lift that ball, clean it and replace it the next day was a huge benefit. When the ball's got mud on it you simply don't know how it's going to fly. There's a rule of thumb that says if the mud is on the right it will squirt left and vice versa, but it's hard to make the best possible shot – there's just no certainty over how much it will veer off course so the player cannot trust his swing. In this case, it was a pretty big clump of mud and the 10th at Augusta is hard enough without having a mud-ball to contend with. At that stage, he was over par for the round, one under for the tournament, and a long way behind Vijay Singh, the clubhouse leader. To come back on Saturday with the bonus of a clean ball changed his whole mood.

That Saturday, we played 26 holes and Tiger was 10 under par on the day, including a six-under 66 in his second round. He galloped from eight shots behind the leader to a tie for first at 11 under par. And he did that under the most ludicrous circumstances possible.

A lot of what follows has not been written about because people don't want to get offside with those who run the Masters, but what happened that Saturday was a debacle. Normally the third round of the Masters would be played in pairs and everyone would start off the first tee. Because the second round had been delayed, the committee decided to play in groups of three and to start off two tees – the first and 10th. There's nothing wrong with that. The problem was the officials didn't seem to have any idea who was teeing off when and from where.

Confusion reigned – there were no announcements and no one in the scoring hut knew what the tee times were. The message finally came through that we'd be playing in threesomes instead of the usual pairs but the tee times were still not set. Officials started walking around asking players what score they were on. On the putting green they were asking people, 'What's your score? . . . What did you shoot?' Once they had found three people on the same score they would say, 'Right: you, you and you go off together from the 10th tee; you, you and you on the first.' It was incomprehensible they didn't have a plan of any sort in place. They had no idea.

At most normal tournaments, in a situation like this, you're clearly advised of what's going to happen. At Augusta they conduct themselves differently but even by their standards this was completely random. They didn't have a computer printout of the scores – they were finding players as they stumbled across them and rounding them up like cattle. OK, it's the Masters and you know they do their own thing – and that you have to do what they say – but this was absurd.

In my view, the only reason they needed two tee starts in threesomes was because they were so disorganised in the first place. They could have played threesomes off one tee if they'd had a plan, but it was evident they had no strategy.

A measure of how much rain fell was the fact that play had to be suspended at all – Augusta drains better than any course in the world and has an underground vacuum system to dry the greens out, but all their technology couldn't cope with this amount of water.

The other thing that week was the smell. The place stunk like an abattoir. The stench was almost overwhelming. I'm not sure what caused it – they were forced to scatter a lot of pine straw where the patrons walked to stop the grass areas turning into a mud bath. I think they also put down fertiliser and the combination of mud, pine straw and fertiliser produced a horrendous smell.

Through all this and despite the so-called Tiger-proofing of the course, Tiger won his third green jacket and was only the third player to win back-to-back titles after Jack Nicklaus and Nick Faldo.

———

Tiger Woods called Corey Pavin's 2002 performance in the US Open at Bethpage Black one of the best in major golf history – yet hardly anyone noticed.

There was huge anticipation about the US Open going to Bethpage Black, a public golf course in New York. It was a course we'd all read about but not many of us had seen. It was famous for the fact that people would sleep in the parking lot to be at the front of the queue to get a tee time in the morning. With great facilities and reasonable green fees it was in high demand. There was a certain intrigue about going there to play a US Open, especially as it was going to be the longest course in US Open history.

Not only was it formidable in length, the weather was terrible – it rained all week, which meant the short hitters had almost no chance.

In 2002 Tiger was still one of the big bombers on tour. He was young and injuries hadn't yet slowed him down. Along with John Daly, who was stupidly long, he was often at the head of the field in the driving distance statistics.

At the other end was Corey, a superb wedge player and excellent putter but one of the shortest hitters in the game. At 42, slightly built and with a golf game from another era, Corey was absolutely overwhelmed by this course. He didn't even hit it far enough to reach some fairways. On the 10th, it was a carry of 240 yards over deep rough to put the ball in play – he couldn't hit it that far on the fly so he aimed down the 11th fairway. On another hole he aimed to hit it down the narrow walkway players used to get from the tee to the fairway. And when he did get it in play, he was forced to hit fairway woods into most of the par-4s.

He shot 74-75 to make the cut. As we walked off, Tiger said, 'We might have witnessed one of the greatest performances in US Open history.'

Corey thought it was ridiculous – short hitters will gripe when the course is long, that's to be expected, but in this case he was justified. And while he was unhappy about how it was forcing him to play, he tried his absolute best and earned Tiger's utmost respect.

Another chapter in the burgeoning rivalry between Tiger and Sergio Garcia played out in New York. Sergio was going through a weird phase where he took an inordinate amount of time to prepare for his shots. He would stand over the ball for what felt like an age, all the time gripping and regripping the club. Fans in New York are an unforgiving mob and don't tend to follow the usual decorum associated with golf – they absolutely hounded him about this stalled swing, counting 'one . . . two . . . three' every time he got ready to play.

The fans were also heckling him about his girlfriend at the time, tennis star Martina Hingis, and some of the jibes were pretty ripe – but that's New York. They were yelling rubbish at Tiger too, but he blanked them out and got on with it.

Sergio, however, couldn't block it out, and while I felt sorry for him for having to endure all this he didn't help himself by giving the finger to one heckler and then getting into a verbal altercation with another. He dug a bigger hole for himself in the New York mud by complaining about the weather.

After the first round he was right on Tiger's tail, shooting 68 to Tiger's 67, but he had to go out in the worst of the wet conditions on Friday afternoon when he shot a miserable 74 to fall seven shots behind Tiger, who had a 68 in more tolerable, but still bad, weather that morning.

Whereas Sergio should have knuckled down to his work on all fronts, he said after his round that if Tiger had been out in the ghastly afternoon weather, officials would have called off play. Utter nonsense.

To his credit, Sergio battled back in the third round, despite the crowd making noises like a baby crying, shot 67, and earned his place in the final group with Tiger on Sunday. When Tiger got to the locker room on Saturday night, he found a note from Sergio, apologising for his foolish remarks on Friday. Given they were set to play together in the final round and Sergio had already felt the wrath of Tiger, it's no surprise he took a remorseful approach.

The crowd seemed to appreciate Sergio's fighting qualities from Saturday and were more forgiving on Sunday – maybe they were hoping for a challenger to come after Tiger, but it wasn't going to be Sergio: his fight evaporated and Tiger won by three shots from Phil Mickelson.

Once again, talk of a grand slam was on the cards and more than that – what was once a half-joke about stopping Tiger turned into an actual question: How *do* you stop Tiger? He had won seven of the past 11 majors, which was a mind-boggling statistic.

––––––––––

The third day of the 2002 British Open dawned beautifully fine and I started the day running in brilliant sunshine along Gullane Beach on the east coast of Scotland. It was so warm I had my shirt off.

It felt like it was going to be a good day at Muirfield. Tiger was right where he wanted to be, two off the pace on a crowded British Open leaderboard. The chance to replicate what Ben Hogan did almost 50 years earlier and win the first three majors of the year was possible.

By Saturday afternoon the morning run on the beach was completely forgotten – it was the coldest I had ever been in my life.

I could blame myself for the disastrous 10-over-par 81, Tiger's worst score in a major at that point, but the forecast gave no indication the day was going to turn so badly.

We simply weren't prepared for the arctic blast that swept across Muirfield. If I'd known the weather was going to get that bad, I would have packed Tiger's golf bag with extra towels, hand-warmers, full rain-suits – but we didn't even have a wet-weather glove.

It was a freak thing. This weather came from nowhere, but that's the British Open – nature can take its toll in the blink of an eye. The fact we stayed out there and had to battle through this bone-chilling weather put paid to Sergio's suggestion that Tiger got preferential treatment. If you were playing an ordinary round of golf you wouldn't contemplate going out in that weather, but we got caught in it and there was no reason to come in – there was no lightning, the greens were not under water – so we had to play through it.

It was the coldest I've been on a golf course. My hands were frozen stiff and I couldn't even hold a pencil. When I'm doing yardages, I'm meticulous in writing down the numbers to make sure there's no mistake, but I couldn't even turn the page of the yardage book – I could barely operate.

Tiger wasn't the only one caught in this foul weather but those with slightly later tee times were able to prepare better and had less time in the worst of it. Tiger's score reflected how bad the conditions were – and he's one of the best bad-weather players I've seen. He loves the challenge of playing in tough conditions – freezing cold or oppressive heat – as he knows it will get on top of others and prides himself on being able to handle it better than anyone else.

I was never one to worry much about the conditions. A wet day is when a caddy earns his money because you need three hands. You've got to keep the clubs dry, keep the player dry, dry off the grips, hold the umbrella – you forget about your own needs and do all within your power to keep your player equipped and on task. But to do all that properly you need the right gear in your bag and I was caught out that day.

Tiger showed what could have been possible when he shot a 65 in the final round but it was not enough and the grand slam dream of 2002 was over.

The feeling at the end of the 2002 PGA Championship was unusual. For the first time, Tiger finished runner-up in a major. In the back of his mind he knew it was inevitable – he was intimately acquainted with Jack Nicklaus's record and knew that for all of his 18 wins, he was second 19 times in majors. Still, it was a strange feeling, especially as the tournament had finished in such an emotional fashion.

One of the reasons golf is so great is every once in a while a completely unexpected major winner comes along. In my time, I've seen guys like Ben Curtis, Shaun Micheel, Todd Hamilton, YE Yang – even fellow Kiwi Michael Campbell – have the best week of their life when it matters most.

Joining the list of improbable champions in 2002 was Rich Beem. When I see players like Beem and think about the disparity between them and Tiger in terms of how they strike a ball, I'm usually convinced their swing won't hold up over 72 holes of major championship golf. The pressure at majors is a quantum leap from ordinary tour events and more often than not these guys don't hold on.

Rich Beem was a happy-go-lucky character who had been a used car salesman. He seemed to have a lot of fun playing the game. He withstood the pressure of Tiger charging at him over the final four holes at Hazeltine. Tiger made four birdies on the trot to make an improbable chase nearly possible – but ended up one shot short.

————

A year earlier, at the end of the 2001 PGA Championship, where David Toms denied Phil Mickelson yet another major, Tiger told me he was thinking of ending one of the longest relationships of his career.

Butch Harmon had coached Tiger since he was 16 but in late 2001 he was starting to get on Tiger's nerves. To me, there's no question Butch has the best eyes in golf, even to this day. He's uncomplicated and doesn't have all this fancy equipment like TrackMan. He does it by eye and has a tremendous ability to help a player by simply looking at him.

Tiger was playing so well and was in such control of his game that it seemed like a strange move to part ways with Butch. But it wasn't Butch's coaching ability that started to rankle – it was what he did when he wasn't coaching Tiger.

As the coach of the world's best player, Butch had become famous in his own right and in Tiger's eyes he got a bit carried away with it. Tiger is an extremely private person and Butch is the opposite – he's open and voluble and talked a lot in public about coaching Tiger. He didn't breach any confidences but he used Tiger's name in conversations and this irritated Tiger immensely.

Tiger would hear him on TV saying, 'When I was with Tiger . . . When I did this with Tiger . . . I was practising with Tiger the other day . . .' Tiger felt Butch was trading on his name, taking advantage of their association. It wasn't professional enough for Tiger's liking. I could understand the reasoning but it was also a difficult decision. Butch had been with him since his amateur days and had taught him a lot about the tour, a lot about life. He was a mentor to him as well as a coach and it was difficult to part ways but that's what Tiger felt he needed to do.

The problem was he didn't tell Butch any of this.

A normal person would have talked to Butch, explained that his actions weren't appropriate, said, 'This is how I like things done, this is not how I like things done.' But Tiger is not a normal person when it comes to relationships. His default mode is to cut all communication and avoid any conflict when he gets annoyed with someone. If he thought you'd said something or done something inappropriate, his reaction was to put the mute on.

Often this shut-down mode was like a game – and he did it to me at times – to see how long you could tolerate dealing with a stone wall. Butch got the silent treatment for about a year and took quite a while to realise this was more than a game.

Once Butch cottoned on, he was quick to approach Tiger and have it out with him and they formally parted ways in August 2002.

Tiger is now onto his fourth coach, Chris Como, after stints with

Butch, Hank Haney and Sean Foley. I think he's changed trains too many times and now instead of being the driver he's the ticket collector.

Reading about some of the shots he hit at The Players Championship in 2015, for example, it sounds as if they were godawful shots. He hit the trees off the 1st tee – to do that requires the quickest of quick hooks. On the 8th he hit so far short of the hole he was in the creek. I can't even picture where that creek is. It's so far short of the green, it's not even in the yardage book and he hit there.

It became fully apparent to me just how bad Tiger's struggles had become when I went back to caddy for Adam Scott in 2015.

At St Andrews in the British Open, Tiger's tee shot on the 1st hole was so fat he left a huge divot. That's the easiest tee shot in golf – it's just an iron to a massive fairway. So to hit it fat – behind the ball – is an indication of the mental battle he was fighting. When I got to the first tee with Adam I turned to Ivor Robson, the starter, pointed at the gouged turf and said, 'There's no doubt whose divot that is.'

Tiger had every faith in Butch's coaching ability and right now, in my opinion, if he wants to get his game back on track he needs to go back to Butch, who will make a rescue plan quicker than anyone else and create a swing process that's easy for Tiger to implement. Some of these swing changes he's been through recently are not straightforward to put into practice, but I think Butch could put a plan in place that Tiger could instantly get comfortable with and which would take his swing back to his natural move.

Tiger had huge success with Hank Haney, you cannot deny that, and again with Sean Foley, but each time he's gone a little bit further away from his natural technique to the point now that he's gone too far. If he genuinely wants to break Nicklaus's record, he needs to start over and go back to Butch – that is the only way I can see him winning 19 majors.

But in that transition period after he and Butch parted ways in 2002, Tiger had the skill to manage his own swing. He would rely on his mates like Mark O'Meara and John Cook and a couple of other buddies he played with at his Isleworth club. He'd ask them, 'Can you take a look at this?' and use their feedback to work on his swing.

I was a pseudo-coach on the odd occasion when I would say, 'You need to do this,' or, 'Try that.' When I caddy for someone for long enough I build a mental picture of how they swing a golf club and I can keep track of the intricate moves that can make a difference or act as a quick fix.

Golf is a game of confidence and if I could come up with one thing that might be a remedy to give Tiger some confidence, I would offer it up. It might be what Tiger would call a 'Band-Aid fix', but it would get the job done. There would be times on the range before a round when he wasn't hitting it that well and I'd be thinking of all the keywords I'd said before, or he's said himself, that could get him through that day or week.

A lot of people question why he rebuilt his golf swing three or four times when he was playing better than anyone else, but I admired him for that. He was relentless in his quest to improve. Even when, under Butch, he was playing better than anyone in the history of the game, he still felt like he needed to change. It takes an enormous amount of self-discipline to modify a swing, and each time he altered something there was a down-spiral. To live through that takes a lot of mental toughness and self-belief.

Tiger is stubbornly determined and at some point after splitting with Butch he decided he could go it alone without a coach. He believed in his own understanding of swing mechanics and what worked for him, what his pitfalls were, his checkpoints, and what he needed to look for when he lost his internal compass. And because he's so stubborn, he will stick with a technique or method for much longer than most people would. If he decides to do something, he will give it time – he won't force the issue. He's prepared to wait and not let frustration get the better of him. As a result of this determination, he was prepared to forego a swing mechanic for the next two years and in retrospect it's no surprise his game suffered.

CHAPTER 9
TAKING THE MICK OUT OF PHIL

Yes, I once called Phil Mickelson a 'prick'.

Twice, actually.

Once at a dinner in 2008 in New Plymouth, a regional town in New Zealand, which made it into the news, and again when a reporter asked me to verify that I had in fact used that word.

One thing about me: I tell the truth. I could have denied making the comment at the charity function in New Plymouth but that would have been lying.

Phil and I don't get on. That's the bottom line. Some of Tiger's angst with Phil has rubbed off on me but I have my own reasons for not sending him Christmas cards.

Tiger's rivalry with Phil is well documented and much of it hinges around an interview Phil did with *Golf Magazine* in 2003. When asked about his relationship with Tiger, Phil said, 'In my mind, Tiger and I don't have issues between us . . . Well, maybe one. He hates that I can fly it past him now [off the tee]. He has a faster swing speed than I do, but he has inferior equipment. Tiger is the only player who is good enough to overcome the equipment he's stuck with.'

Tiger had endorsed Nike since turning pro but had only switched to Nike clubs – bar his putter – in 2002, and at that point in his career had won two majors with the Nike clubs and six majors with the Nike ball.

This was a huge story because equipment deals in golf are worth vast sums of money. Phil's comments infuriated Tiger because he had a vested interest in Nike and had been involved in the research and design of the clubs and balls. It was not like he was handed clubs and told, 'Here, use these.' He was part of the process.

The statement was certainly detrimental to Nike but to be fair to Phil he was trying to make a valid point – he just failed to express it the right way. Nike, as a new company in the golf industry, was starting from scratch and up against established companies that have decades of research and development behind them, so it of course took some time for them produce clubs exactly to Tiger's liking, especially the putter.

All the same, Tiger had an incredible run when he switched to Nike. It's hard to say he could have done any better, but I often wondered if he had kept playing Titleist whether that domination could have been even greater. There's long been a stigma attached to Nike – a lot of players use Nike equipment only for short periods before switching back to a more established brand. There was lots of talk on tour about players who signed to Nike and then turned their back on the 'swoosh' – Lucas Glover and Trevor Immelman are two major winners who ditched Nike.

Even when Rory McIlroy first added Nike's swoosh to his gear, there was no question he struggled as he sought to fine-tune his new equipment.

Titleist produces the number-one ball in golf, hands down. When Tiger first started using the Nike ball, there was lots of debate about how it was a ball not available to the public and that got people asking questions about its legality. He even had a stash of balls stolen from a golf course one day.

It was certainly legal – there's no way Tiger would dream of playing with non-conforming equipment. And there was nothing overly special about it, either. It suited his club speed and the spin he put on the ball, which was unlike anything any other player since Greg Norman could generate. People were regularly asking me for Tiger's golf balls – even other caddies – and I had no problem giving these balls away because he wasn't hiding anything.

But, beyond his comments about Tiger's association with Nike, I had my own reasons for disliking Phil Mickelson. The feeling was mutual.

I admire the guy as a player but there's no doubt he has rubbed me up the wrong way. My problem is that he thinks he knows everything. He lords over people – he once tried to tell me the rules of cricket for crying out loud!

Phil is also a legendary gambler. At the 2002 Ryder Cup, I had to take some gear back to the locker room before going out to watch the rest of the team in action and, to my disbelief, there was Phil sitting in the locker room on his own, putting bets on American football when he should have been out supporting his teammates – a no-no in my eyes.

His dislike of me probably dates back to the 2005 Ford Championship at Doral.

In 2004, Tiger was playing in Dubai. We were in the gym one morning watching the golf from America where the Ford Championship was being played. Among the prizes for the winner was a Ford GT sports car.

'What are we doing here in Dubai?' I asked Tiger. 'That course at Doral is tailor-made for you. We should go there next year so you can win that Ford GT, which you'll have to give to me because you're sponsored by Buick.'

The following year Tiger was in a dogfight with Phil for the Ford Championship title. It came down to the last hole with Phil having to make an impossible chip to force a playoff, which he almost pulled off.

After the presentation, I was standing by the scorer's hut and as Tiger walked past he threw me the keys to the Ford GT, a car which I've still got to this day – it's a valuable collector's item.

A couple of weeks later I ran into Phil, who was a bit larger than he is now, and I said, 'Sorry about that Ford GT but it's lucky you didn't win it – you wouldn't have been able to fit in it.'

My animosity towards Phil came back to bite me in the bum in

December 2008 when I made those injudicious comments about him at that charity dinner in New Plymouth. But there was more to the story than a simple rant at a dinner. It harks back to the Ryder Cup in 2004, when United States captain Hal Sutton made the grievous mistake of pairing Tiger and Phil together at Oakland Hills.

This pairing made no sense to anybody whatsoever. In the Ryder Cup there has to be chemistry between players and these two were like oil and water. They stood on opposite sides of the tee and made zero effort to communicate with each other. It was beyond awkward.

Remarkably, despite the tension and having lost to Colin Montgomerie and Padraig Harrington in their morning match, Tiger and Phil were all square with Darren Clarke and Lee Westwood with one hole to play in the afternoon foursomes, where players take alternate shots.

On the 18th, it was Phil's tee shot and Tiger was set to play the second shot. In these situations the players would normally have a strategy planned out beforehand, so whoever is on the tee would try to hit the ball to a position that best suited his partner. Since these two weren't talking to each other there was no strategy in play. Tiger and I positioned ourselves slightly forward of the tee and waited for Phil to play. I thought the best shot for him off the tee was either an iron short of the bunkers or a driver over the bunkers. The only club he shouldn't hit was a 3-wood.

When I saw what club he had chosen, I said to Tiger, 'Phil's got three-wood – that's probably not the best choice. Why don't you go over and have a chat to him?'

'I'm not going over there,' Tiger said. 'If you think it's the wrong club, why don't you go over and tell him?'

'I'm not going back there to say anything to that prick.'

What I didn't know was that someone in the gallery was listening to our conversation. What's more he was from New Zealand, but I only learned that four years later when he turned up at this charity dinner and started baiting me about the incident. He'd heard exactly what I'd said.

A roomful of people now knew I'd called Phil Mickelson a prick.

I didn't try to downplay it or pretend it didn't happen, as that's not what you do in these situations – there's no point in making a fuss and it was supposed to be a fun event. But a reporter from the *Taranaki Daily News*, a regional New Zealand newspaper, was there and included the Mickelson comment in a feature about me that appeared in their Saturday edition.

To be fair to the newspaper, the line was just that – a single line – well down the story. They didn't make a big drama of it and probably had it in context. And there it might have ended . . . except that on the other side of the world a leading golf journalist must have had a Google alert set up for anything to do with Tiger and suddenly my comment was making headlines on the *Guardian* website in Britain. All hell broke loose.

When New Zealand's national weekend newspaper, the *Sunday Star-Times*, rang on Saturday morning to confirm the story, I couldn't deny it but tried to explain why I said it. All that happened was that I embellished the original story – and again it took an instant journey around the world's news websites.

I called Phil and apologised to him. He said he understood – that he's been in the same situation speaking to a room full of people and could see how it happened. We cleared the air and accepted that we'd never be best of mates. After I apologised, we then spent about 30 minutes discussing how he could improve his relationship with Tiger, something I found highly amusing.

It was some surprise, then, that when I arrived in the United States for Tiger's first tournament of 2009 – the World Match Play Championship in early March at Dove Mountain in Arizona – Phil was waiting for me and put me on the spot in front of a TV crew.

It was Tiger's comeback tournament following knee surgery in 2008. We knew there was going to be a lot of media interest and decided to get out on the course with the birds on Tuesday morning for practice. Besides, Tiger always wanted to have his practice rounds at daybreak on the Tuesday and Wednesday before a tournament. As soon as the sun came up, we were off. In my first few years with Tiger, no one else was doing that and it was great fun to play the golf course with no marshals, no spectators and no other players. These days if you turn up at 6:30am, you have to queue up to get on the course – it's so hard to be the first one out and you're never alone.

On this day, we were in the car park at 5:30am when I noticed Phil was there too, which is highly unusual for him. As I got Tiger's bag out of the car, Phil came over and acted in a manner that suggested we hadn't had that one-on-one conversation over the phone.

'Are we good?' he asked. He did all this as a TV crew filmed the interaction. For both Phil and a TV crew to be there, at 5:30am, seemed more than a coincidence.

CHAPTER 10
TALKING BACK

R ight from the get-go, Tiger and I seemed to click – especially on the golf course. We made good decisions and the banter was great.

As Tiger once put it in a press conference: 'Stevie is really positive and upbeat – he knows exactly what buttons to push to get me going. What those buttons are . . . are between Stevie and myself. He has the gall to tell me what he thinks when I'm feeling uneasy about a club and he's not afraid to get in my face, which is nice – he has a lot of confidence in his ability as a caddy, which is reassuring.'

At the 2003 Masters, I did more than 'get in his face' – I got right up his nose.

Tiger had arthroscopic knee surgery in the off-season but came out of his rehab in the same old form – winning at Torrey Pines, winning the World Match Play Championship, and battling flu and wet weather to win Arnold Palmer's tournament at Bay Hill for the fourth straight time, and by an 11-shot margin.

Like the gathering storm that descended on Augusta that year, we rumbled down Magnolia Lane looking for an unprecedented third straight green jacket.

The weather was just as appalling as it had been the year prior. It was wet and there were delays every day, but that was no excuse for

Tiger's poor start. He shot 76-73 and made the cut right on the number at five over. It was his worst start to the Masters, but he charged back into contention with a six-under 66 to be an attainable four shots off the lead. More importantly, there were only four players in front of him and we felt another good round would give him a chance.

On Sunday morning I walked my usual loop of the course. I didn't need to see the entire layout but I wanted to see the pin placements on 1, 2, 3, 7, 8, 9, 14, 17 and 18. I also needed to see where the tee was on 3 and 4. The 3rd tee is sometimes set up in a more forward position, which changes the hole completely, and the par-3 4th has two tees, top and bottom. It was beneficial to know the exact yardage on that hole because Tiger could practise that specific shot on the range.

Tiger started 4-4 to be one under and only three off the lead after Jeff Maggert started 4-5. I knew if he made a fast start and got his name high up on the leaderboard, other players would take notice of him coming and feel the pressure.

I'd done my assessment on the 3rd: with the tee forward, there was a chance to bomb a driver close to the green. It was a no-brainer in my mind, as there was no danger in attacking the hole – the only mistake you could make was a wide and right but even then there was a chance to make a par. A good drive would leave a simple chip and putt for birdie. We needed to attack.

'I like driver here,' I said. To this day I think driver was the only play. When I look back on the round, all the big hitters took driver there.

Tiger ummed and ahhed about it, preferring a more conservative approach, but I made my argument again and he eventually decided to take driver . . . and hit the worst shot imaginable, flaring it way right into an impossible position.

He was furious at himself and seething at me. His rage level lifted to nuclear when he botched the hole completely, making a double-bogey six. Another bogey on the 4th hole meant his tournament was over.

From the 4th tee to the 9th fairway, not a word was said. Nothing. I was getting the freeze treatment and it was miserable. For the best part of two hours he didn't speak and, to make matters worse, he was deliberately walking fast to stay in front of me, minimising all interaction. His play reflected his mood and he fell further and further down the leaderboard – making bogeys at the 7th and 8th to compound our mutual misery.

No one can walk quicker than me going up a steep incline so on the hike up the 9th fairway, I made a calculated move to walk as fast as I could – I wasn't going to let him get ahead of me. As we were walking up, I launched my verbal spray.

'Pull your head out of your arse and start behaving like an adult,' I said. 'If you're going to carry on like this it's a waste of time.

'What I said back there on three was in your best interests. Driver was the best play and when the round's over and you look back you'll know it's the right play, but you hit a bad shot and through your frustration you made six when you could easily have made four from that position.

'Sure, you can blame the poor shot on me but ultimately it was you who made six from a position you should have made four from, so pull your head out of your arse and get on with playing this golf tournament.

'If I'd given you the wrong club and it cost you double bogey, then fair enough, but don't hit a shitty shot and tell me it's the wrong club. I don't mind you saying it's a poor club selection if you hit a good shot and it turns out wrong, but don't blame me when it's the right club selection but a poor shot.

'Get your shit together and stop acting like a child.'

I was only three years into caddying for him and it was the first time I'd dressed him down and got stuck into him. Having been around him for some time and seen how people operate around him I knew nobody ever spoke to Tiger like that. Those around him were not prepared to challenge him and many were sycophants.

I'd given it some good thought and decided the best course of action was to tell him a few home truths. Once I'd started, though, it didn't stop – and it had some bite. When I finished ranting it did cross my mind that this was similar to the incident with Greg Norman in Japan and it was possible I was going to get sacked again over an argument about a driver on a driveable par-4.

I wasn't thinking of the future – I was trying to do the best possible thing at the time, regardless of the outcome. The way I spoke to him, truth be told, I was expecting him to say at the end of the round, 'That's you done.'

That wouldn't have bothered me because I said what I felt had to be said. It was ridiculous what was happening out there – this was the final round of a major championship and while we were out of contention it was still important to put on a good show and for him to do the best he could, and for me to do the best I could on his behalf.

As we skulked off the 18th green he said to me, 'Sorry for what happened out there. I appreciate you saying something. I needed that.'

We moved on as if nothing had happened but my words to him on the 9th had been overheard and led to speculation that Tiger was going to sack me. He put that to bed pretty quickly by issuing a statement and later explained: 'We're both extremely competitive, and we're both pretty fiery . . . I know Stevie is out there trying as hard as he can. And he's not always right. But I know he's only out there trying to help me win. And I appreciate that.'

———————

Tiger won five times in 2003 but none of them were majors – and many of the wins were based on great putting.

At the PGA Championship, his putting was brilliant and prevented a bad tournament turning into something diabolical. Yet his 12-over total was his worst major championship result and meant it was our first season together without a major.

There were lots of questions raised about his swing and whether he'd made a mistake to part ways with Butch the year before. Other questions circled about whether his new girlfriend, Elin Nordegren, was a distraction. Tiger didn't let anything distract him. He had the best mind you can imagine. He's got compartments upstairs where he can hide away the paraphernalia of his life. Emotions or redundant

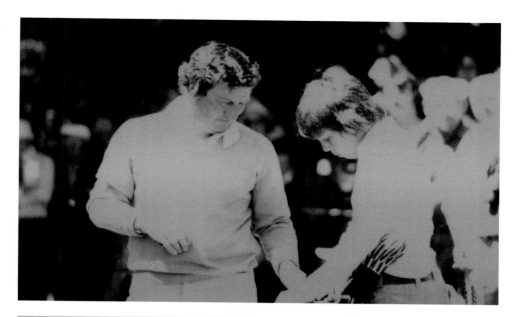

Top: My first proper caddying job was with legendary Australian Peter Thomson at the 1976 New Zealand Open, when I was just 12 years old.

Steve Williams Collection

Above: I fell in love with cars about the same time I fell in love with golf, and it's a passion that's stayed with me all my life.

Steve Williams Collection

Top: Most of my teenage years were spent on the golf course.

Steve Williams Collection

Above: I worked with Terry Gale in Asia during the 1980s and still count Terry's win at the 1985 Malaysian Open among my best.

Bob Thomas/Getty Images

Top: I joined Greg Norman in 1982 when I was still a teenager. This photo was taken at the Hong Kong Golf Club.

Steve Williams Collection

Above: Life with the Great White Shark was fantastic. He won frequently and treated me like his young brother.

Phil Sheldon/Popperfoto/Getty Images

Top: I still believe Greg Norman might have won the 1989 Masters had I been able to convince him to change his club selection in the 18th fairway.

Augusta National/Getty Images

Left: In 1990 Raymond Floyd was poised to become the oldest Masters winner in history, but he lost to Nick Faldo in a playoff.

Augusta National/Getty Images

Top: Fanny Sunesson has been a good friend of mine since we met on the European tour in the 1980s.

Steve Williams Collection

Below: Australian Ian Baker-Finch has remained a close friend for 30 years, and we enjoy catching up at tournaments. This photo was taken at the 2015 British Open.

Steve Williams Collection

Left: Winning my first national speedway title, the 2005 Super Saloon Championship.

Steve Williams Collection

Below: Retiring from fulltime caddying in late 2014 gave me time to focus more on speedway. This is Jett and me celebrating a win during a summer of great racing.

Graham Hughes, SportsWeb Photography

Left: Kirsty and me with Jett on our wedding day.

Steve Williams Collection

Below: Winning the 2010 New Zealand Saloon Championship.

Steve Williams Collection

Top: Tiger Woods' vital par putt on the 17th hole in the final round of the 1999 PGA Championship at Medinah. It was his second major title and our first together.

Phil Sheldon/Popperfoto/ Getty Images

Below: Tiger Woods winning the 2001 Masters to complete the Tiger Slam: holding all four major championship trophies in the same year. It's a feat that is yet to be repeated.

Stephen Munday/ ALLSPORT

Top: I was so proud to bring Tiger Woods to my old home course, Paraparaumu Beach Golf Club, for the 2002 New Zealand Open.

Nigel Marple/Getty Images

Left: Tiger's win in the 2006 Open Championship at Royal Liverpool was incredibly emotional, coming just three months after his father, Earl, passed away.

Photosport

Following pages: One of the bravest and most inexplicable wins I witnessed was in the 2008 US Open at Torrey Pines, when Tiger triumphed in a playoff over Rocco Mediate – despite carrying a ruptured anterior cruciate ligament and fractures in his left leg.

Harry How/Getty Images

At the 2013 Open Championship at Muirfield, Tiger and Adam Scott were paired together in the final round, and I took the opportunity to give Tiger a piece of my mind. The commentators assumed we were making peace.

Rob Carr/Getty Images

Above: I regard Adam Scott as a genuinely good bloke. I decided to caddy for him because I knew I could make a difference to his game.

Mark Ralston/AFP/Getty Images

Following pages: Adam Scott's win in the 2013 Masters broke Australia's jinx at that famous tournament, and I was rapt to play a significant part in it. I knew that Adam's putt for victory on the second playoff hole broke more right to left than he thought, so he adjusted his line, sinking the putt and winning the tournament over Angel Cabrera.

Simon Bruty/Sports Illustrated/Getty Images

A good caddy does much more than just carry the bag. That said, on an average tournament day I'm weighed down with more than 18 kilos of gear.

Scott Halleran/Getty Images

thoughts that in most people would jump around in their head, he was able to lock them up and keep his train of thought on a singular track that seldom derailed.

I believe his phenomenal play between 2000 and 2002 had also taken its toll – the focus needed to win the grand slam in particular took a lot out of him. In that era he had no trouble peaking for the majors, but in 2003 and 2004 he didn't manage to hit those peaks. There wasn't a major week in that period where his form looked unbeatable. For many reasons, but no particular reason, he was at odds with himself and while he managed to win on the PGA Tour he couldn't find a way to put himself into contention on a Sunday in a major.

I'd learned my lesson from my time with Greg Norman, and with Tiger I tried to ensure we kept a professional distance in our private lives. Despite that, we had quite quickly become close friends. It was a surprise, though, when the phone rang in the middle of the night in my Japanese hotel room in November 2002.

The last time my phone rang in the middle of the night in a Japanese hotel, it was Greg Norman ringing to sack me. This time it was Tiger waking me up.

'You got a minute, Steve?'

'Ah, yeah. What's up?'

'Come to my room.'

I didn't know what to expect.

'Have you ever thought about getting married?' he asked when I got there.

Where the hell is he going with this?

'I think Kirsty is really good for you and I think you should seriously think about getting married.'

Marriage advice from Tiger Woods? I was gobsmacked.

We had talked about our relationships – he'd met Elin in 2001, a year after I'd met Kirsty. He met Elin through golf – she was a nanny for Swedish professional Jesper Parnevik – and I met Kirsty through golf as well. Soon after I established the Steve Williams Foundation, I hosted my first charity tournament at Waikanae Golf Club, in the next town up the road from my home course, Paraparaumu. Kirsty's dad was the club president and she played in the tournament. I spent the day at one of the par-3 holes, greeting each player as they came through and having a chat. I remembered Kirsty coming through and later, in the clubhouse once we'd had the dinner and finished the formalities, she was helping her dad clean up. We started chatting at the bar and a romance blossomed from there.

I was racing in Napier the following week and not being one to take a backward step, I invited her to come along. She didn't know anything about motor racing but was soon hooked on the thrill.

Kirsty was working in New Zealand when I met her but was soon transferred to London, which made it easier to develop a burgeoning relationship – she could make trips to the States and we would sometimes be together in Europe. One of the reasons I'd not contemplated marriage was the frequent travel and nomadic nature of my job. A couple of serious relationships had proved hard to maintain, thanks to the travel and time apart. Kirsty was the first girlfriend who understood me, what I did and how I thought.

I'm highly driven: a perfectionist in constant pursuit of the best possible performance. My commitment to Tiger was total. His obsession became mine. I wholly bought into the chase for 18 majors – I wanted to be the guy who caddied for the man who broke Jack Nicklaus's record. I thought about it incessantly. The scenario, as he broke the record, had played out in my head so many times I was sure it would happen. It was going to be one of the ultimate moments in golf history. And I was going to be there.

Even back in New Zealand, when I should have been turning off and shutting down, I was thinking all the time about how we could get better. The next major was seldom relegated to the back-burner – it was front of mind as I plotted ways around the course, strategising the best possible score. I was obsessed, no two ways about it. And I was fanatical to the point it was detrimental to other aspects of my life. I let standards slip, such as not staying in contact with my friends and family as much as I should have. Yet Kirsty understood that – and, at the same time, helped me understand that this fixation on Tiger's goals was harmful to the rest of my life.

When Tiger suggested I propose to Kirsty, I was stunned but it also opened my mind. In many ways, Tiger was actually giving me permission to stop being infatuated with his goals at the expense of my own life.

Tiger is seen as completely self-obsessed but he could be incredibly caring. Whenever I came back from a summer in New Zealand he asked about my family, about Kirsty, about my racing. He was genuinely interested in Kirsty, and later, my son Jett. That might sound like normal behaviour but golf pros are an unusual bunch – they tend to be selfish and it's not uncommon for them to bypass asking you anything about your personal life or interests.

Once I had Tiger's permission, so to speak, I started thinking about how to propose to Kirsty. I couldn't picture myself going about it the 'proper' way – that wasn't me. I'm not the romantic type.

Eventually, I decided to be myself. I was racing that summer in New Zealand and before one race I asked my crew chief to make sure Kirsty was standing by the safety fence, close to the track as I rolled past. I'd made a sticker that read: 'Marry me Kirsty' and stuck it to the outside of my car. On one of the warm-up laps I drove slowly past the safety fence so Kirsty could read it. Fortunately, I got the thumbs up.

> I had no inkling he was going to propose. In fact, I didn't want to be there. It was my birthday and I didn't want to go racing on my birthday – but Steve cajoled me into going along because he had this plan.
>
> When he drove back into the pits and got out of the car, he said, 'Well, will ya?'
>
> I told him, in front of all these people in the pits, that he had to ask me properly . . . he didn't go down on one knee but he did pull out a ring and popped the question again.

When I told Tiger how I'd proposed, he just laughed, and said, 'I always knew you were a redneck.'

CHAPTER 11
UNDER PRESSURE

A t the end of the 2004 US Open at Shinnecock Hills, New York, Tiger and I had both had enough.

A wretched week had tarnished my image. I was called a bully, a boor, a thug . . . you name it, after I kicked a camera belonging to a news photographer and took another camera away from a fan who happened to be an off-duty police officer.

It was just as bad for Tiger: a public spat with his former coach Butch Harmon over the quality of his golf swing turning into a verbal serve and volley. And as if to prove Butch had a point about the deterioration in Tiger's uncoached swing, he shot 10 over for the tournament – miles back.

A hell week was an exclamation mark on a tough two years – he'd now gone eight majors without a win.

We were almost back to Tiger's rented house when he pulled over to the side of the road, stopped the car and said, 'Stevie, I think I've had enough of golf. I'd really like to try to be a Navy SEAL.'

The year had started in jarring fashion, as Tiger endured the agony of seeing Phil Mickelson claim his first green jacket at Augusta.

Phil was his arch-rival and to see him finally win a major gnawed away at Tiger because, like everyone else, he knew that once Phil won that first major, he had the ability to win again and again.

He definitely struggled to deal with Phil finally breaking through. Some of the language he used wasn't pretty, but to me the bottom line was that he didn't like seeing Phil win and would do his best to make sure it didn't happen again.

Phil had the better of him again at Shinnecock Hills, finishing second to Retief Goosen as Tiger floundered – his battle with the golf course compounded by Harmon's public critique of his swing during his commentary on Sky Sports Europe.

Constantly using Tiger's name while working for Sky Sports irritated Tiger as it was the kind of thing that got Butch sacked in the first place. This time he'd taken his Tiger-baiting too far.

After Tiger shot a poor 73 in the third round, Harmon said, 'Tiger Woods is not playing well. He is not working on the right things in his golf swing, although obviously Tiger thinks he is. He should have felt, "I could win this tournament by six, seven, eight shots." That was the old Tiger Woods. But for him to stand there at every one of his interviews and say, "I am close, I feel really good about what I am doing," I think it might be a bit of denial.'

Tiger was fuming. He later told a press conference, 'I don't understand why he would ever say anything like that, especially when we've been as close as we are. And we've resolved everything, I thought. I thought everything would have been cool. For him to go off and say things like that, I don't understand where he's coming from. It doesn't do himself or anyone any good.'

Tiger's swing had been the subject of debate since he'd ditched Butch. There were still wins on the regular tour but often they came with what he called his B and C games, where he relied on willpower and putting to close out a win. The problem was the majors – after his sensational run from 1999 to 2002, his pursuit of the magic 18 majors had stalled.

I kept records and statistics of every tournament round Tiger played and his performances in majors definitely declined in 2003 and 2004.

Over his 16 major championship rounds in 2000, he played a

solitary round over par. In 2001, he had four rounds over par; in 2002, two rounds over par. But in 2003 that ballooned to 10 rounds over par, and in 2004 it was eight rounds over par. With hindsight, it's clear that not having that extra set of eyes looking at his game in those big weeks was to his detriment.

All the great players are said to 'own' their swing. Like a fingerprint, the way they move the club is intrinsic to them. Tiger badly wanted to 'own' his swing and while it was a noble pursuit, by the end of 2004, after 10 majors without a victory, it was evident he wasn't getting there.

For my part, the week at Shinnecock Hills was equally frustrating.

I'd previously copped a fine for taking a camera off a fan at a skins game in California in 2002. There, the bloke was taking pictures during the players' backswings all day. I'd told him numerous times not to do it, and he didn't give a damn. The last hole was worth $200,000, and Tiger needed to get up and down from a bunker to stop Phil Mickelson from winning the cash. The guy clicked on Tiger's backswing, he flinched, hit a poor shot, and Phil scooped the money. I was pissed off this guy had ignored my request, costing my boss – and me – money. As we walked across a bridge toward the clubhouse, I spotted him and asked to look at his camera. The fool let me take it, and I duly dropped it into a nearby pond as I walked across a bridge. Tiger paid for the camera and my fine from the PGA Tour.

But the trouble at Shinnecock Hills started on the practice range.

'Can you can go and tell that guy to stop shooting?' Tiger asked, waving me in the general direction of the photographer.

The snapper moved at my request but a minute later he was back, this time hiding behind a water cooler. I moved him on again but he then popped up behind a tent. Whenever he was asked to stop, he moved somewhere else and continued to shoot.

When he showed up on the 10th tee, our first hole for the day, and I could hear him clicking away through Tiger's practice swing, it tipped me over the edge. I loped across to where he was positioned on the ground and kicked his camera.

It was the wrong thing to do but my job was to give Tiger a level playing field against the other players. He had more photographers and media following him than any other player and not a day went by without someone trying to take photos of his golf swing – especially with swing sequence cameras. I would challenge anyone to walk a week with Tiger – from practice, to the end of the tournament – to see for themselves how difficult it is. My job was to make sure his work environment was as distraction-free as possible – and I did that, though on this occasion I admit I took the wrong road towards a solution.

In the final round I also took a camera of an off-duty cop – I didn't know he was a policeman at the time, of course – but I don't regret it, as cameras are banned from the course unless the photographer has the right press credentials. He shouldn't have been able to get that camera onto the course. Security hadn't done their job properly so I had to do it for them.

As bad as that week had been for us both at Shinnecock Hills, the last thing I expected was for Tiger to announce he wanted to quit golf to join the Navy SEALs. I was so stunned, all I could think to say was, 'Don't you think you might be a bit old for that?'

As I understood it, he knew someone who could get him in. Either through his dad's military connections or because the name Tiger Woods opened doors that would be locked to the rest of us, he was adamant he could get in with a special dispensation. He'd done his homework and was deadly serious.

I could see he was intrigued by the Navy SEALs – he read about them a lot, habitually watched documentaries on them, and could recite you a list of missions they'd accomplished. I think his military obsession also stemmed from his dad's service in the armed forces – Tiger was extremely proud Earl had been a green beret. In my view, a part of Tiger wanted to carry on that family military connection.

What stopped Tiger running off to join the SEALs? I'm sure his many multi-million-dollar sponsors would have had something to say about it if he had quit golf. Plus he was engaged to Elin, with a wedding planned for the end of the year.

Instead, over the next three years, he took part in various military-style training courses. This included basic training in underwater diving, parachute jumps, and mock warfare. He once showed me the marks where he said he was hit with rubber bullets while playing war games in what was called a 'kill house'. The excitement in his voice as he described the intricate details of this military training left me in no doubt as to how much he loved this military simulation.

Tiger's fascination with the SEALs extended to an almost god-like adoration of these military warriors, whom he regarded as the ultimate human beings – both physically and mentally.

I told him that if he looked at himself he would have seen one of the greatest sportspeople of all time, but he didn't see himself like that – he didn't think being a golfer was significant in the grander scheme of life. I think he saw himself as others had seen him growing up – a slightly nerdy, skinny kid. He seemed to want to change that image by changing his physical look – that's why he was starting to get into his gym work: he wanted an athletic, finely tuned body. His gym sessions were already increasing in intensity and he was fixated on building muscle. I believe he wanted to be as mentally tough as these warriors but he also wanted the physique. As a result, he became addicted to his exercise regime, which he religiously carried out morning and evening, every day.

Psychology also played a part in this military diversion. He was at the pinnacle of his career and lived constantly under the spotlight. I can't comprehend how, from 2000 to 2002, when Tiger was playing unbelievable golf week-in and week-out, and winning every second major, he dealt with all the demands placed on him. Every day and from all directions, people would intrude on his life, wanting something from him. He received a lot of threats that weren't made public – they came on an almost weekly basis for years. I wouldn't wish that life on anyone.

I'd often wonder what he did to relieve the pressure. He loved watching cartoons but that was a short-term mindlessness that wasn't going to be enough to take his mind away from the pressure of being

A REV-UP FROM TIGER

I'VE BEEN A FITNESS FREAK MY WHOLE LIFE. I'd run and swim whenever I could – but I'd not been one for the gym until I started working for Tiger. At a World Cup tournament in Kuala Lumpur, I had my first gym session with Tiger. The challenge was that I did the same routine as him but with lighter weights. The next morning I couldn't even lift the toothbrush to my mouth I was hurting that bad.

One thing Tiger taught me was to strive to be better. I'm grateful to have been around a person whose self-discipline and work ethic rubbed off on me. Over the years I got fitter from being around him because I learned to push myself harder. In training I sometimes got into a routine, such as doing a 10km run knowing it was going to take about 42 minutes. That's what I'd come to expect of myself and I was happy with that – but Tiger would say, 'No, Stevie – you can do better than that. You can push yourself,' and I'd go out and improve.

Tiger Woods. When he raised the prospect of joining the Navy SEALs, I could understand it – he was looking for an outlet, an escape from the intense scrutiny.

I'd already noticed how his mind had started to wander on the course. He didn't have the same focus he'd had at his peak. He didn't suffer burnout as such, but he did become a little more fragile. Little things that had previously been water off a duck's back started to irritate the hell out of him, and his temperament took a slide. From the people screaming out in the gallery, the people wanting autographs, people pushing and shoving and being bad-mannered around him . . . a person can only accommodate that kind of mental and physical intrusion for so long. He had a reputation for not signing autographs, but when he did stop to sign there would often be a stampede. I'm not exaggerating when I say little kids were getting knocked down in the rush. Professional autograph-hunters would also send children out to have stuff signed on their behalf. But he would not refuse to sign an autograph if it was asked for nicely. It irked him when a piece of paper was shoved in his face with someone yelling, 'Sign this.' Once it developed a *Groundhog Day* feel, his dislike for the baying masses grew more intense.

Tiger also loved a challenge. No test of skill or willpower – no matter how trivial – was ignored. From Navy SEAL training to a game of ping-pong; from playing golf in brutal weather conditions to completing a physical challenge – even silly games became mental endurance tests. He loved pizza, so we had a bet he couldn't eat pizza for 30 days. I liked Sprite, so the challenge was whether I could go without it for a month. He was up for anything that stretched him mentally or physically.

The Navy SEALs thing, in my eyes, fell into this domain – it was a fresh challenge that encapsulated all the markers he loved to measure himself against: fitness, denial, mental toughness, with the added factor that you could get hurt.

The risk associated with jumping out of airplanes or playing combat games that involved rubber bullets and physical confrontation took him to a place that golf couldn't. He considered himself an athlete but couldn't prove his athletic prowess the way a footballer could in a physical confrontation. The injuries he got from Navy SEAL training – and they were often quite serious – were worn like badges of honour, such as the bruising from rubber bullets that made a substantial welt on his skin through protective clothing.

A number of injuries he picked up in his career, in my view, were not injuries you would receive from a golf-related training programme designed for core strength and flexibility – they were injuries that came from high-impact training. I only trained with Tiger in weeks when he was playing tournaments and in those weeks he would do training specifically related to golf, so I didn't bear witness to his extreme training and cannot pinpoint how his injuries happened. But, for a guy who was so fit and so strong, it was surprising he had so many injuries. To his credit, he would often play through pain and prided himself on how much pain and suffering he could endure but it was also an unnecessary burden, probably caused by his need to prove himself as a warrior.

The Navy SEAL fixation eventually ended in 2007, when there was a meeting between myself, Hank Haney, his new coach, and his manager Mark Steinberg. We decided something had to be done about this military captivation. Mark took Tiger off for a long conversation that finally put an end to this extracurricular activity.

Taking into account all the factors influencing him – his father's military background, his fascination with extreme training, his obsession with the SEALs and his need to have an outlet away from golf – it still shocked me that he was, at one stage, prepared to put aside his lifelong ambition to beat Jack Nicklaus's record of 18 majors.

On the flipside, he'd won eight majors in the eight years since turning pro, and he was ahead of schedule in his quest, considering he wasn't yet 30 and had a good 12–15 years of good golf ahead of him.

Perversely, in hindsight, I think if he could have taken a sabbatical from golf and undergone the 30-month Navy SEAL training course it would have been better for him in the long run. He might have returned to golf reinvigorated, mentally refreshed and hungry.

And he might have got something out of his system and prevented his humiliating fall from grace five years later.

CHAPTER 12
GREATEST HITS

I 'm constantly astounded by how many thoughts can go through my head in the short time a golf ball is in the air.

As the ball left Tiger Woods' club on the 16th hole during the final round of the 2005 Masters, my head was spinning with possibilities – centred mostly on the fact that Tiger was going to cough up the Masters to Chris DiMarco and his major drought would extend to 11 on the trot.

'That's left,' was my first thought. 'That's wet – we're done here.'

'Hang on, that's got a lot of hit on it. It might catch the bunker.'

'No. Shit, that's going over the water, over the bunker . . . what's over there?'

The first thing Tiger says to me is, 'Where's that?'

'It's long left.'

'What's over there?'

'I don't know, I've never been there. I've never looked there.'

Of course, I'm supposed to know the golf course inside out so it was embarrassing to say I didn't know the lie of the land in the area his ball had headed to. But truly, no player I'd seen had hit it that far long and left of 16, and I'd not bothered to scout that corner because, given the relatively short length of the hole and where you're supposed to be aiming, you simply didn't expect any player to be over there.

I quickly strode ahead of Tiger, desperately trying to get someone's attention in the TV tower behind the 15th green to see if they'd seen where the ball ended up. I was worried because I wanted to tell Tiger it was dry but I wasn't entirely sure. Eventually someone from the broadcast team told me it was safe and I was relieved to confirm that with Tiger because he was on edge at that point.

As we approached the ball, I thought, 'We can get away with a four here, and with an excellent shot we can have a makeable putt for three.' But the most likely outcome was a bogey, which would have us fall back into a tie with DiMarco or even fall one behind, as he had a birdie chance coming up.

What followed is perhaps the most viewed, most talked-about golf shot Tiger ever hit. The aim was to play the ball into the slope above the hole and have it roll back down towards the flag. The danger was that if he didn't get the speed right or hit it too far up the slope, it would race past the hole and possibly go into the bunker below.

'Stevie, see that pitch mark,' he said, pointing to a faint discoloration where a ball mark had been repaired. 'If I land the ball on that pitch mark do you think it will roll back down and end up underneath the hole?'

'Yep, that looks as good as anything,' I said.

I focused on that pitch mark – he landed it right on the target, hitting a coin-sized mark from 45 feet. It rolled down the hill with good speed. My mind raced along with it, 'We can make par here, we're going to be OK.'

'Wait on, this has got great speed, there's a chance it will go in . . .'

'. . . no, it's stopped right on the edge of the hole. Tap-in par.'

'Wait . . .'

The ball sat on the very edge of the hole for what felt like an eternity. It was balanced on the threshold long enough for the crowd to fall momentarily silent – before pandemonium erupted as the ball gently dropped into the hole.

It was the most excited I've ever been on a golf course. The only negative was that Tiger and I were so pumped that we made an absolute hash of a high five – we didn't even connect.

BEST SHOTS I'VE SEEN

1. **1985 AUSTRALIAN OPEN, ROYAL MELBOURNE:** Greg Norman's driver from the fairway to set up eagle on the par-5 14th.

2. **2002 PGA CHAMPIONSHIP, HAZELTINE:** Tiger Woods' 3-iron from the bunker on the 18th.

3. **2000 CANADIAN OPEN, GLEN ABBEY:** Tiger Woods' 6-iron from the fairway bunker on the 18th.

4. **2005 MASTERS, AUGUSTA:** Tiger Woods' chip-in on the 16th.

5. **2008 US OPEN, TORREY PINES:** Tiger Woods' putt on the 18th to get into a playoff with Rocco Mediate.

6. **2013 MASTERS, AUGUSTA:** Adam Scott's putt on the second playoff hole to win the green jacket.

7. **2006 BRITISH OPEN, ROYAL LIVERPOOL:** Tiger Woods holes his second shot, a blind shot, for eagle on the 14th.

8. **2008 US OPEN, TORREY PINES:** Tiger Woods' second shot from a bunker on the 9th fairway while playing the 15th hole in a playoff with Rocco Mediate.

9. **1992 MASTERS, AUGUSTA:** Raymond Floyd's 'impossible' chip-in for birdie on the 14th.

10. **2013 AUSTRALIAN OPEN, ROYAL SYDNEY:** Adam Scott's second shot to set up eagle on the par-5 12th.

From the draining feeling of first thinking the ball was in the water and he would make five, to thinking we might get away with four, to the hope of making a three to the absolute delirium of making a two . . . it was some journey! After all that noise and excitement there was no way DiMarco was making birdie so suddenly Tiger was ahead by two with two to play.

He needed both of those shots as he finished bogey-bogey to fall into a playoff with DiMarco – and those last three holes in regulation were typical of what had been a topsy-turvy tournament.

DiMarco had led Tiger by four after the second round, trailed him by three after 54 holes and then ended up even after 72, as Tiger played the back nine in poor fashion. Tiger described it best: 'I'm throwing up on myself.'

He hadn't been in that situation before – where he'd been in total control of a major championship and stumbled – but some of it was down to having a new coach in Hank Haney and being caught in between the introduction of Hank's new swing pattern and reverting to his old habits under pressure.

DiMarco made a clutch putt to save par and force a playoff and had all the momentum as we headed back down the 18th for the playoff. Sensing Tiger needed a rev-up, I said, 'Remember, you're Tiger Woods, eight-time major champion. This guy hasn't won one – show him why you've won so many.'

A birdie on the first playoff hole gave Tiger his ninth major and he was halfway to his goal.

————

While that chip-in on 16 is probably the most talked-about and replayed shot that Tiger played, it only makes number four on my all-time list.

The best shot I've ever seen in my life belongs to Greg Norman and typified Greg's swashbuckling, daring approach to golf.

The 1985 Australian Open at Royal Melbourne had been reduced to 54 holes, thanks to some wild weather. The wind was up on the last day making conditions incredibly tough, too. Going into the final round,

Greg was in a four-way tie for the lead, and when he reached the 14th hole he made a bold play to try to distance himself from the field.

After a pure driver to the middle of the fairway of a long par-5 that played dead into the wind, I was stunned when Greg asked for the same club again in the fairway. To this day I cannot envisage how it was possible for him to play that shot – it kept low initially, under the wind, but it lifted just enough to carry to the bunkers in front of the green and ended 20 feet from the hole. The resulting eagle was the two-shot buffer he held at the end of the tournament.

The reason that shot is so special is that I cannot think of any other player who would even *try* to play that shot, let alone make it – when you work for golfers you learn to picture what shots they can accomplish and that was one shot I never thought possible from Greg or any other golfer to this day.

The 2002 PGA Championship at Hazeltine featured another golf shot, this time by Tiger, that I can quite safely say no other player in the world could replicate. It was so good that Ernie Els, who had recently won the British Open, took a white towel out of his bag and waved it in surrender.

On the 18th hole in the second round, Tiger hit his drive into a bunker. The ball was so close to the left edge he had to stand as if pressed against a wall and, even then, the ball was much closer to his body than it would be for a normal swing.

The green was about 200 yards away and he had a 3-iron. I was thinking, 'There is no way this ball is coming out of there.' Blading it into the lip was the most likely outcome and the only possible result was disaster. And if he somehow managed to get it out of the bunker, he still had to get a 3-iron up over the trees.

On top of that, he was aiming to play a draw from what's known as a hanging lie, where the ball is below the player's feet – a stance that naturally makes the ball fade. The wind was blowing left to right as well – if anything, this shot was going to smash into the grandstand on the right-hand side of the green.

All the signs were telling me he couldn't pull it off. Obviously, I still had a lot to learn. Not only did he execute the shot he'd envisaged, he did it perfectly. He hit that ball with such force that he should have lost his balance and toppled over. I would challenge any player to stay upright in that situation, but he was as balanced as a gymnast on a beam.

The ball landed a few feet from the pin and he made the birdie putt. Over the years, I've learned to picture the possible shots Tiger could make but that one . . . I still can't picture it. When the PGA of America took the championship back to that course some years later, the very first thing I did when measuring the course was go to that spot and try to imagine how he did it. It still didn't make sense then either.

———————

At the 2000 Canadian Open at Glen Abbey, Tiger played himself into a direct contest with a New Zealander, Grant Waite, and had to conjure up one of the best shots of his life to deny my countryman the win.

It was special for me to go up against a fellow Kiwi. There were few New Zealanders on the tour and even fewer who have appeared on the leaderboard. I can remember only three times when Tiger was involved in a pitched battle with a New Zealander – twice against Michael Campbell and this time against Grant.

Grant was obsessed with trying to find the perfect swing – it was a pursuit that reflected his personality. He was a good-looking guy, quite dashing, wore great clothes and was impeccably presented. He took a lot of pride in his appearance and his swing was part of that package – it was beautiful. He struck the ball as well as anybody, but if he looked back on his career he'd probably wish he'd spent more time on his putting rather than perfecting his swing because he was a bit erratic with the flat stick. You can get away with not being a great putter as long as you're perfect from tee to green, but no one, not even Grant, can hit the ball perfectly all the time.

That week in Canada, though, was one of his excellent ball-striking weeks and he was deep in this contest against Tiger, who was one shot ahead coming down the 18th fairway.

Grant drove it up the fairway and popped it on the green to give himself a long eagle opportunity. It looked like he might force a playoff after Tiger's drive found a bunker.

With any other player in that situation – with water between them and the green – you'd ask, 'Do you want a lay-up yardage?' to give them the option of the bail-out shot. In most situations the conservative option is best: hit the ball back into the fairway and back yourself to hit a wedge shot close enough to have a decent chance at birdie. Assuming Grant's long eagle putt was unlikely to go in, Tiger could easily win taking that option and the worst result was possibly a playoff.

Tiger's mentality, however, was to assume his opponent was going to pull off the unlikely. He would mentally prepare himself for his rival to do the unthinkable – that's why Tiger didn't show any emotion if a rival holed an unlikely putt or made a chip from off the green. In his head he'd already lived through the worst possible scenario and accepted all possibilities.

In this case, he'd mentally 'conceded' that eagle putt to Grant and was now playing the hole as if he needed an eagle himself to win.

It was raining quite heavily and when that happens the ball sits down a bit in the bunker, making it that little bit harder to get clean contact. He had 192 yards to the green, with no margin for error. Short was in the water, long was in the back trap and dead. The landing area was only a few paces deep. It had to be 100 per cent. His 6-iron was pure and pitched close to the flag before settling off the back of the green. He made a chip and putt for a birdie, which was good enough for a one-shot win after Grant made his four.

––––––––––

I hate to think how much beer was spilt by the fans surrounding the famous island green on the 17th hole at the Tournament Players Club in Sawgrass, Florida, the day Tiger made the 'impossible' putt at the 2001 Players Championship.

The island green is like a Roman coliseum. The players live and die by whether they can hit that green. You're happy to be anywhere on there so the crowd doesn't hand you your ego on a plate. If you miss, the ball is in the water and you have to suffer the ignominy of hitting from the drop zone in front of a bellowing crowd.

In the third round on Saturday, fans had been there since the gates opened at 9am and by late afternoon, when Tiger lined up his putt, they were pretty animated. The putt broke left on the top part of the green and then dived right down a ramp to the lower portion of the green – by the time it reached the hole it was going so fast there was a serious risk he could have putted it right into the water.

As the putt tracked towards the hole, I could see the spectators all rising to their feet – all holding their beer – and when that ball went in the hole and they instinctively threw their hands in the air, beer went everywhere.

CHAPTER 13
CAMBO STANDS HIS GROUND

I walked off the 18th green at the 2005 US Open suffering the most complex mix of bitter disappointment and overwhelming excitement.

Tiger had made a late birdie but it was too little too late after poor bogeys on 16 and 17. He was going to finish runner-up.

I rushed through the formalities with Tiger after the round before dashing back to the 18th green to watch a New Zealander win the US Open for the first time.

I was the first person to greet Michael Campbell as he came off the green as my country's second major golf champion, and the first in more than 40 years. Bursting with pride, I gave him a hug and told him, 'Michael, that's the best sporting achievement by a New Zealander, ever.'

I repeated that claim to the media and got ridiculed for it but I stand by it today. Everyone said, 'What about Edmund Hillary climbing Everest?' but I know how hard it is to win a US Open and I know how much harder it is to win a tournament like that when Tiger Woods, one of the greatest athletes the game has known, is chasing you. I wasn't born when Bob Charles won the British Open in 1963 – and I'm certainly not taking away anything from him – but bearing witness to something that hadn't happened in my lifetime was an unparalleled experience.

This was the ultimate tournament for me. I love seeing New Zealanders play on the tour and one of my dreams had been to caddy for a Kiwi capable of playing at the highest level. That didn't happen, but the next best thing was going head-to-head with a fellow New Zealander while caddying for Tiger. While we weren't paired with Cambo on the final day of the Open – he was in the group behind us – it was the strangest, most exhilarating feeling for me when it came down to a battle between Tiger and Michael.

Pinehurst No. 2 suited Tiger beautifully. He was playing well coming into the tournament so I thought he would be in contention. Cambo, on the other hand – not in my strangest dreams did I think he would be in the mix as well.

For him to even line up in the tournament was a remarkable story. He had to come through a qualifying event at Walton Heath, not far from where he lived in London, but even then he almost skipped it as he was tired after playing four weeks in a row and wasn't sure there was much point in showing up for his 7:30am tee time on Monday. His wife Julie and caddy Michael Waite, another Kiwi, convinced him he had nothing to lose and urged him to show up and see what happened.

Even then, he needed an eight-footer on the last hole to qualify and had some luck when his playing partner, Steve Webster, putted first on a similar line to give Cambo a good read.

Once he got to Pinehurst, in North Carolina, Michael played incredibly well to be four shots off the lead going into the final round but no one expected Retief Goosen, the defending champion, to do anything but grind out a third US Open victory on the Sunday. Retief was at three under and three clear of Jason Gore and Olin Browne, neither of whom had US Open credentials. Michael and Mark Hensby, an unheralded Aussie, were four back.

Tiger, at six back, was a contender but Goosen, if he could shoot somewhere around even par, probably had too much of a buffer in most people's eyes. Greg Norman had this number in his head; he said if you were within seven shots of the lead on Sunday you could win a major. I don't know why he said seven precisely, and not six or eight, but I came to believe seven was the magic number because the Sundays of major championships spared no one. Those days were an incredible test of mental endurance and skill – you can play well and still shoot three or four over. Tiger bought into that theory – for him to be six back felt like he was right in contention and he thought he could win it.

If you'd told anyone on Sunday morning that Goosen was going to shoot 81 in the final round, they'd probably have you locked up. And he wasn't alone – this was a multiple-car crash – his playing partner, Gore, had 84 and Olin Browne self-combusted with an 80.

The leaders' spectacular descent happened so fast that by the 6th hole Cambo was leading. All around him players were falling by the wayside and when Tiger launched one of his trademark back-nine charges it became a two-man race. Tiger got within two shots of Michael with three to play. Cambo later said that when he heard the roars for Tiger's birdies he pretended the crowd was calling out for him. That's typical of Cambo – his mind works differently to most people.

Like most, I didn't expect Michael to win the tournament. I couldn't see him chasing down Retief, but when Cambo's in contention he's an unusual player in that he responds well to any heat applied to him. Once I saw his name clear at the top of the leaderboard, I told Tiger he would have to lift because Michael wouldn't falter coming down the stretch.

In that sense, Michael's a strange player – one of the strangest I've seen, to be fair. When he was on form he could play as well as anybody in the game. The flipside was he could also be as bad as anyone who's played the game. But when he was in the mix he was not intimidated by anybody. Tiger fired his best shots but Michael was bulletproof that day.

Where Tiger failed to put pressure on Cambo was on the 16th green, where he had a straightforward chip and putt to make par and stay in the game, but his chip was bad and his bogey gave Cambo the breathing space he needed. That fluffed chip cost Tiger a chance to press for the win but ironically it probably helped him win the next major at St Andrews.

Tiger, as good as his short game was, was terrible at old-fashioned chip-and-run shots. It was an area of his game that needed some work but which he neglected. I told him afterwards, 'If you can learn to chip and run, you can win at St Andrews. You have to practise that shot.' And for the next three weeks leading up to the British Open, that's all we did. The victory at St Andrews was built on the loss at Pinehurst.

Not long after the US Open, I caught up with Michael. I told him I had one piece of advice: be wary of getting caught up in all the hype that comes with winning a major. When you win one of these crowns, opportunities come flying at you from all directions. 'There's two roads to go down,' I said. 'One is to take all those opportunities and cash in on your new-found fame to make your fortune, or put all that aside and do the very best you can to win another major championship and to become one of the true greats of the game.'

It's an elite club of players that has two or more majors. So many guys win one and with it comes the great downfall as they get offers left, right and centre – appearance fees to play overseas, to run clinics, to speak at functions, to host events . . . it's relentless and if you say yes to every opportunity that gets thrust under your nose, your life gets turned upside down pretty quickly. And it takes a toll on your game because you get tired and don't practise as hard as you should.

I told Michael I believed he was good enough to be one of the players who carry on and win another major championship if he focused on his golf. Unfortunately, I don't think Michael made the right decisions after that US Open. Bad habits crept in and his game dipped south.

Tiger later told me that not long after that US Open, he'd bumped into Michael who said to him, 'I don't know how you do this all the time.' And that was his problem – he struggled to cope with the multitude of distractions and obligations that came his way.

It's times like that in the merciless world of golf that you have to surround yourself with the right people, because every man and his dog wants a piece of you. Many players rely on their managers or agents to do the right thing by them but those managers have a vested interest in seeing the player make as much money as possible – they get a slice of every pie and I think there are some irresponsible agents and managers out there who don't do the right thing by the player.

––––––––––

Practice rounds at St Andrews for the 2005 British Open carried an echo of that 16th hole at Pinehurst – on each hole, Tiger put balls down from short of the green to rehearse his chip-and-run shots. The great thing about Tiger is that if you tell him something he needs to work on he *will* work on it – he *will* improve and he *will* show you. That week, his touch was impeccable with the chip and run and he continued his domination of the St Andrews course to clock his 10th major.

That event was Jack Nicklaus's last British Open and I'll never forget that wonderful portrait taken on the Swilcan Bridge of Jack, Arnold Palmer and Tom Watson. That bridge is one of the greatest landmarks in golf. Every great player in the world has walked those 10 or 15 steps and I love the romance that came with seeing Jack stop there and pose for photos.

I was fortunate early in my career to spend some time with Jack. He and Greg Norman became good friends after Jack took him under his wing when Greg first played in America. As a result, I was lucky to be part of the many practice rounds Jack and Greg played over the years.

I watched him like a hawk whenever I was in his company, trying to learn anything I could from the greatest player the game had known. I even took notes when he said or did anything that I could learn from, because you don't get to be that good without having something special that sets you apart from other players.

What stood out above all else with Jack was that he stuck to his game plan unless he was forced to make a change by circumstances outside of his control. If he decided the best way to play a given hole was 1-iron then 6-iron, then that's what he did. The only reason he'd change was if the weather dictated terms and he couldn't hit the 1-iron to the desired spot on the fairway. There's a lot to be said for that – if he was going to lay-up, he was laying-up no matter what state the tournament was in. His course management was flawless. He was the best strategist of his

MAKING THE CUT

NEXT TO TIGER WOODS' GRAND SLAM IN 2000–1, his next greatest achievement was making 142 consecutive cuts. To front up week after week, year after year, in a cut-throat environment and continuously finish in the top 60-odd that get paid each week requires incredible focus. Tiger plays about 20 tournaments a year and from 1998 to mid-2005 he made the cut in each and every event he played. There are some players whose entire careers don't last seven years and a player who makes every cut in a season would be considered to have had a fantastic year. Many critics, when they assess Tiger's career, overlook this phenomenal streak. It ended at the Byron Nelson tournament in 2005, where the first two rounds were played on two courses. One, Cottonwood, was considered the easier of the two but Tiger disliked it. And he was having one of those days where nothing seemed to go his way; with nine holes to go he was right on the cut line. On each hole he played, the size of the media contingent grew. They were there for one reason only — to see Tiger stumble for the first time. There was a distinct feeling of vultures hovering around us. He needed a par on the 18th to play the weekend but after finding a bunker, his 15-footer for par sat on the lip. His shoulder slump was matched by the raised eyebrows among fans and media — this was something novel to write about. Perhaps the best measure of how stupefyingly good he'd been in making 142 cuts was the fact that the record for the longest active cut streak on tour then fell immediately to Ernie Els: 20 tournaments. Tiger's 142 will never be beaten. And I doubt anyone will even get close to the next best, who are Byron Nelson (113) and Jack Nicklaus (105).

era. His control of ball flight was incomparable. In his prime, he could hit the ball a lot higher than other players but he also had a rifling low shot for playing in the wind.

My brother Phillip, who also caddied for a time, had the pleasure of carrying Jack's bag in Australia. When I learned Jack was coming down to Australia, I asked him, 'Have you got a caddy?'

'As a matter of fact, I haven't even thought about it,' he said.

I mentioned my brother and Jack was kind enough take him on – something I'm quite jealous about even now.

Once I was caddying for Raymond Floyd at a skins game, an exhibition event in Hawaii that also featured Jack, Lee Trevino and Arnold Palmer – four of the greatest players in golf history. Raymond won the event and afterwards Jack came to me and said, 'Steve, you're one of the best caddies. What you do out there is excellent.'

Coming from Jack Nicklaus that was special.

On the final day of the 2005 PGA Championship, Tiger Woods was the clubhouse leader at two under par when play was called off due to darkness following a weather delay.

Tiger cast his eye down the leaderboard and made the call, 'Let's go home.'

I wasn't going to argue, whatever the boss says I do, but I agreed with his assessment. Plenty took an opposing view and blasted Tiger for flying home from New Jersey on the Sunday night.

A handful of players had to come back the next morning to finish their rounds. Phil Mickelson was four under with five to play; Steve Elkington and Thomas Bjorn were three under with three and four to play respectively. Tiger figured it wasn't feasible for those in contention to play badly enough to fall back to his score of two under. The forecast for Monday morning was no wind and the course would be soft from the rain – at least one of those guys ahead of him was going to hang on and win.

That's exactly what happened, with Mickelson staying at four under to win by a shot from Elkington and Bjorn. If any other player in Tiger's position had decided to go home, no one would have said a thing. But anything Tiger did – not matter how irrelevant – was turned into a drama of some description and this was another example of the unrelenting scrutiny he faced.

I got caught up in the micro-analysis during the first round of the tournament, when Tiger shot himself out of the contest with an opening round 75.

At the 554-yard par-5 18th, he hit a low hook that smashed into a tree and landed in a gully near a water hazard. It took us ages to find the ball because no one saw it land. At one stage, Tiger asked the gallery if anyone saw a splash, suggesting it might have gone in the water.

Lots of people joined the hunt for the ball and I eventually found it buried in soft ground. Tiger begged the officials to be able to lift his ball out of the plugged (or submerged) lie, arguing there was no way the ball, after bouncing off a tree, could possibly have ended up plugged – someone must have stood on it. If that was the case, he was entitled to lift the ball and replace it as near as possible to where it was embedded. But the rules officials said he had to play it – an impossible option – so he took a penalty drop.

The next day I was dumbfounded to see a local paper report that it was I who'd stepped on the ball. The writer said he'd reviewed the video footage and that I was the only person who'd been near the spot where the ball was eventually found.

'Williams was walking along the creek's bank when he made a step and quickly appeared to pull back his foot – perhaps as if he had stepped on something. He then located the ball,' the paper had stated.

If I'd stepped on the ball, Tiger would have been penalised one shot and I would have admitted it. I'm not a cheat. I knew I hadn't stepped on the ball and wasn't comfortable with being accused like that – but that is the kind of non-stop vigilance that follows Tiger everywhere he goes.

———

The only time in my long career when I missed a week caddying was when my son Jett was born in late 2005. I'd not been sick, slacked off, or taken a mid-season holiday until that momentous occasion. The event I missed was The Presidents Cup where Billy Foster, who had been Lee Westwood's caddy, filled in on Tiger's bag, causing speculation I had been sacked.

I first heard the name Jet when I was working in Japan, where the Ozaki brothers were real celebrities. Jumbo (Masashi), Jet (Tateo) and Joe (Naomichi) were all great guys and I spent a lot of time with them. Maybe it's the petrol-head in me but I've long thought Jett (with two ts) was a great name and told Kirsty that if we had a boy he was going to be called Jett. When I saw Jet Ozaki after I became a dad, I told him I'd got the name off him, which he thought was hilarious.

CHAPTER 14
BACK FROM DESPAIR

Tiger Woods fell into my arms and wouldn't let go. I instinctively moved to separate from him – his victory hugs were traditionally short and sweet – but as I tried to break free his embrace tightened and I realised this wasn't the Tiger I knew. He was sobbing uncontrollably. He'd lost it completely. I'd never seen him like this – ever.

I'd seen him relieved, exhausted, spent, beaten up and wrung out but, until that moment on the 18th green at Royal Liverpool after the 2006 British Open, I'd not seen him publicly reveal even a glimpse of real emotion. His mind was like Fort Knox when it came to guarding his feelings. I'd come to expect that he would maintain an even keel in public – letting go completely was not part of his repertoire.

The year started on a different emotional plane. After Tiger had taken the longest non-enforced off-season break of his professional career – a whole 24 days – he came back in late January to his favourite course, Torrey Pines, with a new Nike driver in his bag and sprayed the ball all over the course.

He dumped the new driver after that first round and played better – barely doing enough to scrape into a playoff with Nathan Green and

Jose Maria Olazabal, both of whom were the masters of their own demise as they handed Tiger victory.

Despite the win, albeit a messy one, there was no reason to think he wouldn't be at his best at the next stop, the World Match Play Championship at Carlsbad, California. Yet for some reason his first round opponent, Stephen Ames, a Trinidad-born Canadian, let his confidence get the better of him and was derogatory to Tiger, saying pre-match, 'Anything can happen, especially where he's hitting the ball.'

In match play, the minimum number of holes you need for a result is 10. The best possible result is to win 10 and eight, meaning a player wins all 10 holes and claims victory with eight holes remaining. That's not something I've ever seen but I did witness a nine and eight victory: when Tiger obliterated the upstart Ames. Tiger was on a mission that day, winning the first nine holes on the trot before halving the 10th for the most comprehensive win imaginable.

A master of vengeance, Tiger was asked after the round if he'd been aware of Ames' pre-tournament comment, and whether he had any reaction: 'Nine and eight,' is all he said.

A win the following month, in a playoff against Ernie Els in the Dubai Desert Classic, was the fourth playoff victory in a row – he'd beaten John Daly at the WGC-American Express Championship in San Francisco, Kaname Yokoo at the Dunlop Phoenix in Japan, as well as Jose Maria Olazabal and Nathan Green at the Buick Invitational.

That changed at the Ford Championship at Doral in March with a wire-to-wire win. We were on a high and, despite a couple of so-so performances, we aimed for the 2006 Masters in April, confident of winning again.

'Take this putter and break the fucking thing,' I said to Mark Steinberg as Tiger and I walked off the 18th green at Augusta.

We'd gone into the final round of the Masters two shots behind Phil Mickelson, poised to deliver a showdown of epic proportions. Tiger badly wanted to win this one for his dad, who was terminally ill with cancer. He knew Earl didn't have long to live and thought this would be the last chance to win while 'Pops' was still alive to appreciate it.

Maybe he pushed too hard to get it done for Earl – it wasn't a great final round from a noted king of closing and it was his putting that let him down. Sometimes he would have days when he didn't putt as well as others but he could often dig his way out of it. But that day he had a tough time on the greens – and if you lose your confidence out there at Augusta it's an impossible place to get it back.

As we passed Steinberg, I made the joke about breaking the putter – and of course someone overheard it and it ended up being a headline. When you're being yourself and making a joke like that, there's invariably someone eavesdropping and only too willing to turn it into a story.

As if that wasn't bad enough, as defending champion, Tiger then had to endure the ceremonial presentation of the green jacket to his arch-rival Mickelson.

––––––––––

After the Masters, I headed back to New Zealand to prepare for my wedding on 21 April. Kirsty and I had invited Tiger and Elin but, knowing Earl was very ill, it wasn't certain Tiger would make the trip. As he revealed at a press conference later that year, he actually talked it over with Earl.

'I asked Dad, "Hey, Pop, do you think I should go?" He said: "I'm not going anywhere. Get your ass out of here. Go be with Stevie. That's where you need to be."'

Tiger and Elin stayed with us for a week at home in Huapai, a small rural community in west Auckland. It was difficult to keep Tiger a secret – though to be fair we didn't hide behind drawn curtains. Tiger and I did quite a bit of running on the streets around Huapai and it was soon obvious to most people in town that there was a celebrity in their midst. We had media camped outside our front gate and we had to hire security to keep them at bay.

I had a great day when Tiger caddied for me at South Head, a beautiful golf course where I am a member, near the south head of Kaipara Harbour on the rugged west coast north of Auckland. Tiger was dumbfounded when I told him they had only one fulltime greenkeeper and one part-time greenkeeper. In contrast, his home course at Isleworth has about 30 staff. He understood it was a little country course but he couldn't believe how great it was and how well-groomed the greens were.

The other thing I arranged that week was a celebrity stockcar race. I drive saloon cars when I race in New Zealand but I love the stockcars, where racers work in teams with lots of banging and crashing. 'Gladiators on four wheels' I call them. I showed Tiger YouTube videos – he was humming to have a crack at this.

He got the hang of how the cars handled during a mid-week practice day at Huntly, a track about an hour's drive south of Auckland. Race day on Saturday proved very popular, though we almost didn't make it to the racetrack. We set off down the motorway in plenty of time but soon ran into a massive traffic jam. Luckily, I knew a guy who owned a helicopter company, so we abandoned the car and took a chopper to the track.

Competing with the likes of New Zealand rugby captain Tana Umaga, and local motor-racing legends Greg Murphy and Paul Radisich plus other top stockcar drivers, was a huge thrill. Tiger quickly adapted to the crunch-and-crash tactics and thrived on the physicality of racing, though he couldn't believe how sore he was the next day. He took one big hit but also dished out a decent thump of his own, which broke a guy's rib. That was Tiger though – super-competitive no matter the challenge.

And, of course, Tiger was my best man on the big day. When asked about his trip to New Zealand ahead of the 2006 US Open, a few weeks later, Tiger told media the following:

> It's always special to be a part of a wedding but also to be the best man. As close as Stevie and I are, you see us on the golf course, but away from the golf course, actually it was a little bit of a tear-

jerker . . . I get emotional talking about it because they're near and dear to my heart. It's quite an honour for them to ask me to be a part of something so momentous in their life and something that I will always remember and always cherish the rest of my life.

For our part, as amazing as the experience was, looking back I wish we'd handled things a bit differently, as the week became more about Tiger than us. Kirsty certainly thinks we made some mistakes.

It wasn't as nice as it could have been. We put too much thought into how it was for Tiger and Elin and how we were going to look after them and keep things private. For instance, we didn't let anyone bring cameras to our wedding because we wanted their privacy to be protected.

That wasn't Tiger's doing – it was our choice. Both he and Elin said, 'Don't worry about us – treat us like anyone else,' but it was hard to ignore the fact we had this global figure at our wedding.

I would love to do it again and make it about ourselves . . . one day.

Less than 10 days after our wedding, Earl Woods died.

Tiger lost more than a father when Earl passed. He lost an incredible mentor who knew his son's game better than anyone.

Earl would often be in town where Tiger was playing tournaments but had a strange habit of staying in a hotel and watching the golf on TV rather than coming out to the course. I wondered why he travelled all that way to watch it on TV . . . but that was Earl.

Earl had an innate feel, an almost sixth sense, for Tiger's putting and would often give him little tips – he knew Tiger's putting as well as anybody and if Tiger was struggling he would make a call to Pops and ask him if he could see anything amiss. Earl, even watching on TV, had a fantastic eye for small details no one else would notice.

Earl was astute, sharp and to the point – he left you in no doubt he had a military background. There was a lot written about how he would mentally test a young Tiger by trying to distract him on the golf course. It's been described by some as mental torture – but Tiger only ever talked fondly of the challenges Earl would put in front of him. He thought they were brilliant and lived for those tests.

Perhaps the biggest challenge he had in life came with Earl's death. It hurt him deeply and it took him a long time to get over it.

When Earl passed away, I rang Tiger's secretary to say Kirsty and I were coming for the funeral – it was a rushed trip because the funeral was to be only a couple of days later. I didn't have much to do with Tiger at the funeral but he was grateful we made the trip.

He told me there that he was going to take some time off, which I found unusual because it was the opposite of what Earl would have expected. Earl's tough nature would have insisted Tiger kept playing through whatever difficulty presented itself.

When he did come back for the 2006 US Open at Winged Foot in June, it was obvious he was incapable of playing well – his mind wasn't on golf. He'd made a mistake to come back for such a big event – he wasn't ready to play at the level he was used to, and nowhere near the level needed for a major championship. The emotional shock and lingering grief were too strong to overcome and it was definitely the least focused I'd seen him. It was the first time I'd seen his mental toughness let him down. In fact, I would have described him as brittle and not with it – he couldn't compete and it was no surprise that he missed the cut at a major championship for the first time.

When we got to Liverpool for the British Open a month later, the first thing I did was to take a quick run around the course so we could start to build a plan for our first practice round.

The course at Hoylake was as hard and fast as I've seen for a British Open. It was baked dry, like concrete. At his previous tournament, the Western Open in Chicago, Tiger was back to normal and he'd hit his long irons as well as I'd seen him. My first thought on seeing the course was, 'Given how well he's hitting his long irons, if we can avoid these bunkers then we've got a chance.' If you hit into the steep-sided bunkers, the chance of a double bogey looms large – often you have to play out sideways and sometimes even take two shots to get it out.

A player who's driving it well could try to thread the needle and split the bunkers. That would shorten the course considerably but comes with increased risk. Taking an iron off the tee to eliminate the risk meant playing into the greens from much further out, which presented its own problems as it was hard to get long-iron approaches to stop on the firm surfaces.

Back at the house we were staying in, I gave Tiger a quick overview and we looked at both options in our practice round – some irons off the tee, then some drivers – and formulated a plan to hit long irons and avoid the bunkers.

What followed over the next few days is one of the all-time great performances in golf. Tiger took a relatively easy golf course and made it reasonably hard by taking such a conservative approach off the tee. To shoot 18 under over four rounds as he did that week was entirely possible, just not from the positions he was playing from, as he conceded distance off the tee in order to avoid the shot-eating bunkers. He outplayed the field and he did it by playing a golf course that was completely different to what anyone else was playing.

To do that, he had to have his game absolutely dialled in. His focus – which had been so wayward at the US Open – was as rock-hard as the fairways underfoot. To keep hitting short of bunkers and playing dozens of approach shots from around 200 yards, when he could have been hitting from 120 or 130 yards, took supreme discipline. I was rapt that, like Jack Nicklaus in his prime, he had come up with a game plan and stuck to it.

That tournament brought another memorable Tiger–Sergio show-down, though this was as much about the unusual attire Sergio chose to wear in the final round when paired with Tiger in the final group. A highly anticipated battle between these two rivals almost disintegrated as soon as the fans, media and other players saw what Sergio was wearing: nothing but yellow. Honestly, he looked like a giant canary. It's fine to wear something that brings you attention – a lot of players are sponsored by clothing companies and there is interest from a fashion viewpoint in what they wear. And some clothing outfits will script what their player is going to wear if they want to promote a certain line. But if you're going to send out a player dressed like a cartoon character you'd better be sure the player can perform to a standard that ensures the outfit doesn't become the talking point. Whoever came up with Sergio's wardrobe had a lot to answer for. It was no surprise someone entirely in yellow turned to custard in the heat of battle – and there were plenty of jokes about the big cat and Tweety Bird.

As had been the case at St Andrews when Tiger won there in 2000, the final day had been overcast until we walked down the 18th fairway, when the sun burst through and turned the sky a spectacular colour. Knowing what Tiger had gone through while grieving for his father, and knowing how disciplined he'd been – exercising the very mental strength Earl had ingrained in him from a young age – I was overcome with emotion.

As the sun illuminated us on the fairway, I turned to Tiger and said, 'That's your dad looking down on you.'

I was the one in danger of losing it – I was cut up with emotion and close to tears – but Tiger held it all in check until he'd holed his final putt. That's when the grief, relief, joy and immense pride flooded out of him as he wrapped his arms around me and held on for dear life.

Once he'd calmed down and absorbed the magnitude of what he'd done, all I could see was happiness. It was a joy I hadn't seen in him for a long time. He was radiant – rapt with his performance, and with Elin, who disliked being in the limelight but on this occasion was at the back of the green so she could be there for him.

As if a burden had been lifted from him, Tiger followed that win by playing with a freedom I'd not seen since his majestic days through 2000–02.

While he loved his father deeply and had taken some time to come to terms with Earl's death, once the grieving period ended with the outpouring of emotion in Liverpool he started playing with an air of self-confidence that I hadn't really seen before. There was a feeling now that he was his own man. He no longer had Earl to fall back on –

he was completely in control of his own destiny, relying on his own judgement and decision-making.

He was newly married and his career crossroads of 2004 was a thing of the past – he was no longer thinking of becoming a Navy SEAL, even though he kept up the training for another year or so. It felt like he was moving forward as a golfer under his own steam.

Over the years, I've lost count of the number of times Tiger had a must-make putt that took any route except straight to the bottom of the cup. When he slid his blade through the ball on what should have been the final shot in his second round at the 2007 PGA Championship at Southern Hills, I was certain the ball's destiny was to finish in the hole – and for Tiger to become the first player in major history to shoot 62, a chalk mark next to his name he desperately wanted.

To this day, I don't know how his birdie putt stayed out of the hole. From my perspective – standing below the hole – it looked in the whole way. I was thinking, 'Here it comes,' and was primed to jump in the air and celebrate when the damn thing horseshoed around the hole and stayed above ground. I couldn't believe my eyes. Whenever I've seen the replay over the years I still can't work out how it missed.

As disappointing as that lost opportunity was, it set Tiger up for a 13th major win, which came amidst a run of wins unparalleled in modern history.

From the British Open, he won the Buick Open, PGA Champion-ship, WGC-Bridgestone Invitational, Deutsche Bank Championship and WGC-American Express before coming in second in Shanghai and Japan, winning the Grand Slam of Golf and finishing the year with a win in his own tournament, the Target World Challenge.

In the 11 stroke-play tournaments after he missed the cut at the US Open, Tiger won eight times and clocked three seconds. In total, he won 11 of 21 tournaments and was runner-up in another three. His PGA Championship win took him past Walter Hagen and into second place on the list of all-time major champions. He was only 30.

CHAPTER 15
THE GREAT LIMP TO GLORY

Sometimes I would get a premonition or a gut feeling about a shot. Call it intuition or instinct, but there were times with Tiger that I had a clear vision for a shot – I saw it in my head, saw him hitting it and saw how it would turn out.

Standing over his third shot on the 72nd hole of the 2008 US Open at Torrey Pines was one of those moments. I measured out the yardage and, based purely on those numbers, the club he needed was a sand wedge. But I knew that wasn't the *right* club. I told him he had to hit his lob wedge – a more lofted club that under normal circumstances wouldn't cover the distance he had in front of him. The arguments for and against were batted back and forth for some time – way longer than we normally talk about club selection – but we had to get this right and it took me a long time to convince Tiger of my vision. He wanted to hit the sand wedge. Based on pure fact, it was the correct club to select, but I saw him hitting that club too far past the hole and he'd be left with a tricky putt to make the birdie he needed to join Rocco Mediate in an 18-hole playoff. I knew the right play was lob wedge.

What I said next I vowed I'd never make public.

That 2008 US Open was Tiger's dream tournament. He'd played at Torrey Pines as a teenager and it had been an integral part of his golfing development. He had an almost irrational love of that course. It's a good track with some spectacular views but not the greatest layout I've seen – far from it.

I'd not seen him more fixated on a single event. From the moment in 2002 when the United States Golf Association announced that the tournament would be played there, he wouldn't stop talking about it.

'Stevie,' he'd say, 'I'm going to win that tournament.'

It had more meaning for him than any other tournament I'd caddied for him – even more than going for the 2001 Masters, when he needed to win to get four majors in a row. He was consumed by it. Whenever we played there in the regular season tournament that Torrey Pines hosted, on two courses in January, he was thinking of where the pin placements were going to be for the US Open, how the tees would be set up, where they would grow the rough . . . this was his Holy Grail.

If Tiger hadn't been so infatuated with Torrey Pines he would have taken the advice of his doctor and had full reconstructive knee surgery after the 2008 Masters, which would have ruled him out of action for the rest of the year – meaning forfeiting the chance to win at Torrey Pines.

Tiger's left knee had been injury-prone for years. He had surgery in 1994, as a teenager, to remove benign tumours and scar tissue. In 2002, he had cysts removed and fluid drained.

How he so badly damaged his knee in 2007 is still something of a mystery to me. The official line is that he injured it running on a golf course after the British Open – but both his coach Hank Haney and myself were of the firm belief it was an injury caused by his Navy SEAL training, which he'd finally shelved.

Whatever the cause, he had played in pain through the latter part of 2007 and into 2008 but it hadn't stopped him winning – just the opposite. He started 2008 by winning the Buick Invitational, played at the same Torrey Pines venue that was to host the US Open, triumphed in the World Match Play Championship, won at Bay Hill (again) and was fifth at the World Golf Championship event at Doral.

For the second year in a row he was runner-up at the Masters, this time falling well short of runaway winner Trevor Immelman.

It was then he decided to have someone look at his knee. Arthroscopic surgery cleaned up some cartilage damage and allowed the specialist to look further inside the joint. Bad news. His knee was wrecked. But he didn't tell anybody how badly damaged it was until after the 2008 US Open.

While Tiger was happy to show off his war wounds – like the bruises from the rubber bullets – he wouldn't openly complain about how much pain he was in. I'd often see him limping or wince in pain but he didn't gave much away; showing any sign of weakness was not part of the deal. Once he'd had his knee cleaned up after the Masters, he told me he would eventually have to undergo some other surgery but didn't tell me exactly what the damage was – he kept that to himself.

Turns out he had a classic anterior cruciate ligament rupture with associated stress fractures in the tibia. He needed a knee reconstruction. He figured he could put off surgery until after the US Open. Nothing was going to stop him playing in this event.

Even then, with only eight weeks between the arthroscopic surgery and the US Open, it was touch-and-go as to whether he would be ready in time.

Tiger was extraordinary in his early days – no matter how long a break he had, he could come back as if he hadn't been away. I wasn't concerned when he came to a tournament after a long break, but this was totally different. When I got to Torrey Pines on the Sunday ahead of the Open, it was clear to me that he was in no fit state to play a game against his mates, let alone contend for his national crown.

On the Saturday prior to my arrival, Tiger played with Hank Haney at Big Canyon, where he was a member. Hank told me he lost eight golf balls in nine holes and that he was struggling to walk.

The plan when we hit Torrey Pines on Sunday was to play 18 holes, but we got through only nine because he was in so much pain. Given his physical pain and equally painful form with club in hand – five days out from the start of the tournament – I couldn't see any point in playing.

Both Hank and I, from what we'd seen, agreed this was going to be a futile exercise. He could barely walk and his swing was all over the place; his ball flight was awful – it was like a wounded bird and wasn't covering any distance. But we kept our concerns to ourselves because we knew how much he wanted to play and nothing we could have said would have deterred him.

Admittedly, he got a little bit better with each passing day but there was no proper practice done – he played as many holes as he could handle each day and got regular treatment from his physical trainer Keith Kleven.

The US Golf Association came up with a novelty for the first two rounds at the 2008 Open. They decided to group players together according to their rankings rather than in a random draw. The players ranked 1, 2 and 3 in the world played together, as did 4, 5 and 6, and so on. It was a way of creating a marquee group for television – in this instance, it was Tiger Woods, Phil Mickelson and Adam Scott.

Knowing how fractious the relationship was between Tiger and Phil, Mike Davis of the USGA rang both players to make sure they were OK with it.

Phil, like Tiger, is a southern California native and is hugely popular in that part of the world – he too wanted to win at this 'home' event. Going head-to-head with Phil for the title fuelled some of Tiger's ambition. He knew how much Phil wanted to win. Adam, like Tiger, was also injured, thanks to having his hand slammed in a car door by a mate. He played the tournament with a broken bone in his hand.

My mantra around major championships is that they are not won by the highest number of good shots hit but by the least number of bad shots. When Tiger butchered the first hole at Torrey Pines on Thursday, making double bogey, I was convinced the number of bad shots would pile on top of each other and prove insurmountable.

While Tiger's renowned for being a cool, calm, clinical finisher who doesn't flinch under pressure coming down the stretch, he is equally notorious for being a bad starter. He's like a racehorse that has a great heart and will find a way to win a close contest but at the same time cannot handle the starting gates, getting fractious and bombing the jump.

Anxiety was the main reason he was so bad early in his round at majors. If you don't care you don't get nervous – and no one takes more pride in his performance than Tiger Woods. He's a bundle of jangling synapses on the first tee and through the years he's hit some horrendous opening shots. And that's despite the fact that his routine on the practice range is to not leave until he's perfected the shot he wants to play on the first tee.

Yet when he gets to the tee, that practice feel gets lost in the tension. To be fair, when Tiger arrived at any first tee there was a lot going on – there was more bustle, more people, more anticipation and he gets too tightly wound up. As a result, he's hit some incredible wides off the first tee – and this one at Torrey Pines was wider than most. Once he's on the course and going, that tension gets left behind.

Based on how he practised and how badly he missed that first tee shot, I thought there was no way he could break 80 in that first round. But he'd had so much success at Torrey Pines and his willpower was so strong, plus he was able to call on all the great memories he had at that course and reignite his muscle memory for good swings. Somehow, he shot 72 – and that's with two double bogeys on his card. More surprising than his 72 was the fact it left him reasonably high on the leaderboard – as badly as he was playing, no one else played that well either.

On the second day, which started on the 10th tee, his play was worse than day one. Midway through the round he was two over par and three over for the tournament, and a long way off the lead. It wasn't going well.

Back on the first hole, he would have repeated his previous day's double bogey were it not for a lucky bounce that kept his ball out of trouble. But it still left him with an awkward second shot, standing on a cart path with his ball lying on hard dirt. He was wearing metal spikes, which made it tough to swing off a concrete path as he couldn't get any grip with his feet. As he hit the ball – and it was a good shot – he almost collapsed in pain.

This was too much to bear. To see him in so much anguish was awful – he was visibly close to tears. We were so far back at that stage, I thought it was a waste of time to continue.

'Is it really worth it, Tiger?'

'Fuck you,' he said. 'I'm winning this tournament.'

As if to prove his point, he limped up to the green and knocked in his birdie putt. What followed was a succession of long-range birdie putts for a front nine tally of 30, one shy of the best nine-hole score in US Open history. Incredibly he finished the day tied for second place, behind Stuart Appleby.

I didn't know what was harder to comprehend: that he was in contention or that he had managed to physically survive this self-inflicted torture. I had serious doubts as to whether he could keep going, but he had a late tee time on Saturday and that gave his trainer extra hours to work on the knee and get him ready to hobble around for a third time.

Robert Karlsson, Tiger's playing partner in the third round, called it the 'freakiest' round of golf he's seen. For all the magic I'd seen Tiger conjure up, it was hard to beat the last six holes of the third round – the atmosphere was electric and the unexpected kept turning into reality.

He'd started the day with another double bogey at the first, and so-so golf for the next 11 holes – yet he wasn't falling that far down the leaderboard as no one, bar Rocco Mediate, was rising to the challenge.

The situation was just as ugly on the 13th when he slashed it so far right the ball landed in an area where people were buying hotdogs and soft drinks. He got two good breaks there – he was allowed a free drop as there was a TV tower between him and the hole, so ended up with a better line for his second shot. He also got to drop the ball where people had been walking so he ended up with a relatively good lie. His 5-iron was almost perfect – it flew a little bit too far, perhaps – and he had an eagle putt, albeit from at least 60 feet. I was holding the flag and Tiger was so far away we couldn't have held a conversation without shouting. The putt was all downhill and with a huge break from right to left. His chances of making it? About 5 per cent. In it raced.

On the 17th, he again blasted the ball way right, but this time hit a poor recovery and left himself an awkward chip on a steep slope from deep rough. The stance was so bad and he was in so much pain that he was almost standing on one leg when he hit a shot that came off the club far too fast. The ball was destined to run well past the hole but hit the flagstick about a foot above the ground and dived into the hole.

That was a five he somehow turned into a three and all he could do was laugh. If it was a game of cards, you'd swear he was playing with a marked deck – every time he had a bad hand he'd come up trumps. From bad shots he was not only getting out of trouble but gaining on the field.

An eagle at last with two perfect shots and another long-range putt gave him the clubhouse lead. The noise from the crowd was overwhelming; the buzz of excitement palpable. Tiger could hardly walk and had no right to even be playing, yet he was leading the US Open with 18 holes to play. And it wasn't as if his leg was getting better – if anything, it was getting worse.

My main worry on Saturday night, after all that excitement and adrenaline, was whether he would be able to bring the same energy and focus to the final round, or would he fizzle out?

Tiger's overnight lead – one ahead of Lee Westwood and two ahead of Rocco Mediate – vanished in two holes after, yes, another double bogey at the first followed by a bogey.

The final round seesawed, with Tiger, Rocco and Lee taking turns in front as birdies and bogeys cancelled each other out. Rocco was in the group ahead and when he made a par-5 on the 18th, both Tiger and Lee knew what they had to do – eagle to win, birdie for a playoff.

An eagle was out of the question when Tiger hit his tee shot into a bunker. He knew he could make four if he laid it up to around 100 yards but his second shot was awful, rolling into the rough 96 yards from the front of the green. He was disgusted with himself.

In that situation, after a quick club throw and burst of swearing from Tiger, I'm not thinking of what's gone wrong: I'm thinking about what happens next. Wherever the ball goes, as a caddy I know what I have to do. I'm thinking of the best way to play the next shot to achieve the best result.

We had a lot of discussion over how to play that shot. He wanted to hit his 56-degree sand wedge and I wanted him to hit a 60-degree lob wedge. The yardage said sand wedge but my first thought was, 'This ball is going to fly – it's going to go further than it normally does.' And I knew he was pumped up.

If he opted for the sand wedge it was a fiddly shot to get the right distance for a makeable putt and he would likely end up behind the hole, offering the lowest percentage putt. But a full swing with a 60-degree wedge could scramble onto the front of the green and he would have a putt he could make. I argued my case but wasn't winning.

I finally played my trump card.

'Tiger, you have to absolutely trust me on this one,' I urged. 'And if I'm wrong, fire me. I know how much this means to you, so if I'm wrong just fire me.'

He was with me. He bought into my vision for the shot but we'd taken so much extra time over the discussion I was now worried he was out of his routine. I was as nervous as I'd been after making that call on the putt on the 17th hole at the PGA Championship in 1999. He'd placed his trust in me again, but my job was done: he now had to execute the shot the way I'd envisioned it.

He couldn't have hit it any better. It was on the green 15 feet away. The hard part was over. My job was safe and he had what he wanted: a birdie putt to stay alive.

Once we were on the green there was no doubt in my mind that putt was going in – I saw it going in before it reached the hole. It was destiny. Even though the green was bumpy and the ball was bobbling all over

MY TOP 10 HOLES

I am a huge fan of short, testing par-3s and driveable par-4s that offer risk–reward scenarios.

1. **ROYAL MELBOURNE,** composite 5th, par-3.
2. **KINGSTON HEATH,** 15th, par-3.
3. **AUGUSTA,** 12th, par-3.
4. **ST ANDREWS,** 11th, par-3.
5. **PARAPARAUMU BEACH,** 16th, par-3.
6. **ST ANDREWS,** 9th, par-4.
7. **RIVIERA,** 10th, par-4.
8. **ROYAL MELBOURNE,** composite 6th, par-4.
9. **KINGSTON HEATH,** 15th, par-4.
10. **ST ANDREWS,** 10th, par-4.

the place, it was fated to fall in the cup. It limped as badly as the man who hit it, but it stayed true to its line for long enough to catch the edge of the hole and drop.

No matter what happened in the Monday playoff over 18 holes, it was going to be a fantastic story for the media. If Rocco won, it was the perfect fairytale of the underdog battler who had the week of his life and beat one of the game's best.

If my man won, it was another chapter in the legend of Tiger Woods.

A year earlier, Rocco was found lying face down in a car park. A long-standing back injury, which had needed surgery in the past, flared up and left him immobile on the ground. He had to ring for help. That he was here now, standing toe-to-toe with Tiger, was testament to his character. And just as Tiger had been undergoing therapy for his knee each night, Rocco was getting his back treated – they were two wounded warriors.

Rocco was a fan favourite. He had that everyman American look. I wouldn't describe him as athletic – he looks more like Mr Normal – but he's funny, friendly and engaging, and people could relate to him. I knew the playoff wasn't going to be all about Tiger. Rocco was going to have his share of the fans. The big question was how Rocco would handle the pressure.

Tiger is synonymous with red. In the last round of a tournament, a red shirt has become his trademark. It comes from his Thai mother, Kultida, who taught him red was a lucky colour in her culture.

When we saw Rocco that morning on the practice range wearing a red shirt it was awkward to say the least.

'Nice fucking shirt,' Tiger said, trying to make light of it while half-hiding how annoyed he was.

Rocco claimed he wore red because it was the only clean shirt he had – perhaps he thought Tiger would wear a different-coloured shirt because it was a Monday. Whatever he was thinking, Tiger only saw a red rag. When I saw the bristling reaction, I knew it was beneficial for us that he was so pissed off – that's when his desire burns all the brighter.

Rocco is a chatterbox and Tiger – well, he's not exactly known for small talk. Rocco tried a few times to spark conversation but soon realised he was talking to himself. It put him off his stride and his rhythm was also out of whack – he was playing quite fast. When Tiger marched three ahead after 10 holes, a 14th major seemed a foregone conclusion. But Tiger coughed up a couple of bogeys at 11 and 12, and Rocco, sensing a change in the air, suddenly sprang to life and rattled off two birdies, only one of which was matched by Tiger. A three-shot lead had vanished in four holes. At the very moment Tiger looked like he'd taken the playoff by the scruff of the neck, Rocco wriggled free of his grasp and started to play his own game.

On the 15th, Tiger had one of those drives that sails way right. He was so far right that he ended up in a bunker on the 9th hole – this playoff was suddenly in danger of spiralling out of Tiger's control. Rocco had knocked his approach close and a two-shot lead looked possible.

From his position in a bunker, with trees in front of him and an awkward angle to a green that sloped away from him, I couldn't see how Tiger was going to hit the 15th green. Nor could Rocco. Never one short of something to say, Rocco later said of the shot that followed, 'I've run out of words . . . he was hitting it from Pluto.'

It's one of the best shots you can imagine under pressure, from a bunker on another fairway, over trees where you can't see anything, and he put it on the green to make a par four to keep the deficit to a single shot. Not many players could ever hit that shot, let alone in the cauldron of a US Open playoff.

Once more, we came to the 18th and, once more, Tiger needed a birdie to tie Rocco and take the playoff to a 19th hole. There was less drama this time – he hit the green in two and made a simple two-putt birdie to Rocco's regulation par five.

When the playoff finally ended on the 91st hole, the USGA was accused of rigging it in Tiger's favour. The playoff rules said that if scores were still deadlocked after 18 holes, the players had to go to the

7th hole, a dogleg right that perfectly suited the power fade Tiger had been hitting all week. It was the worst possible hole for Rocco, who liked to play a draw. The format had been set months in advance and for some crazy people to bombard the USGA with accusations they'd cheated to make it easier for Tiger was plain ignorant.

That said, there were no two ways about it – the hole was set up perfectly for Tiger and poorly for Rocco, who hit his tee shot into a bunker and his second into the grandstand from where he got a free drop, but he was still in a tight spot. We identified that if we hit the green, a two-putt par for four had a better than even chance of winning and that's how it played out – with Rocco missing a 15-foot par-saver to hand Tiger the title he'd craved for so long.

'Told you so,' he said to me as we embraced.

Outside of when he won at Augusta in 2001, to hold the four major titles, I hadn't seen Tiger so elated. After six years of hearing him tell me, 'I'm winning this tournament,' it was incomprehensible that he'd pulled it off. As I've said before, it's not the greatest number of good shots that wins a major title, but the least number of bad shots – and what made this victory all the more remarkable was there were so many bad shots.

That afternoon, I drove up the freeway to LA to catch a plane home. I was still trying to fathom how he'd won and more importantly how a score of one under par was good enough to make it into the playoff. It didn't seem possible for him to win the tournament the way he was playing, yet whenever I looked at the leaderboard and saw that no one was making a move, that didn't seem right either. Whatever Tiger did – as poorly as he was playing – his main rivals did the same. He had no right to be in contention – he could hardly walk, was in unbearable pain, and was hitting it all over the place. There were bad shots on every other hole. I think the rest of the field had been too conservative – the golf course was hard but it wasn't so hard that one under par should have been the best score. Someone should have been able to go on the attack and post a lower score, but no one did.

I think Rocco best summed the week up in *Are You Kidding Me? The epic battle between Rocco Mediate and Tiger Woods for the 2008 US Open*, the book he wrote (with John Feinstein) about the tournament: 'It was the golf experience of a lifetime, bar none. It was five days of controlled, semi-controlled insanity. Especially on Monday, it was crazy on Monday.'

I can't disagree. It was one time in my life when I wished I could have been in the background as a neutral observer, watching this magic unfold rather than being in the thick of it.

If I'd done that, however, I would have missed the experience of a lifetime. I felt like I'd undergone a complete metamorphosis. I started the week in complete denial of Tiger's chances, yet with every painful step, every audible crunch of his damaged joint, every awful shot – all of which should have further convinced me of his inability to win – my doubts became fewer and my belief intensified. His mantra – *I'm winning this tournament* – became mine. We were winning this tournament. We did win this tournament.

For me to be part of one man's hell-bent determination to win, and to have played a significant role along the way, was like being Tensing Norgay alongside Edmund Hillary on Mt Everest. It was the hardest, most gruelling, most painful thing Tiger had done and I couldn't have hoped to play a more vital role in helping to achieve that goal.

CHAPTER 16
GIVING BACK

I t was Greg Norman who first made me aware that it was possible to use fame to improve the lives of other people.

It was 1988 and we were playing at The Heritage tournament in Hilton Head, South Carolina. Greg had been approached by an organisation called Thursday's Child, which grants wishes to children suffering cancer. Jamie Hutton was a 17-year-old suffering from leukaemia. His wish was to meet Greg Norman.

Thursday's Child flew Jamie and his mother from Wisconsin to Hilton Head to meet Greg and watch him play. Greg was moved by Jamie's situation and took a shine to the youngster. Jamie was supposed to fly home on Sunday morning – he had a long trip ahead of him with stopovers at Atlanta and Chicago – to be home in time to undergo a bone marrow transplant on Monday. Greg told the family to change their plans, stay for Sunday's final round, and he would fly them home in a chartered plane that would take them almost door to door.

Greg started the last day of that tournament four shots back but blazed through the front nine with four birdies to get the lead. He had a six-foot putt on the last to maintain a one-shot advantage.

'This one's for Jamie,' he said, and drilled the putt.

He gave Jamie the tournament trophy to keep and then we all piled into Greg's limousine to go to the airport. It was an emotional and memorable day and it's stayed with me as proof that you can influence someone's life by doing something good.

That sentiment lay dormant for many years until Earl Woods suggested I think about starting a charitable foundation. He figured I was popular in New Zealand through the caddying and car racing, and that I'd be able to raise money for a good cause. He outlined to me the dos and don'ts of running a foundation and how it should work.

When I started the Steve Williams Foundation in 2000, it was fairly small in scale and my aim was to encourage junior golfers in smaller, less well-off provinces of New Zealand, such as Northland, Southland and the East Coast. The Foundation put money into junior development programmes and sponsored selected individuals to travel overseas and compete.

When I met Kirsty she took a leading role in the Foundation, but after a few years we found the programme wasn't as rewarding as we wanted it to be. Whenever we gave a grant it came with guidelines as to what we wanted – it was as simple as a quarterly report with feedback on what had been done with the money. Basically, we wanted to know the money had been useful. The recipients were terrible at giving feedback – some did, but too many didn't – and we were quite disappointed. It was an eye-opener for us to give money to organisations and individuals and for them not to take the time to write back to us with any feedback.

Despite the disappointments, I was very proud to be made a Member of the New Zealand Order of Merit for services to youth sport in 2007.

We were really blown away that others had noticed our work. To go to the ceremony at New Zealand's Government House and sit with all the other famous people who had done amazing things was really quite special and made us both feel incredibly proud of what we had achieved.

Ironically, just six months after being named on the honours list over Queen's Birthday weekend, we changed direction.

I was set to race my car in a coastal New Zealand town, Gisborne, on Boxing Day, so we had to set out on Christmas Day to make the long trip from Auckland. Kirsty wasn't at all happy about being dragged along on this road trip on Christmas Day. On the drive down, she decided she wanted to do something in the spirit of Christmas and locked onto the idea of brightening the day for all the children who were in hospital in Gisborne. Being Christmas Day, there weren't many shops open so we did the best we could, which was to buy as many chocolates as we could get our hands on and take them to the kids in hospital.

A lot of these children didn't have much in the way of family or were from poor backgrounds – and the delight on their faces as they received the chocolates was a real buzz for us. As were driving away, Kirsty had an epiphany: 'We have to do something bigger and better than this.'

When Tiger underwent his knee reconstruction in mid-2008, I was freed up to put a lot of energy into fundraising for Starship Children's Hospital in Auckland. Our goal was to give them $1 million. I donated $500,000 of my own money and set about raising another $500,000.

One thing people regularly ask me is, 'What's the highlight of your career?' Until then I would have picked something golf-related. But now I can safely say I will never experience anything as uplifting as the day we opened the new oncology unit – cutting the ribbon to a unit that bears my name was such a wonderful feeling. We spent a lot of time in that hospital and it's an astonishing place to be. To see these poor kids fighting for their lives and knowing you are doing something to help, however small, gave me a new perspective on life.

From that point, we stopped funding golf and focused on sick children. Kirsty started contacting a few different charities to see what we could do.

Andrew Young, the CEO at Starship, got back to me and said, 'We've got this one project we need help with.'

He took Steve and me through the children's cancer ward of the hospital, and we were quite sad to see the way it was set up. A hospital that was designed to have two children per room with space for parents to stay now had up to four children in a room, and if parents wanted to spend the night they had to sleep on a mattress on the floor.

In one room, there was a baby, a toddler and a teenager – it wasn't right. And the stats showed that the teenagers were the most disadvantaged – they were dying at a higher rate than other kids – and the thought was that many of them were giving up because the environment was so morale-sapping.

Today there are two separate sections – one for younger children and one for teenagers – plus a completely separate isolation area with clean, filtered air. Everyone has their own room and there's a bed that pulls down for parents. When you're a child, you don't want to be left alone in hospital. There's a TV lounge, a games room, a nice kitchen . . .

Over the years, we gave a lot of money to golf and helped a lot of kids. But with the work we've done at Starship, we're still getting emails to this day from people who are just so grateful.

We're currently helping to raise money for a bigger isolation unit at Ronald McDonald House, which offers support to families of sick children. I also try to help young mini-stock drivers aged 12 to 16. Like the golf donations, all we ask is that these kids report back to us on how the money has helped them. And the motor-racing kids have been far more productive in terms of reporting back to us.

The revenue streams for the Steve Williams Foundation include guest-speaking, which I do, and corporate golf tournaments. A lot of other charitable organisations also ask me for auction items and when I agree to that, the deal is 50 per cent of the money goes to the charity and 50 per cent to our foundation. We don't take any money out of it ourselves – we pay for our expenses but they are minimal because we do it from home, so nearly every dollar we raise goes back out to people who need it.

I thought the fundraising might fall away when I stopped caddying for Tiger and lost some of that profile I'd built up over the years, but since I've been retired it's got even busier – almost to the point where it's hard to find time to schedule events.

Another area of my life in which I try to give back is speedway.

As kids, my dad would take my brother Phillip and me to Te Marua speedway in Upper Hutt, north of Wellington, on Saturday nights. I was fascinated with the speedway bikes – back then in New Zealand we had superstars such as Barry Briggs, Ronnie Moore and Ivan Mauger who competed regularly at Te Marua. But when I first set eyes on a car bearing the number 21, driven by Ian Taylor, my love of the sport soared to a new level.

Ian had immaculate machinery. His cars were just beautifully presented and I couldn't wait for him to come out on the track in car number 21. And when he was out there, I couldn't take my eyes of this car. I was hooked for life and 21 became my favourite number – almost to the point of obsession. If I went for a run it was 21 minutes out and 21 minutes back. If I was swimming it was 21 lengths.

Years later, Ian's son Stephen started competing out of Wellington with the same number 21 car his dad drove. When I got to know Stephen, I asked to meet his dad. As I drove up to his house, the grounds were as immaculately presented as his cars used to be 40 years earlier. It was one of the biggest thrills of my life to meet this guy who had been a boyhood hero.

After I started caddying, I'd come home to Auckland for the summer and would venture out to Waikaraka Park Speedway. In contrast to the almost perfectly detailed cars belonging to Ian Taylor, this time I was captivated by an absolute lunatic of a driver – Clark Proctor – who drove with no fear at all. He wasn't interested in finishing a race – he was there to see how many cars he could take out.

I got chatting to him one night and over time we talked more frequently, before one day he said, 'You seem very interested in this. Do you want to give it a go?'

'I don't know anything about it.'

'Well, I'll build you a car.'

'Um . . .'

MY LUCKY NUMBER

AT THE NEC INVITATIONAL AT FIRESTONE COUNTRY CLUB IN 2000, my number 21 came into play as we approached the finish of the tournament. Tiger played phenomenally well – shooting 61 in the second round – and was walking to victory. Coming down the last he was 20 under par and 10 shots clear of the field.

On the tee, I grabbed his glove and wrote '21' on it because I wanted him to get one more birdie and get to 21 under. The only problem is that it was almost dark. In any other tournament, play would have been suspended because of it but Tiger was so far in front the result was a foregone conclusion. No one wanted to come back on Monday morning to play one more hole. He was paired with Hal Sutton, who had a flight booked that night to go to Jamaica. The sun was long gone when Tiger said to Hal, 'Do you want to finish?'

'Yep, let's finish,' Hal said.

It was so dark we couldn't see the flagstick from the fairway. Around the green, people were holding lighters and in the car park they had turned on their cars and pointed the headlights at the green to help us finish.

For Tiger's approach shot to the green, I gave him the numbers and he made a swing based purely on theory – he couldn't see the flag. He stiffed to about two feet, made the putt in the glow of car headlights, and finished at 21 under.

'No, I'll build you a car – an entry-level car. It's called a street stock.'

That was 1987 and with Clark's help I got hooked on the adrenaline of racing. I started in street stocks, which was a contact class, and as a person who liked to keep everything neat, tidy and well presented, I found it to be a lot of work to keep the car in good shape. It was always getting dinged and bashed. I moved to saloon class and progressed from there.

I have two cars now: a saloon car, which has restrictions placed on it, and a super saloon, which has no restrictions. Each week I decide which one I'm going to run depending on what events are on. My team is called Caddyshack Racing and I employ one guy who works fulltime on my cars.

Eventually I became good enough to win two national championships – the 2005 super saloon title and the 2010 saloon championship.

That was important to me because for a long time people didn't take me seriously as a driver. I was always regarded as a caddy who drove cars. When I caddied for Raymond Floyd or Greg Norman, no one paid me much attention in that regard, but once I was caddying for Tiger, even though I'd been driving for more than 10 years, I was constantly introduced at racing events as 'Tiger Woods' caddy', and that annoyed me a lot because I'm Steve Williams the driver! So to win the national championship twice cemented my name as a driver and a capable one at that – not Tiger Woods' caddy.

I won both my titles at Bay Park in Tauranga, which is also where I've had two big crashes – including one where I badly mangled my left hand, which required surgery, after I was catapulted into the air. So I've got a love–hate relationship with that track.

To cement my status as a genuine driver, I also represented New Zealand twice: once against Australia in a trans-Tasman challenge and then in a saloon challenge against an American team.

While it's a dangerous sport, racing my cars is also a great de-stresser for me.

The years caddying for Tiger were incredibly high-stress. Only weeks in which he had a win were considered good weeks – anything else constituted a shit week – and for 13 years I was under that stress. Speedway became my outlet and I loved nothing more than coming home every summer, pulling on a helmet and racing my cars around the track.

It helps that speedway is the polar opposite environment to the PGA Tour. A true blue-collar sport, it's as far away as you can get from the manicured fairways of Augusta and the American country clubs we visit.

One of the things I brought to New Zealand was the concept of Speedweek. It's something I picked up in America and we've been doing it in New Zealand for a number of years now. Each season we race on seven tracks over seven nights and it's an event that alternates between the North and South Islands.

In 2010, Speedweek was in the South Island and was sponsored by DHL. On the Friday we were in Dunedin when we heard news of the Pike River mining disaster, where 29 men died in a gas explosion in a coal mine near Greymouth on the West Coast of the South Island. We had a race scheduled for Greymouth on the Sunday afternoon and as the organiser of the event I had to ask the question: Can we still race?

I talked to the promoter at the track in Greymouth and his initial response was, 'It's a very dark time here,' but then he considered the racing could be something of a distraction from the tragedy and also a way to bring the community together if we handled it properly.

I came up with the idea of having a fundraising race – the Pike River Memorial – which, instead of the usual 20 to 25 laps, would be contested over 29 laps in memory of the 29 who had lost their lives. We started taking donations in Dunedin on the Friday and did the same on Saturday night in Christchurch.

It was during these couple of days that I was chatting with Tiger over the phone and telling him what had happened. A lot of people give Tiger a bad rap for his tightness with money – and it's true he's the world's worst tipper – but in my experience he was also generous in ways people never saw, and which he never made any fuss about. He wanted to help, and said, 'Whatever you guys raise, I'll match it.'

The event itself was a stirring, emotional and eventually uplifting occasion. We started by having every car and support vehicle lined up in the street outside the track; one by one they rolled onto the track in a procession. We knew we'd done the right thing when we left town the next day to drive north for the final stop of the week. Spray-painted on some road metal piled up on the side of the road was a message that read: 'Big thanks to the DHL drivers'. And further down the highway there was another thank-you sign.

CHAPTER 17
THE BEGINNING OF THE END

I've seen a lot of great rounds of golf in my life but the best nine holes I've ever seen was Phil Mickelson's front nine in the final round of the 2009 Masters. He was either hitting it stone dead or making fast, curving putts. Even when he got into trouble on the 9th – deep in the woods – he found a way out and made par after playing his third from a bunker for a front nine of six-under-par 30.

He was absolutely on fire and Tiger was grinding away before sparking into life with an eagle at the 8th and a birdie at the 9th; it felt like there was magic in the air. Two of the world's best players – arch-rivals to boot – charging up the leaderboard at the Masters.

The patrons – you have to call them patrons at Augusta, not fans – were noisy and full of anticipation that they were watching something special.

'I would say it was the most fun I've ever had on a golf course caddying,' Mickelson's caddy, Jim Mackay, would later say.

Ultimately, both Tiger and Phil would fall short with back-nine mistakes – Phil's dramatic charge came to an undignified end when he gave his ball a drink in Rae's Creek on the 12th for a double bogey, while Tiger bogeyed the last as they finished three and four shots back respectively.

He didn't win but Tiger's performance at Augusta showed me his repaired knee was strong, his form was good – it was going to be a great year.

Looking back over that 2009 season, in which he only once finished further back than 11th – an almost inexplicable missed cut at the British Open – it seemed like the momentum was again building to overhaul Nicklaus's major record in the next two or three years.

To give you an idea of how well he was playing, here is a list of Tiger's placings in 2009 after taking more than six months off for surgery: 9-6-4-1-8-1-6-1-cut-1-1-2-2-11-1-2-6-1.

The disappointments were the slow start at the US Open at Bethpage Black, where his opening 74 on a waterlogged course left him too far off the pace and he could only manage sixth, and the missed cut at Turnberry for which I largely blame myself. I didn't sleep for two or three days afterwards because I felt my mistakes led to him missing that cut.

It all came undone in a stretch of six holes in the second round, during which he lost a ball and shot seven over par, eventually missing the cut by a single stroke. This was the first time he had missed a cut properly in a major. The year his dad died he teed it up at the US Open because he was eligible to do so but his focus was obviously elsewhere.

At Turnberry, the problem – in many ways – was a decision to play what he called a strong 3-wood, which made it easier to hit a draw. He planned to use it off the tee in the second round, as it would be better in the windy conditions than the weak 3-wood he'd used in the opening round.

My concern was that he wasn't hitting the strong 3-wood well enough in practice but my mistake was to keep letting him hit it during the round, even though it was patently obvious it was leading to bad shots.

He didn't hit the ball that well but my advice was poor and I contributed to a round that went pear-shaped in a hurry.

'Well, that is surprising,' Tom Watson said, when he learned Tiger had missed the cut. 'It seems like he's been playing awfully well this year. But when you're not confident about where you're hitting it and you start hitting it sideways a few times, then it gets to you. I don't care how good you are – it gets to you.'

Nothing seemed to get to Watson – at 59 he was leading the British Open and I don't know what was more shocking, that Watson was leading or Tiger had missed the cut.

I was back home at the end of the tournament and, like everyone, I was mesmerised by the prospect of Watson winning a major championship at 59 – it would have been one of the greatest sports stories of all time.

The beauty of Tom Watson is that even in his 60s, he swings the same as he did when he was 30. And even though he's battled through the yips with his putter, he's stayed true to what he's always done – he hasn't gone to a long putter, hasn't changed his grip, hasn't gone cross-handed. He's old-school and has old-time values. Most other players, if they'd been in the state he was in, would have changed something, but he kept doing exactly what he'd done and struggled through it. I admire him for that.

Anyone who loved golf was pulling for Tom Watson at that 2009 British Open. It's such a shame he missed his par putt on the last as he didn't have the youthful legs needed to handle the four-hole playoff against Stewart Cink. He seemed to melt, going from looking bulletproof to vulnerable in the twinkle of an eye. It was a sad end to a compelling tournament – even Stewart, who richly deserved a major title after blowing the US Open in 2001, looked guilty for winning.

Because of Tiger's poor performance – to which I contributed – I suffered a rare bout of low confidence in myself, which carried over into Tiger's next tournament, the Buick Open at Warwick Hills.

Again, I didn't do a great job and it was reflected in Tiger's score – a one-under-par 71 on what was a relatively easy course. My thinking was a bit negative and I was down on myself. I was talking to Kirsty after the first round and she gave me a much-needed wake-up call – the confidence boost I needed.

After that chat, I went out of my way to be more positive and upbeat. Tiger shot 19 under par over the next three rounds to win.

––––––––––

As much as Tiger loved winning, what he loved even more was a challenge. He wanted to be tested – as much as his beloved dad used to test him on the golf course when he was a kid.

One battle he absolutely relished was the final-round showdown against Padraig Harrington at the WGC Bridgestone event in 2009.

During Tiger's injury-enforced layoff, Paddy had won the last two majors of 2008 and was now regarded as one of those players who could challenge Tiger's dominance. While the big cat was away, Harrington had come out to play and proven himself as a skilled player with a heart to match his formidable work ethic. But no one had yet seen him head-to-head with Tiger until that final round at Akron.

Harrington had a three-shot lead going into the Sunday but Tiger wiped that out within an hour. Harrington, as expected, fought back and had his nose in front by one shot as they played the par-5 16th, where a rules official ruined it for all and sundry.

Harrington had been regarded as a slow player and someone you didn't want to get paired with, as he could be frustratingly deliberate. He had improved over the years but his reputation stayed with him. In this instance, we had fallen only slightly behind the group ahead of us but there were only three holes left to play and we were well on target to finish inside the allocated broadcast time of 6pm.

John Paramor was a rules official who, I felt, had something against Tiger. It seemed he would put Tiger on the clock nearly every year at the British Open. Tiger was a patient player but not slow, and rules officials failed to take into account the extra time it takes to get around a golf course if he was in contention. There are extra TV people, more media and photographers, bigger galleries, beefed-up security – there's more time needed to get everything in order. We were invariably waiting for people to settle. It's frustrating to be put on the clock when it's not your fault.

Paddy Harrington had been warned to speed up earlier and once we were being timed there was a risk of a one-shot penalty (a punishment Paramor dealt out to 14-year-old Chinese amateur Guan Tianlang at the 2012 Masters).

With the tournament in the balance, Paddy seemed to overreact to the news that he had to pick up the pace and started to rush – getting himself into trouble by hitting his third shot over the back of the green. His thinking was not helped by Tiger having stiffed his third shot to have a tap-in birdie coming up to at least draw level. The real disaster came with Paddy's fourth shot. With a good chip he could have made par, or bogey at worst, and we'd still have a contest. In rushing, he skulled his fourth across the green and into the water and ended up taking an eight while Tiger made four.

Paddy definitely played out of his comfort zone once Paramor intervened. I felt sorry for him, I really did. It was a great battle: two players at the top of their game. Tiger was up for it – he was relishing the prospect of winning a fierce contest, and for that to be interrupted by a rules official was hugely disappointing. Who knows what the result would have been had they kept playing at the normal pace, but I know for certain that Paddy wouldn't have made an eight if he hadn't been put on the clock. It's the first time I'd ever felt sympathy for a player Tiger had beaten. When a rival folds under pressure from his opponent, that's the nature of the game – but this was an outside influence.

We finished that round at 6:03pm, three minutes outside the time allocated. If Paddy hadn't taken three extra shots on the 16th because he was harried, we probably would have finished at 6pm on the dot.

The fallout from that was a story in itself. Tiger was quite critical of Paramor in his press conference. Many felt he should have been fined for criticising an official, but nothing happened – which led some media to speculate that the PGA Tour had thrown Paramor under the bus.

Having said that, slow play is the biggest problem in golf – for professionals and amateurs alike. It should not take over five hours for three professionals to complete a round of golf. There are well-known serial offenders out there and top of everyone's list is Kevin Na.

I'd heard all the stories about how slow Na was, and how players would look at the leaderboard and if they knew they could avoid playing with him the next day they would do their best to do that.

Bizarrely, given how long I'd been on tour, I'd not yet experienced the torment of playing with Na. That changed at the Deutsche Bank Championship in 2014 when Adam Scott, Chris Kirk and Na were paired together in the opening two rounds, which were held on a Friday and Saturday.

There were only 100 players in the field, as it was one of the season-ending playoff events for the FedExCup, and in small fields the pace of play is significantly increased.

We teed off the 10th on Friday morning and by the time we were walking off the 13th tee, a rules officials was on his way to see us. We'd played only three holes and already we were on the clock – we were at least a hole out of position.

On Saturday, we got to the 7th hole before the rules officials paid a visit. And this time Kevin started pleading his case, which only cost us more time because he's arguing with the officials. Chris and Adam were exasperated with his carry-on.

Everything Kevin did was slow. And he was so into himself and what he was doing that he had no awareness of the other players around him and how they were feeling. I couldn't stand it.

At the 18th, I said to Adam and Chris, 'Hang around in the scorer's hut after you've signed your cards. I've got a surprise for you.'

Once all three players were in the hut, and when Kevin finished signing his scorecard, I stood in the doorway to block his exit and said, 'Hey Kevin, if you went to a bad movie would you go back and watch it a second time?'

'What do you mean? I don't understand.'

'Just that: if you saw a bad movie would you pay to see it again?'

'No, of course not.'

'Well, watching you play golf is like a bad movie and I don't ever want to see it again.'

He turned to the official and said, 'He can't talk to me like that.'

'Wait on,' I said, 'I haven't finished yet. You're the most inconsiderate player I've ever met in my life and I hope I'm never paired with you again.'

Adam and Chris at this stage have got their heads in their hands trying to hide their laughter. The story quickly looped around the course and I even had a couple of rules officials come up to me and say, 'Well done, that needed to be said.'

When YE Yang asked me where in New Zealand I lived, I thought he was trying to make small talk to settle his nerves as he faced the prospect of playing with Tiger in the final round of the PGA Championship at Hazeltine in 2009.

When I told him I was based in Huapai, west Auckland, I was stunned to learn that he knew exactly where it was. He used to practise at the driving range on the Coatesville–Riverhead Highway, he told me. That's just down the road from where I live. I often pedalled past it on a bike ride. Yang was like many young Koreans who come to New Zealand or Australia to hone their games in cities flush with good golf courses and great practice facilities. He'd prepared for his showdown with Tiger on my very doorstep.

All the same, I knew nothing about him and as the round evolved I struggled to marry up the seemingly opposing facts – that an unheralded Korean who used to practise down the road from my house in New Zealand was dishing it up to Tiger Woods.

No one at this stage had succeeded in coming from behind to beat Tiger on the final day of a major. Bob May, Chris DiMarco and Rocco Mediate had come the closest by forcing playoffs.

Tiger had a two-shot lead going into the final round and major number 15 looked a foregone conclusion – especially when I saw where YE Yang was hitting it. It was obvious he wasn't going to overpower the golf course so he was going to have hit it arrow straight and putt exceptionally well to win.

And exceptionally well is exactly how he played – making a chip-in eagle at the 14th to take the lead – while Tiger faltered, making bogeys on the last two holes to lose by three.

It had been the first year, to the best of my knowledge, that Tiger had played pain-free – he was healthy, hungry and playing incredibly well. I thought this could be the year where he made huge strides towards his goal of 18 majors . . . but it didn't happen. The year ended without a single major.

It was also the first time where his usual ability to peak for majors deserted him. He won at regular intervals during the year but for some reason he'd lost the knack for lifting himself to a higher level for the biggest tournaments. Despite how well he was playing in general, it felt like something was ruffling his immaculately honed focus.

I knocked on Tiger's hotel room door as arranged.

It was Sunday, 15 November 2009 and we were in Melbourne, Australia. I was calling by to collect his gear ahead of the final round of the Australian Masters at Kingston Heath.

Whenever I stayed at the same hotel as Tiger, he would usually give me a key to his room and I'd let myself in to pick up his golf bag. On this trip, however, he brought a couple of old mates with him and I wasn't given a key. So during the week, I'd normally knock on the door and walk in. But this Sunday morning the door was locked and my repeated knocks got no response.

'Maybe he's in the shower or on the phone,' I thought, and waited a few minutes before knocking again. Still no answer.

After I'd been there 10 minutes I thought, 'This is getting weird. There's a chance we'll be late to the golf course.'

Tiger was normally so punctual, I figured something must have changed his routine and wondered if he'd already gone downstairs without me.

I rang security to see if he was waiting for me in the lobby.

'No, he's not here,' they said. 'We're waiting for you – you're late.'

Finally, after 15 minutes – which for Tiger is like being an hour late

– the door opened and I immediately knew something was different.

He had friends there but they were dressed as if they'd recently come in from a night on the town. Tiger had a suite with a number of bedrooms and there was more than enough room for them all to stay, but I thought it was odd that they'd elected to go out all night and then disturb Tiger in the early hours of the morning when he was due to play the final round of a tournament.

Tiger looked the same – I didn't notice anything unusual about him – except he wasn't ready to play golf and seemed a bit preoccupied.

He told me there'd been a change of plan and he was packing up all his gear now and would be going straight to the airport from the golf course in a helicopter without calling back to the hotel to shower and change.

Again, I thought, 'This is strange,' but by now everything was starting to seem a bit weird. And besides, we were running late.

It was the first time in 10 years that Tiger had played in Australia. There was a huge amount of anticipation about it and I was excited he was getting a chance to play at Kingston Heath, which I think is one of the best golf courses in the world. Architecturally, it is superb.

The weather was perfect, the course was perfect, Tiger played impeccably and I had a great time. There were heaps of New Zealanders in the crowd, too – I kept hearing them yell out 'kia ora' wherever I went.

In many ways, I got as much of a buzz from this tournament as from winning a major – I'd caddied a lot in Melbourne, knew my way around the place, and had spent a lot of time there when I was getting set up as a young caddy. Next to having Tiger come to Paraparaumu, it was the closest thing to being at home. I was delighted Tiger was able to win the tournament and pick up the gaudy gold coat that is the Aussie answer to Augusta's green jacket.

But the joy of winning dissipated in the strangest fashion. No sooner had Tiger fulfilled his media obligations than he fled to the airport in a chopper, leaving me to head back to the hotel on my own.

As I was driving, I got a text from Mark Steinberg which read, 'There is a story coming out tomorrow. Absolutely no truth to it. Don't speak to anybody.'

———————

In the back of my mind, one thought often replayed, over and over, without an answer: What did Tiger do with himself to get rid of the stress that built up in his life?

He loved the gym work and, before he got injured, the Navy SEALs training. I figured that addiction to the gym was where he got rid of many of his frustrations. And when I say addiction, I mean just that: year by year he got more and more hooked on working out.

When you live so intensely in the public eye, you surely have to have something else away from the spotlight that gives you pleasure – and it turns out I was wrong about the gym.

The one question I'm now regularly landed with is: How could you not know about Tiger's multitude of mistresses? It's a valid question – it's one I would ask myself if a scandal of Tiger-like proportions happened to another caddy's boss. How could I spend so much time with him and not have an inkling this was going on?

The answer, in a roundabout way, is that Elin didn't know either. Only a handful of his oldest buddies actually had any idea this was going on. I didn't know because Tiger didn't dare tell me. We had such a strong bond and working relationship that there was no way he could let me in on what was happening – he knew my values and that I would have zero tolerance for that kind of behaviour. I would have told him straight away that I condemned that kind of activity and, unless he stopped, there would be no conversation – that would be the end of us.

On top of that, Kirsty and Elin had become close friends and Tiger would have been aware of that as well.

———————

When Mark Steinberg sent me that text following the Australian Masters, I had no idea what to expect. When I first got back to New Zealand, there was nothing going on.

The story being chased by the *National Enquirer* about an alleged affair with Rachel Uchitel – who had been with him in Melbourne – was still developing. Steinberg's warning to say nothing wasn't a problem because no one was asking.

That all changed once Tiger slow-crashed his SUV into the fire hydrant just outside his house on Thanksgiving night. He was fleeing an angry Elin, while dosed up on sleeping tablets, after she discovered he had been cheating on her. Before long, my phone wouldn't stop ringing.

I distinctly remember what I was doing when I heard he'd been involved in an accident – I was in a paddock slashing the grass and listening to the radio through headphones. I knew only what everyone else knew at that stage: that Tiger Woods had been involved in a car accident close to his home but the details were sketchy.

Any story involving Tiger got blown out of proportion, so I was happy to wait for more details. When later reports said there were no serious injuries, I relaxed and waited to hear from him. Tiger and I had been regular communicators and I figured he would contact me soon enough. A few days later, in late November, he emailed to say that he was in a spot of bother and would be in touch.

I didn't hear from him again for four months.

Every other bugger was calling me, though. The media were incredibly disrespectful with constant calls asking for information. There was no let-up. I got frustrated over that period – the media feeding frenzy was relentless. It seemed like each new day broke with another story about Tiger and in response to these daily revelations someone would want me to comment.

I was angry at him for what he'd done – especially what he'd done to Elin – but regardless of the morality of the matter, he was still a friend in trouble and I was going to stick by him.

I did that even though people were accusing me of being an enabler, an accomplice, saying I was lying when I stated clearly that I knew nothing about this. For months on end, my life was absolutely miserable.

People in my local community would front up to me at the shops and call me a liar to my face, and ask, 'What are you doing with him?'

That summer I won the national saloon car title and the next time I raced at my home track there was a grand parade of champions, which I led out. I was sitting on the roof of my car with Jett beside me, holding the trophy – and all I could hear were boos. Jett turned to me and asked, 'Why are these people booing you Dad?' He was five years old and it was impossible to explain to him why it was happening – it was embarrassing and humiliating.

Even when Jett returned to school at the end of the summer he'd come home and ask, 'Why do people say you're bad?'

It wasn't easy for Kirsty, either.

> There was a lot of anger and blame directed at Steve. A lot of people thought he was doing it too and that he and Tiger were going out together – it was a difficult time but I never doubted Steve and neither did Elin. Both Elin and I understood that Tiger knew very well that Steve was the kind of guy who would have told Elin about his cheating, had he known.

I repeatedly asked for Tiger's management to release a statement that would clear me of any involvement in this lurid news. They simply wouldn't do it because there were others in his group who knew exactly what was going on, and management felt they couldn't single out one person as innocent.

Angry, frustrated and hung out to dry, I was also in limbo about when I would next work. Tiger had taken an indefinite break from golf and I had no idea when he'd be back – or if I'd be working for him again. Quitting wasn't an option as I felt incredibly loyal to Tiger – this was the toughest time of his life and I wasn't going to ditch him. The uncertainty came from the total lack of communication from Tiger's team. It didn't bother me that he hadn't said anything because he had told me he'd be in touch when he was ready – though admittedly that was an email and I'd rather have had a phone call. But I think Mark Steinberg or one of his lackeys could have been more forthcoming and more understanding of my situation. All I got was silence.

At one stage, one of the many women who claimed to be a mistress said she'd met me when I was with Tiger in Las Vegas – that got broadcast on radio in New Zealand and picked up in the papers. It was despicable reporting. I was giving my side of the story but no one seemed to care and comments like that from some bimbo on the other side of the world trying to get her 15 minutes of fame made me look like a fool. I begged Tiger's team to say something in my defence, but they wouldn't.

We took a family holiday to Australia's Gold Coast in February, staying in an apartment right on the beach. One morning, Jett and I walked down to the beach for a swim – I was in my board shorts only, no T-shirt. Suddenly, there's a reporter and photographer there wanting a comment on the televised statement Tiger was about to give. That's how far this media machine was prepared to go – we couldn't even take off to Australia on holiday without being hounded by the press. I couldn't say anything. I had no idea what he was going to say that day anyway. The next day there's a shot of me in the paper running across the road without a shirt on – and people wonder why I would get upset.

I didn't see the need for Tiger to make that televised statement – I didn't think a public apology was warranted. Yes, he needed to apologise to the people closest to him – his family and friends, me, Kirsty, his sponsors – but to hold an internationally televised press conference to say sorry to the world? That was way over the top.

It was a peculiar thing to watch too, as he was so awkward in his delivery and choice of words. I turned off the TV thinking, 'That's not the Tiger I know.' It was heavily scripted with nothing natural about it. It would have been more appealing to me, to his fans, to the other players, if he had spilled his heart out honestly. I've never asked him but I'm positive this was not his idea – it was obvious to those who knew him that it was not something he would choose to do.

That statement was also made while the World Match Play Championship was on, prompting many players to criticise Tiger and his team for showing no respect to his fellow professionals. Ernie Els, an elder statesmen on the tour and someone who held Tiger in high regard, called him selfish to make his statement on a Friday while the tournament was on.

'I feel sorry for the sponsor. Mondays are a good day to make statements, not Friday. This takes a lot away from the golf tournament,' Ernie later said.

Others thought the whole thing was a payback to Accenture, which sponsored the tournament but was one of the first companies to ditch its personal sponsorship of Tiger.

'That was the first thing we all thought of, like he is sticking it to Accenture – and that the PGA Tour is part of it all,' said another player, making reference to the fact that Tiger was allowed to make his statement at the PGA Tour's headquarters.

I think these pros had a right to be upset – that statement didn't need to be made during a tournament, let alone an important one like a World Golf Championship event. There was no doubt a better time to hold that broadcast. Anyone who made such a comment was justified. I don't think anybody thought it was the right time to be doing it.

There was still no indication as to when he'd come back to golf and I had to make up my own mind, as no one from his company gave me any clue as to what was happening. Knowing Tiger and knowing how much he loved Augusta, I didn't think he'd skip that tournament but I had no idea if he was practising or not. It was only at the 11th hour that I found out he was playing.

———

Tiger finally rang me on 23 March. He had already sent me an apologetic email when he was in rehab. It was heartfelt and meaningful; he was open, honest and remorseful and it reinforced my thinking that because I was so straight up and had such strong values, he felt couldn't tell me what was going on with his affairs.

It was good to actually hear his voice over the phone. I told him I was sorry to hear what he'd been going through and he was again apologetic to me.

I didn't have any sympathy for him over what he'd done. I believe you're in charge of your own actions and I have no sympathy for people who get addicted to drugs or gambling or sex. People make choices in their lives and he had chosen to do this. But I did have sympathy for the way he'd had to suffer in front of the world when others would have been able to sort out their mess in private.

I also told him that before I came back to work we had to sit down and have a long chat as there were some home truths I needed to say face to face. There was no question in my mind that our relationship – and his relationship with the game of golf – was going to be different when we got back together for the Masters in two weeks' time.

After we chatted he immediately phoned Kirsty and apologised to her as well. While Kirsty wanted to give him a piece of her mind, she was appreciative of the fact he'd at least made an effort.

> While I appreciated that it would have been hard for him, I didn't thank him for the call. Elin was and is a very good friend. I told him how upset I was about what he had done to Elin and the children, and then asked him to clear Steve's name in the media, as we were still getting a lot of hate mail and the media were still hassling us. When he told me he couldn't, I asked why not, and he told me that if he cleared Steve's name, the media would start asking if anyone else knew, and they did, so basically he was covering their butts and letting Steve suffer.

Through this period, there was one person who was incredibly helpful to me – former All Blacks rugby coach Laurie Mains. Laurie was one of those people I'd met along the way – he's a big golf fan, was a big Tiger fan – and we had struck up a friendship.

He'd had experience dealing with rugby players who had been in sticky situations and was a great person to talk to about what was going on. When I told him I wanted to have it out with Tiger face to face, he advised me to list the gripes I needed to get off my chest and not to leave the table until I'd said every word I'd written down.

The list was long – there was a lot I needed to say and it was going to be difficult to tell my boss he had to pull his head in. But I'd done it before and I would do it again before I retired.

I explained to him what had happened in New Zealand and how furious I was at being dragged through the wringer over a scandal I had nothing to do with. He needed to know how difficult that was for me and my family.

I told him it was something that could have been avoided and how bitterly disappointed I was at his people for their total lack of communication and unwillingness to put out a statement saying I had nothing to do with it.

I was adamant that some of his behaviour on the course had to change. He was well known for his bad temper and, while that wasn't pleasant to witness, you could live with it because it ended as quickly as it started. But he had other bad habits that upset me. I wanted him to prove to me he could change his behaviour and show me – and the game of golf – more respect.

One thing that really pissed me off was how he would flippantly toss a club in the general direction of the bag, expecting me to go over and pick it up. I felt uneasy about bending down to pick up his discarded club – it was like I was his lackey. The other thing that disgusted me was his habit of spitting at the hole if he missed a putt.

Tiger listened to what I had to say, the air was cleared and we got on with it – his goal was to be the best player in history and my goal was to keep working as best I could to help make that happen.

CHAPTER 18
BROKEN BONDS

G iven the fact that he hadn't played since November, Tiger's game ahead of the Masters in April was looking sound. And after all the angst, lies, silence, uncertainty and frustration, I was actually excited to be back on the golf course – my only fear was whether Tiger was mentally ready to face what was ahead of him.

That excitement evaporated soon after arrival at Augusta. I could sense immediately the air around us had changed. The attitude towards Tiger, usually deferential and distanced, was replaced by a cool disdain. People all over the world, including his rivals, had lost their respect for him, were no longer in awe of him – his lies and double life had been exposed. He was naked out there. I could feel it too – I'm thick-skinned and don't usually care what others think of me but it was obvious our world had changed. People were looking sideways at me as well. It was an uneasy feeling. I knew other players and caddies were talking about me but I only worried about those who were closest to me – they knew the truth and that's all that mattered to me.

Tiger had been briefed by his management about what to expect from the fans, but nothing had prepared him for the bollocking he got from Billy Payne, the Masters chairman, who ripped Tiger to shreds at his pre-tournament address to the media.

'It is not simply the degree of his conduct that is so egregious here,' said Payne. 'It is the fact that he disappointed all of us and, more importantly, our kids and our grandkids. Our hero did not live up to the expectations of the role model we saw for our children . . . his future will never again be measured only by his performance against par, but measured by the sincerity of his efforts to change.'

I was shocked. Billy Payne, speaking on behalf of the Masters, had no right in my view to give his opinion on the matter, let alone to admonish Tiger for how he conducted his personal life. The Masters has strived to make itself about golf, not about politics or morality – how else could they sustain such a socially unacceptable anti-women stance? I thought Tiger had been through enough humiliation and it was not Payne's job to engage in a bout of finger-wagging from the pulpit.

When Tiger finally stepped out on the golf course, his vulnerability was plain to me. Normally he was oblivious to the crowd but, walking out to the first tee, I could see all his senses were on high alert. He was acutely aware of the people around him and self-conscious about being the centre of attention for all the wrong reasons. He was like an animal sniffing the wind for signs of danger.

While he's one of the mentally toughest guys on the planet, not even he could block out this feeling of being stripped down to his bare bones in public – he looked lost and uncertain.

Surprisingly, the patrons at Augusta were a lot more forgiving than I'd expected. There were a few negative comments, but that was nothing unusual with Tiger, and I was surprised by how many people said, 'Welcome back,' and, 'We're behind you, Tiger.' They were receptive and supportive and seemed to be able to separate the strands of Tiger's life. They may have hated the philanderer but they still loved the golfer.

Even more surprising was the golf he played. He opened 68-70 and was right there after two rounds, doing so while trying to live up to his pre-tournament promise to tone down his bad behaviour, to 'be more respectful of the game', and be more appreciative of the fans. He did all that during the first two rounds – on the Friday he shook hands with a little girl who was sitting on her father's shoulders, he joked with the media. He was relaxed and still played well.

As foolish as it may have been, I allowed myself, given his modified behaviour and an OK game, to believe the old Tiger could genuinely change his stripes. That hope lasted all of 48 hours before Mark Steinberg brought everything tumbling down again.

We were walking from the media centre to the practice range when Steinberg told Tiger that if he wanted to win the tournament he had to 'stop being a nice guy' and go back to being his old self.

I couldn't believe my ears. After all that Tiger had been through, and the fact he had made a public commitment to a less snarling and aggressive Tiger, that he'd promised me he would reform his bad habits, his main advisor was telling him the opposite.

This was the moment in time when Tiger had a chance to turn his image around. It was the perfect opportunity to create a new Tiger – a fan-friendly Tiger who would sign more autographs, interact more openly with fans, be less surly with his rivals, more communicative with those around him – so to hear those words from Steinberg floored me. Right then, something inside me changed. A brick in the foundation of my relationship with Tiger had been prised loose. My immediate thought was, 'I'm not sure I'm going to be around much longer.'

The irony in all this was the fact that, despite his swearing and bad-tempered behaviour on the golf course, having fun was actually important for Tiger. He would constantly remind me it was, at heart, a game and that we were both fortunate to be doing what we loved. Yes, it's serious and there can be some tension but Tiger was also aware he was in a privileged position. When he was playing badly, he would often say, 'If I keep playing like this, it's going to be TW's carwash and you'll be the one polishing cars, Stevie.' He knew life could be a lot worse – something a lot of other professionals from country club backgrounds didn't necessarily appreciate. Some of them don't know what an honest day's work is – they think a hard day at the office is hitting balls for a few hours, going to the clubhouse for a sandwich, fries and a Coke before heading out to play nine holes. I think some of them forget how lucky they are to be making a living out of something they love.

Prior to this Steinberg comment – and despite all the pain and humiliation I'd endured – I still saw myself caddying for Tiger until he gave up. I didn't know when that would be but I knew playing on the Champions Tour, for players over 50, was not on the cards for either of us. Of course, we'd often had a conversation about how many majors he wanted to win and I believed that when he got to his target he would rack the cue – it's just that we were a little unclear on what that target would be precisely. Initially it was 20, and then one day he said, 'No, your favourite number is 21 – we'll get to that.' I came back with, 'No, you're a great Michael Jordan fan – why don't we go for 23?'

It seems like a fantasy now, a childish game, to have assumed so much but there was no reason not to believe he had the world at his feet. And I'd wholeheartedly bought into the Kingdom of Tiger and had set my compass to his goal of breaking Jack Nicklaus's record.

I know now that my single-minded pursuit of Tiger's dream got me offside with a few people. I got blinkered and lost sight of the fact there were more important things in life than being a passenger on an express train hurtling through a long, narrow tunnel towards a destination. The moment Mark Steinberg made that comment, I knew my chances of seeing the light at the end of that tunnel had all but disappeared.

———————

At the same time, Tiger's coach Hank Haney was also thinking of pulling the pin. Hank had long felt that he was treated poorly by Tiger, who often admitted Hank bore the brunt of his famously bad temper.

Hank's moment of truth came two days later, on the practice range before the final round of the Masters.

The previous evening, in Hank's view, Tiger had slighted him during a press conference, effectively blaming Hank for a bad swing when, in his view, it was bad putting that had let Tiger down.

All the same, he woke up on Sunday with a chance to win, which was incomprehensible given everything that had happened in the lead-up. He was four behind Lee Westwood and three behind Phil

Mickelson, which is nothing at Augusta – the deficit could be wiped out in a single hole.

At the range, Hank expected Tiger to be hitting a series of pure practice shots, as was often the case by the fourth day of a major, when his game was grooved.

Hank said Tiger was disengaged, rushing his shots, going about his routine in a sloppy fashion without any care or emotion. And Tiger pretended not to understand what Hank was trying to tell him – even doing the opposite to what Hank wanted him to practise: hitting the ball low instead of high, trying to work on a draw instead of the left-to-right fade that had served him well over the first three days.

Tiger sometimes came to the range and just did whatever he wanted. He could get into his own world and not want any input. He also played a peculiar game where he would hit bad shots on purpose – sometimes to see if the coach was paying attention or to see what reaction he would get. For whatever reason, on that Sunday there was no engagement whatsoever with Hank, who then and there made the decision he was going to quit.

Hank rang Steinberg that night, after Tiger had finished a meritorious fourth, telling him he was done. Steinberg begged him not to 'abandon' Tiger. 'He needs you,' Steinberg said. Hank felt a moral obligation not to let Tiger down so agreed to stay on.

Doubts had been planted in my mind when Mark Steinberg had told Tiger at the Masters to stop being Mr Nice Guy and go back to being himself. But I was prepared to judge Tiger based only on how he treated me and how we interacted. At the Masters, he might have treated Hank poorly but as far as I was concerned there was no noticeable change in how he treated me out there on the course. There was an awkwardness away from golf, which was not surprising, but I was prepared to invest the time required to rebuild that part of our relationship.

When he next teed it up, however, there was a dramatic change in his mood and in his attitude towards me.

To be in contention for the Masters, given all the mental and emotional baggage Tiger dragged behind him, was phenomenal. To play at the Masters under the scrutiny he'd faced and to appear for the first time in front of all those people who knew what he'd done was like undressing in public. I'd long regarded his mental toughness as his biggest asset but at Augusta that week it was beyond comprehension. He'd survived – and that was more commendable than winning.

At this next event, the Wachovia Championship at Quail Hollow, it all came undone. He'd put so much effort into Augusta that he had nothing left to hold back his emotions. His fuse was super-short. Short with me, short on the golf course – I understood why and tried to do the best I could, saying what I had to say, putting up with the anger and frustration. I don't know if something else had happened since Augusta – whether divorce proceedings were under way, perhaps – but he was a different person. His foul mood was embellished by terrible play as he missed the cut by eight shots. His second-round 79 was his worst score since that freezing-cold day at Muirfield in 2002.

The physical and mental strands of his life unravelled further at the next stop, The Players Championship. Not only was his fuse still frighteningly short, but he was in a high degree of discomfort as well, with a neck injury. On the range ahead of the final round, he was in excruciating pain, and I asked, 'Are you sure you want to tee it up?'

'I'll be all right,' he said.

He was impressive when it came to dealing with pain, as the world now knew from the 2008 US Open, and wouldn't dare walk off the course unless he felt he really couldn't handle it – he is such a traditionalist in that sense. But on the 7th hole he'd had enough and walked in.

The next day he spoke to Hank for the first time since the Masters. Hank was still officially Tiger's coach but they'd had no contact for a month and Hank felt like he was being strung along – kept on the books so Tiger had someone to blame for his poor form. On Monday, he sent a text to Tiger saying it was time to find another coach. To Hank's disbelief, Tiger said, 'We're still going to work together.'

'No, we're not. It's finished,' Hank replied.

'We'll talk in the morning,' said Tiger, who then performed his usual press conference palaver by saying he and Hank were working on his swing.

Hank had no choice but to release a statement saying he'd informed Tiger he was no longer working as his coach. Aside from the sponsors who ditched Tiger in the wake of the sex scandal, Hank was the first person in the history of Team Tiger to walk out rather than wait to be sacked.

A month off as he recovered from his neck problem was probably what Tiger needed at that point, and a top-20 finish at the Memorial Tournament when he resumed in June suggested he might be in good shape for the US Open, which was returning to Pebble Beach where he had scorched the field by 15 strokes 10 years earlier.

As it turned out, Tiger was 15 shots worse than he was in 2000, finishing at three over par and three behind winner Graeme McDowell, who finished even-par for the tournament.

His problem was obvious: he wasn't as mentally sharp as he used to be. The dismantling of his life in public was now affecting him quite badly – he still had the determination but he didn't have the patience and focus required to win. Even then, he still had chances to push himself into contention but he couldn't hit that clutch shot or make that vital putt that had previously defined his career. He was simply un-Tiger-like.

As the dire revelations about how low Tiger had sunk in his pursuit of sex were unveiled, sponsor after sponsor deserted him.

Through it all, a handful stayed loyal, notably Nike.

When Tiger used a Nike Method putter for the first time at the British Open at St Andrews in 2010, plenty of people jumped to the conclusion he had been pressured into finally becoming a complete Nike player in return for their loyalty.

Until then, he had stayed true to his long-serving Scotty Cameron Newport 2 putter. To all intents and purposes, it's the only putter I'd ever handled in his bag, as he started using it not long after I was hired. It was probably his most valuable asset. He'd held onto it for dear life.

Nike wanted him to be their guy, head-to-toe, with all 14 clubs bearing their swoosh, but they didn't force the issue. They tried and tried but failed to make putters that had the same feel and look as that Scotty Cameron putter, continuously using Tiger's feedback as they sought to make a club that suited him.

It was highly unusual that he finally decided to put a Nike putter in his bag at a tournament as important as the British Open. But then I'm also certain that he would not have changed it unless he believed he would perform well with it. He'd practised with this putter and felt it was suited to the slightly slower greens at St Andrews that year.

He started well with it – shooting 67 – and it looked like a good move. But his putting performance deteriorated in the second and third rounds. He was three-putting with alarming regularity and it was no surprise when the old friend made by Scotty Cameron came back into play for the final round.

The chopping and changing of the putter was perhaps the first outward sign that the unravelling of his private life was starting to impact upon his performance on the course. At that stage, he'd also been without Hank's input for a good three months. While Hank finally made his resignation formal at The Players Championship, he and Tiger hadn't had any interaction – apart from text and email – since that final day at the Masters in April.

Rudderless in so many ways, it became obvious at the WGC-Bridgestone event at Akron in August how far Tiger had slipped without a constant set of eyes watching what he was doing. The swing he brought to Akron was so broken that it was going to take more than a Band-Aid to fix.

Hank had previously told Tiger in an email that he felt Tiger's thoughts on his swing were like a game of musical chairs and that he might have 'swing ADD [attention deficit disorder]'. Whatever had been going on in practice, it was obvious something had come badly unstuck.

At a golf course where he'd had unprecedented success – a place he felt he owned and where he once shot 21 under by making a birdie in the dark – he was playing as badly as I'd seen him play. His 18-over-par tally was evidence something had become seriously unwired.

He played so early in the morning in the final round that we were able to fly to Whistling Straits, the venue for the PGA Championship the following week, getting there in time for me to measure the golf course.

That Sunday night Sean Foley came over to the house Tiger was staying in and gave us a presentation about his golf-coaching method.

The *New York Times*, in a feature on Foley's unusual teaching methods, wrote: 'On the spectrum of golf instruction, Foley belongs at the egghead, theoretical end . . . he believes in TrackMan – a radar device that measures the speed, spin and flight of the golf ball – the way a surgeon believes in X-rays and MRIs. His conversation is studded with references to fascial chains and kinesthetic submodalities, and in drills, he likes to trick the brain into creating new neuropathways. But he also talks a lot about philosophy (his major in college) and clinical psychology. In his study there are biographies of Gandhi and Nelson Mandela, and the memoirs of Bill and Hillary Clinton.'

The session we had with Sean ahead of the PGA was bizarre to say the least. A lot of the terminology and phrases Sean used were completely alien to me – the way he talked about the golf swing was practically a foreign language. I sensed it got quite overwhelming for Tiger too, and could see he wanted to end the session because of information overload.

Anyone who's going to talk to Tiger about coaching needs to have a pretty good sales pitch and Sean was super-convincing, even if his language was incomprehensible.

Tiger, remarkably, spent Monday, Tuesday and Wednesday with Sean and took on board what he had to say. It was the second major in a row where he was prepared to try something completely radical, after using the Nike putter at St Andrews. Again, I was surprised at this rupturing of a well-honed routine and the willingness to turn his world upside down on the eve of a big tournament. Until then, I'd thought Tiger was simply out of form and struggling with his focus – it turns out he was completely and utterly lost.

Sean Foley definitely turned Hunter Mahan and Justin Rose into better players – they are two of the best strikers of the golf ball and they weren't as good until they came under Sean's tutelage. Whether his method would work for Tiger was an unknown – but Tiger was so far in the wilderness he had to take someone on board. In the few days Tiger had before he teed off, he worked his arse off trying to implement what Sean was telling him. And, to be fair, the difference in one week was huge – if he had played at the PGA the way he'd played at Bridgestone, he wouldn't have made the cut. He hit a huge number of better shots than he did the week before but a tie for 28th was the best he could muster on a challenging course.

The year ended winless, which should not have come as a surprise. Mistresses had exposed him, sponsors had left him, fans heckled him, rivals stopped respecting him, his wife was divorcing him. He'd lost his self-respect, his coach and his swing.

In hindsight, I think he should have taken all of 2010 off and got away from the game, just like he thought of doing back in 2004 when he wanted to join the Navy SEALs. To have got away from all the pressure would have been the best thing he could have done for himself. He made a mistake by coming back so soon, but he couldn't resist the lure of playing the majors at Pebble Beach and St Andrews – they were venues at which he had such a compelling record it was too much of an attraction for his ego to ignore.

And despite what he'd promised to me – and what he later promised the public – about respecting the game more, being better with the fans, being better to the people he worked with, so much about him remained unchanged.

The lingering doubts about my longevity in the job caused by Mark Steinberg's comment at the Masters were still gnawing away at me, but there was also a part of me that didn't want to let him down. We'd had so many good times in the past I couldn't desert him in the bad times.

There was no doubt things were awkward between us. I felt our friendship had been severely tested and it was going to take time for us to regain the strong trust we once shared. We'd had that conversation before the Masters where I was pretty firm with my words and, while we'd moved on professionally, my sense was that was the limit of our connection now: we were in a player–caddy relationship rather than friends. It seemed to me that every interaction carried with it an imperceptible tension. Something had been lost. Lost forever, as it turned out.

CHAPTER 19
OUT OF THE JUNGLE

The Tavistock Cup is a glorified interclub event where pros enjoy themselves in a well-sponsored, low-key tournament. At the 2011 Cup, Tiger was paired one day with Adam Scott, who played superbly well – as well as I can remember seeing him play – and he was using the long putter, much to Tiger's disdain.

I asked Adam why he couldn't transform this kind of performance into a major championship win.

'Adam, what are you doing?' I said. 'Every time I see you playing, you're hitting the ball so well – what's wrong, what's missing, what is it, why are you not fulfilling your potential? What is it, man?'

He didn't have any obvious answers.

I'd long admired Adam – he was a genuinely good bloke and was quick to say g'day or offer congratulations after Tiger had won a tournament, which wasn't always the case with many pros. It's standard practice, when you bump into someone who's won the week before, to say, 'Good on you, well played,' that sort of thing, but Tiger's success seemed to turn people the other way. Whether it was jealousy or the fact that Tiger won so often, a lot of players chose to ignore any success he had.

Adam was one who took the time to come over and give you a little bit more than just a, 'Hey, well played,' and I appreciated that.

A few weeks after the Tavistock Cup, Adam was in contention for the 2011 Masters going into the final round, albeit five shots behind Rory McIlroy, with Tiger seven back. As it turned out, given the way McIlroy collapsed with a final-round 80, everyone in the top 10 had some kind of hope on the back nine.

By chance, Adam and I found ourselves alone on the putting green at the start of the final day, an unusual situation given how many people are usually hanging around Augusta's practice facilities. He was standing on the green alone while his caddy was setting up on the range. I was there waiting for Tiger to come out of the locker room.

For reasons I cannot explain, I started giving Adam a bit of a rev-up, using the same language I used with Tiger Woods the day he beat Chris DiMarco in the 2005 playoff. I told Adam in no uncertain terms he had to go out there and believe he was the best player, that it was his day and to keep telling himself, 'I'm Adam Scott and I'm winning this tournament.' He was shocked to hear it – I could see the surprise written all over his face.

He played incredibly well, shooting 67 in the final round to share the clubhouse lead alongside compatriot Jason Day, with a couple of groups on the course behind them. He'd done his utmost, including making birdies on some of the hardest holes but failing to take advantage of the par-5s on the back nine. But in the minutes that Adam and Jason were thinking about an all-Aussie playoff, and finally breaking the jinx that great golfing nation had endured at the Masters, South Africa's Charl Schwartzel did the unthinkable and made four straight birdies on the last four holes to win one of the most dramatic Masters tournaments I can remember.

Runner-up was Adam's best performance in a major. I know my little pep talk had made a difference when I bumped into his coach, Brad Malone, at the next event, The Players Championship.

'Man, that was unbelievable what you said to Adam. He'd never heard anything like that.'

Call it fate or destiny but there were definitely wheels in motion in April and May at the Masters and Players championships.

Subconsciously, I knew my time with Tiger was close to an end. My relationship with him had continued to deteriorate – an element of trust was missing and we weren't able to relax around each other like we used to. I took the attitude that time would heal whatever it was that had frayed between us but, as I found out over the next few weeks, when I put our so-called friendship to the test, Tiger had nothing to give me in return.

The wheels of fate turned a little faster when Tiger withdrew halfway through the first round at The Players Championship. He'd hurt his knee at Augusta when hitting out from under a tree and when he grumpily pulled the pin on his first round after shooting 42 on the front nine, he said the knee 'acted up' causing a 'chain reaction' through his lower leg.

It also started a chain reaction in our lives. Though neither of us realised it, when he limped out of that tournament it would be the last time we worked together.

———————

Tiger had to take time off but I anticipated he would be ready for the US Open. He'd played every US Open – even when his dad died, even when he had a ruptured cruciate ligament and stress fractures in his leg. He gave no indication he wouldn't play until just nine days out when he announced he was skipping the Open for the first time in his career.

Adam was on the phone straight away asking if I'd be available to caddy for him. I knew I'd had an impact on him at the Masters but was still surprised to hear from him. Plenty of players had asked me to work for them over the years when Tiger was out of action but I was loyal to my boss and the answer was the same each time: no. Helping someone else was not something I'd given any thought to, but this time it was Adam who was after a fresh perspective.

It was an interesting time – I guess I was just taking my chances. In that period I was highly motivated to reach my potential and I was willing to do whatever it took.

There was some reading between the lines required. Steve had given me some words of encouragement before the Masters – which was something he didn't need to do – and that stuck with me. Within a matter of weeks, Tiger Woods was out injured and I was in between caddies. I thought, 'It's time to see what this guy's all about,' and I took the view that if you don't ask you don't get. I was fully expecting Steve to say no but I had nothing to lose. And it turns out Steve was in a position where he was prepared to take a chance.

What attracted me to Steve as a caddy? Like others, I had watched Tiger's twelve years of utter domination of the golfing world and I'd seen the role that Steve played in that. I wanted to get that kind of experience on my bag.

Not many people on tour were that close to Steve when he was with Tiger Woods – he kept a professional distance through necessity. I had the same idea of Steve as everyone else did – that he was forthright and outspoken – but I think I had a better understanding of him than many others because Australians and New Zealanders share a similar mentality, especially when it comes to sport.

He and I also had a mutual respect for each other. And at the time I wasn't afraid to have someone come in and tell me what he thought. I was looking for another piece of the puzzle and part of that was getting Steve's frank assessment of my game.

I called Tiger and explained the situation. He said, 'No problem.' But I soon got a text from Mark Steinberg, which read: 'Do you really think it's a good idea to caddy for Adam?'

I had expected that might happen. Tiger had reconsidered but couldn't bring himself to ring me and discuss it in person, which was typical of his conflict avoidance. At that stage, I'd said yes to Adam on the basis that Tiger had given me his blessing and I wasn't about to turn around and tell Adam that Tiger had reneged. I rang Tiger back, discussed the situation further, explained it was a one-off, and noted that I didn't have any contract that prevented me from caddying for someone else. In the end, he said he was fine with it.

Not that it mattered that much as Adam didn't play particularly well and missed the cut.

The next question was whether Tiger was going to play in the AT&T National, a tournament that benefited his foundation and for which he was the tournament host. A few days after the US Open finished, he confirmed he was out of that as well.

Again, Adam was on the phone. I knew this would probably be stretching it with Tiger but I had another reason for being at that tournament in Pennsylvania – my father-in-law, Ian Miller, and a good mate from Oregon had already planned a trip to the east coast to coincide with this event.

I was looking forward to seeing them there and when you caddy in a tournament there's a few extra perks you can get for friends and family, such as spectator passes and good parking. We were going to take in some motor racing in Pennsylvania as well – a friend of mine raced sprint cars and the venue wasn't far from the golf course. It was a bit of a boys' trip that we were all looking forward to and had planned for some time.

When I rang Tiger for an OK, I explained why I wanted to be there, that it was for personal reasons and since I couldn't be there working for him I'd like to be there working for Adam.

He argued we could still make the trip and watch the golf together as spectators – that I didn't have to caddy for Adam. Well, I argued back, why would I want to do that – go and watch a golf tournament I had no interest in? And why would my father-in-law and my friend want to go to a tournament where I wasn't working? It was more fun to watch golf when you knew someone involved. They wouldn't go to watch a golf tournament for the sake of it – they wanted to follow me around and be part of something I was doing.

I thought I made a cogent argument, and assured Tiger this was purely personal and as a mate I thought he could do this for me.

He eventually relented.

No sooner had I given Adam the green light when Tiger rang back and said, 'Actually, I'd rather you didn't caddy for Adam.'

'We discussed this . . .'

He wasn't happy – and I was furious. I thought it was selfish of him to stop me doing this. My father-in-law had taken time off work to go on this trip; it was all planned. If he'd been a real friend he would have understood.

We were at a stalemate. I wasn't going to budge and he was digging in his heels.

Mark Steinberg then called me and spelled out why I shouldn't caddy for Adam. He said Tiger was concerned I would pass on all the knowledge I'd gained over the years with him and that would help Adam become a threat to him in the future.

That was another conversation that travelled on the road to nowhere – as if I could pass on 12 years of knowledge in a week. I wasn't budging.

A weird thing then happened. I got a text from Steinberg, accidentally sent to me instead of Tiger: 'I've talked to Stevie. I think I've persuaded him not to caddy for Adam.'

He hadn't done any such thing and the whole episode was starting to get a little bit ugly.

Tiger, under the impression that Steinberg had convinced me to say no to Adam, rang back. I told him Steinberg was wrong – I was going to stick to my plan.

'If you caddy for Adam, that's you and me finished,' he said.

It came to me quite clearly then. If he couldn't appreciate the fact that this had nothing to do with him – that I was caddying for Adam for one more tournament only, and for all the reasons I'd clearly laid out – then I wasn't as close to him as I thought I was. He was not the friend I imagined him to be. I told him I wasn't going to go back on my word to Adam.

'Then we're done.'

Ian is a builder and he was in Oregon helping me do some renovations to our house there. When I got off the phone, I climbed upstairs and said to Ian, 'You're not going to believe this – I just got fired.'

Tiger remembers this whole thing differently. He claims he didn't fire me until we met face to face at the AT&T National, on the final day of the tournament, but it was as clear as day to me – after 12 years I'd been fired over the phone. There's no mistaking the language – when your boss says 'we're done' that means the gig is over.

Weirdly, I was happy with that. I'd already come to the conclusion at the Masters in 2010 that I wouldn't be there right to the end, that I would never see him break Nicklaus's record. I'd already accepted it was over and this was a rubber-stamping of the divorce papers. It didn't bother me at all.

———

After the final round of the AT&T National, Mark Steinberg met me and said, 'He's waiting for you in the boardroom upstairs.'

As I walked up, I was rehearsing all the lines I wanted to recite about his selfishness but when I walked in the door his body language stopped me dead in my tracks. Leaning back in a boardroom chair, at one of the most prestigious golf clubs in America, he had his feet up on the table.

I don't know what he was trying to achieve but the negative energy, exemplified by his posture, turned me right off. As soon as I saw him like that, I decided I wasn't going to waste my breath saying anything – I'd let him have his say, then I'd walk away.

It was friendly enough. He told me it was over and wished me luck. He knew at that stage he wasn't going to be playing the British Open and I knew I would probably caddy for Adam there. Tiger and I agreed there would be no formal statement about our split until after the British Open so as not to distract Adam, who didn't need the stress of having to answer a whole lot of questions about it.

I wasn't angry at being fired. That's what happens in our sport. But I'd been angry for a long time, going right back to when the sex scandal first unfolded on Thanksgiving Day in 2009. I was angry at not being included in anything that was going on. I was angry I didn't know what was happening. Angry I didn't know when he might play again. Angry

I was left to hang in the breeze looking like a fool as all these accusations were thrown at me. And I was seething at the way his people blatantly ignored my situation as I was implicated in his wrongdoings.

The way this circus played out, and the way he'd failed to live up to his promise to change his character, had diminished my respect for Tiger and undermined my enthusiasm for his goals and dreams. Yet I'd stood by him out of loyalty. I was steadfast in my support of him despite my doubts – I was not going to be the one who let him down.

But when I asked for a show of loyalty from him, when I asked him to do something for me as a friend – he let me down.

I'd put so much time and effort into that relationship over 12 years, sacrificed so much of myself, but when the walls of my life started to crumble, through no fault on my part, he was unwilling to lend a hand in the rebuild process.

There was nothing there. No support, no friendship.

We'd had a great relationship and we'd had great times, a lot of laughs, it was a brilliant time in my life – and now it had come to the point where we couldn't even have a proper conversation. They say time heals but with Tiger, once he gets rid of you, that's the end of the story. We've barely spoken a word to each other since that day in the boardroom.

———

Adam didn't know I'd been fired but he knew Tiger wasn't going to play at the British Open and was delighted I could caddy for him there.

He was so keen to have me on board that he was there waiting for me at the airport when I arrived in London, something no pro had ever done for me in the past. We jumped in his car and headed down to Kent, which is when I told him it was officially over between Tiger and me.

What I didn't tell Adam was that now I'd finished with Tiger I was thinking of ending my career. I was going to do this one event for Adam and then go back to New Zealand and spend more time with my family, watch Jett play rugby . . . start a new chapter in my life.

But when I saw how excited Adam was at the prospect of my being available to caddy for him fulltime, I started to think of it as a new challenge.

Adam was a totally different character to Tiger. The perception from the outside was that he was too laid-back for his own good and there were questions over his desire, but you don't know what a player's true character is like until you go and work for him – I was curious to see what was there.

During that car ride, which was only an hour or so, we talked about his goals and aspirations and by the end of the journey I was committed to giving it a go with him fulltime. I saw it as a chance to see what difference I could make for Adam – I'd long believed his talent offered great promise, but he hadn't fulfilled it at that point.

———

I don't think I ever got into more trouble publicly than in August 2011.

We were in Akron, Ohio, for the WGC-Bridgestone tournament, one of the best events on the calendar. I had been going there in various guises since the 1980s. I'd worked there for Greg Norman and Raymond Floyd before winning seven times with Tiger Woods, including that unforgettable win in the dark when he shot 21 under.

It's a big tournament in a small town and it has a special feeling to it, and over the years I had met hundreds of genuinely great people there.

Here I was with Adam Scott, who had played almost flawless golf to build a three-shot lead as he stood on the 18th tee in the final round. Adam was wearing all black after a losing a bet with me on a rugby match the previous day – New Zealand's All Blacks had beaten Australia – and it was promising to be a wonderful conclusion to an incredibly difficult period in my life.

It was the first week in August. I had been formally cut free by Tiger about two weeks earlier when he made the delayed statement we had agreed on.

I responded to this 'shock' dismissal by making a statement of my own. There was a degree of smoke and mirrors to all this because for us the news was three weeks old and we had both moved on already. But I took the opportunity to let people know how hard it had been for me over the previous 18 months and how Tiger had failed to earn back my respect following his adulterous behaviour.

As Adam and I walked down the 18th fairway towards a four-shot win, I suddenly realised the crowd was chanting my name: 'Ste-vie, Ste-vie.'

It was bizarre, unprecedented and incredibly uplifting. Adam thought it was weird but cool.

'I didn't know a New Zealander could be so popular,' he jibed afterwards.

After all the heartache, anger and sadness of the past 21 months with Tiger, I was elated and brimming with joy and satisfaction.

Before I knew it, David Feherty, the on-course commentator, had a microphone under my nose and I was being interviewed live on the 18th green. If I hadn't been so highly wound up on emotion, I'd have thought twice and reminded David that caddies don't do interviews.

But he's there with all his Northern Irish charm and wit. I'm high on life and at the end of an emotional and destabilising summer, so it all comes spilling out of me. I unloaded everything I'd been carrying and in so doing completely broke free of my connection to Tiger Woods. That's a part of my life that was over and this victory with Adam was the start of a new chapter.

When I look back on the conversation I can't remember what I said, or how I said it – it was almost babble – but I wish I could go back in time and hit a pause button on myself.

The biggest mistake I made was saying that that week with Adam was the greatest of my life and the most satisfying win of my career. Clearly, it wasn't – there had been much more significant victories – but I was caught up in the moment.

I copped it from all directions over that. Every critic who'd wanted to have a go at me, but perhaps felt they couldn't because they perceived me to be protected by Tiger, used that as a chance to dump their vitriol. I was called every expletive under the sun.

I know I shouldn't have spouted off like that but I also think I shouldn't have been put in that position – to interview a caddy on the 18th green at a tournament is unheard of. But then again, it was unparalleled in golf history to hear the crowd chanting the caddy's name – it was a unique situation and I allowed myself to get caught up in the drama and excitement.

When I spoke to Kirsty she warned me to expect a media firestorm.

> I remember that day so clearly. I was at home watching on TV. I was so excited for Steve, after all the shit that had come his way after what Tiger had done to Elin and the waiting around in the dark while Team Tiger decided what to do, and then finally to be fired over the phone, it was awesome for Steve to go out and help Adam get that win.
>
> But when David Feherty approached Steve and I watched the interview I was gutted. I knew straight away the media were going to crucify him once again, and they did – Steve called me when he walked off the 18th green. I was excited for him and didn't want to put a dampener on what had been an awesome win but felt I had to say something about how that interview was going to come across, and what I thought he would wake up to when the media got hold of it. I basically wanted him to be prepared before he spoke to anyone else.

I apologised to Adam, who, to his eternal credit, was brilliant about it – he understood the situation had got the better of me, which doesn't often happen. He looked me in the eye and said, 'Don't worry about it – we all make mistakes.' He still doesn't have an issue with what happened.

> That whole thing bothered me very little at all. The only thing that bothered me was how the media were going to put it on me in the press conference that followed, but they weren't harsh on me at all.

A lot went into that tournament from Steve's point of view – a lot of emotion – and I didn't hold that against him at all. It didn't affect me in a negative way. Some people said it took away from my win but it didn't. At that stage, I was on a mission and, if anything, I was out to impress Steve and make sure he stayed around. If that's one thing he regrets – he shouldn't.

If I thought that was bad, it was trivial compared to the deep shit I found myself buried under in November.

The annual Caddy Awards Dinner was scheduled to take place during the HSBC Champions tournament at Shanghai. I'd regularly bypassed this dinner – it wasn't my thing – but I got talked into going because they were going to present me with an award for best celebration: for my spiel after Adam's win at Akron.

The whole affair was relaxed – it was a bunch of caddies after all – so the language was ripe and the content ribald. Giles Morgan, the global head of sponsorship and events for HSBC, gave a speech in which he directed the audience to where they could find female companions for the night.

That was the tone of the evening. When I was presented with my award and asked why I'd been so over the top at Akron, I said, 'I just wanted to shove it up his [Tiger's] black arse.'

To me, it was a bit of fun in a closed-shop environment and I didn't feel it was racist or malicious, but when someone in the room posted it to Twitter it spread around the world like wildfire.

Being accused of racism hurt me deeply – especially as I'm part-Maori – and many writers and bloggers jumped to conclusions, failed to do any research, or got the completely wrong end of the stick, saying that I had called Tiger a 'black asshole', which is completely different and completely wrong.

Mark Steinberg texted me to 'acknowledge their disappointment' but Tiger, when he had a chance to dig the knife into me in public, didn't, which I respect him for.

'Stevie is certainly not a racist – there's no doubt about that. It was a comment that shouldn't have been made and certainly one he wishes he didn't make,' he later said.

As you can imagine, this was a firestorm of epic proportions. The abuse I got because of that was horrific – it was so bad we had to close down the 'contact us' page on my website, because people were pouring out the most vicious kind of hate, which poor Kirsty had to read.

I couldn't believe the size of the media pack waiting for me at the airport in Sydney, where Adam and Tiger were playing the Australian Open the following week. But on the golf course the fans were seeing the lighter side of it.

Adam was urged to sack me, the PGA was told to fine me. Neither happened. Adam was under a lot of pressure but he remained supportive, and was unequivocal when he said: 'I have discussed this matter directly with Steve and he understands and supports my view on this subject. I also accept Steve's apology, knowing that he meant no racial slur with his comments. I now consider the matter closed. I will not be making any further comment.'

I felt bad for Adam. he'd hired me in July and by November I was the centre of two global news stories, which didn't reflect well on him, but he was steadfast in his support.

There was one more chapter in the Tiger relationship left to play out that year – The Presidents Cup at Royal Melbourne pitted an International side, captained by Greg Norman, against an American team, led by Fred Couples.

Given my fallout with Tiger, there was a lot of talk about what would happen if Adam and Tiger got paired together. I felt quite uncomfortable reading about it in the papers – and there was a lot written about it. Greg, as captain, said, 'It had to be done,' and decided to get that match out of the way as soon as possible. So on the first day he matched Adam and KJ Choi against Tiger and Steve Stricker.

While I was nervous about the match, it's fair to say I enjoyed the outcome – Adam and KJ gave Tiger and Steve an absolute bath, beating them 7 and 6.

Over my years with Tiger, I knew how much he hated to lose in any match-play event, whether it be the Ryder Cup or Presidents Cup, and he hated it even more when it was a team format, because at least when he was playing singles he felt he could control things more. That day, knowing how much he hated to lose, watching his face as Adam and KJ made putt after putt was something I'll always remember.

CHAPTER 20
A NATIONAL HERO

There are only two losses that keep me awake at night – but Adam's disaster at the 2012 British Open, where he blew a four-shot lead with four holes to play, isn't among them.

Raymond Floyd's near miss at the 1990 Masters, when I didn't speak up on the 17th hole in the final round, bugs me to this day. It's one of the very few times in my life that I didn't speak up.

The other is Greg Norman's miss at Augusta in 1989, when I couldn't convince him to play the shots I wanted.

If anything, even though he became only the second player after Jean van de Velde to squander a 54-hole lead of four shots or more at the Open, Adam's performance for 68 holes at Royal Lytham & St Annes was the opposite of heartbreak – it further instilled in me the belief that he was a major winner in waiting.

And if anyone ever suggests to me it was a choke – or that I made a mistake on the 18th – I will give them short shrift. Adam birdied the 14th, the hardest hole on the course that day, by hitting a perfect drive down a tight fairway riddled with potential disasters. If he was feeling the tension, he wouldn't have made birdie at that hole.

That put him four ahead of Ernie Els, who also had a couple of holes to play. What happened next was like a slow-building avalanche – a bit of bad luck, one bad putt, one bad iron shot, and one bad decision.

On the 15th, Adam was unlucky to see his ball roll into a greenside bunker. He hadn't played a bad shot as such but ended up with an awkward stance – one foot in the bunker, one foot out – and hit a good shot. Not a great shot, but he left himself work to do for par. He didn't manage to get up-and-down and made a bogey. That's one shot gone, but no big deal – move on.

The 16th is the easiest on the course. He could have driven it on the green that day, but that play could just as likely have brought bogey into play if he'd driven it badly, so we opted for a 6-iron/sand wedge combination. He misjudged the second shot a little bit and it came to rest 20 feet behind the flag but that was still OK. No need to panic: make two putts and get out of there – but he three-putted after his par-saver took a look in the hole but stayed out.

The 17th was the one poor shot, and it came after we'd heard the roar for Ernie Els' birdie at 18. It's a big green and he had no right to miss it left. Another bogey and, with Ernie's birdie, it was level-pegging.

From the 18th tee, we knew par was needed for a playoff. I liked either driver or a 2-iron off the tee – blast it past the bunkers or come up short of them. The only club I didn't like was 3-wood. He asked me what I thought and I said 2-iron. He considered it and rejected it. Adam was totally locked on the 3-wood and couldn't see any of the other options. He thought it was the club that was going to get him the best outcome. It was the first time I'd been with Adam when he'd had the chance to win a major championship, and whenever it's the first time for something like that you're not entirely sure how the player is going to react. I could have argued more firmly but didn't want to put any doubt in his mind by questioning his decision, which he'd made after processing all the relevant information. He'd made three bogeys on the trot and I didn't want to force him to hit a club he wasn't happy to have in his hand.

He committed to the 3-wood but hit it into a bunker. He still had a par putt for a playoff but left it outside the hole. He sank to his knees and all he could mutter was, 'Wow.'

Honestly, I didn't lose any sleep over that. I knew he could win a major championship one day – he'd played 68 great holes of golf and then in the last four holes hit one bad shot, made one bad decision and had a three-putt. Nothing more dramatic than that. I knew our time would come.

If there was one thing Adam and I were still struggling with at the Open, it was our decision-making process.

It usually takes player and caddy a while to arrive at a process that plays out without any explanation or misunderstanding. It wasn't quite there at the British Open but by the end of 2012 we'd nailed it and had created a way of working together that we were both happy with.

With most players I've caddied for, the process is that I'll give yardage and other relevant information, suggest a club and describe the shot he needed to hit. With Tiger, he would take that on board and come back with his decision, and if we differed there might be a short discussion before he committed to his club. I started that with Adam but, as we learned more about each other, it turned out Adam preferred that I gave him all the relevant information, which he would digest before making his club selection and then asking, 'Do you agree with that?'

Adam described it as learning to 'not tread on each other's toes'. By the time we got to Augusta for the 2013 Masters, we were on the same wavelength and had our moves down pat.

When I first worked for Adam, at the 2011 US Open when Tiger was injured, I discovered one of the problems that was holding him back.

That week he played 18 holes on the Saturday before the Open, another 18 on Sunday, followed by more golf on Monday, Tuesday and Wednesday. By the time he reached the first tee on Thursday, he was spent – it was no wonder he missed the cut.

I urged Adam to play less golf and to also take a leaf out of Tiger's book and stay away from the crowds – rent a house, hire a cook, stay out of restaurants, keep off his feet, avoid people who would sap his energy when he was out.

That week, we had the perfect situation. Adam, his father Phil, swing coach Brad Malone, manager Justin Cohen and myself, all together in a house with a live-in chef. I'd stayed with players before but not in this kind of relaxed atmosphere with such great camaraderie.

On the back of his Royal Lytham disappointment, Adam had been working tremendously hard on his game – he'd got a taste of it and hungered for it badly. After we played nine holes on Monday and nine holes on Tuesday, with Ernie Els and Louis Oosthuizen, Ernie's caddy Colin Byrne said to me, 'I don't bet on golf often but if you put those two nines together, that is the best round of golf I've seen at Augusta – your man is a good chance this week.'

He was playing as well as he could possibly play. The trick now was to not waste it all at practice. When a player is in command of his game, the temptation is to practise more to further ingrain the moves, but that can have the reverse effect. Too much time spent mucking around on the practice green or hours whittled away at the range can cause a player to lose something intangible but integral to his swing. Sometimes, you need to close it down. If you overdo it – it slips out of your grasp.

During a tournament, I often get a song stuck in my head – that week, it was Supertramp's 'Dreamer'. One of the lines in that song asks if you can do something out of this world. That's what I was repeatedly singing in my head – and wondering, 'Well, can Adam do something out of this world?' He couldn't be more ready. There was no question in my mind it was his time.

He played impeccably all week – I counted only two bad shots for the entire tournament, or, in other words, about 98.5 per cent of his shots were great.

He came to the 72nd thinking he had a putt to win the Masters.

When that birdie rolled in I saw a new side of Adam – he was amped to the max. To anyone who ever questions his desire or his motivation, I'd say watch the replay of that moment. He was as animated as I'd seen him, screaming, 'C'mon Aussie!' at the top of his lungs. He thought he'd won the tournament. He thought that putt was the winning shot, but I knew he was going to have to calm down pronto. Back on the fairway behind us, I could see Angel Cabrera from the waist up, which meant he had driven it a mile and had only a short iron into the green. I knew he was going to attack the pin – Angel doesn't know any other way.

I quickly said to Adam we needed to get back to ground here because we might have a playoff coming. On cue, Angel stiffed it to two feet. Playoff.

And I knew we had a fight on our hands.

Argentina's Cabrera is known as El Pato, which means duck in Spanish, because of his splayed feet – but he should be called The Bull. Immensely strong, the barrel-chested Cabrera wouldn't look out of place in the front row of his country's Pumas rugby team.

I felt a kinship with Cabrera. His early life, while more severe than mine, had similarities. He was working as a caddy when he was 10 – needing money to help support his family. To this day he interacts with the caddies a lot more than most players and is quick to buy them a beer.

He's a friendly, easy-going guy who happily puffs away on his cigarettes without caring too much how it comes across on TV. As a player, he stands up and free-swings. There are no nerves involved in his play and you have to take him seriously when he's in contention, because he won't back down and he's prepared for a fight.

He'd proved his major championship mettle when he battered the notoriously difficult Oakmont Country Club into submission on his way to winning the 2007 US Open, and he'd claimed the 2010 Masters in a three-way playoff over Kenny Perry and Chad Campbell.

The strangest thing happened in the playoff – it was as if Greg Norman was with us, guiding me and Adam, helping him to avoid the mistakes Greg had made there in the past.

On the first playoff hole, the 18th, Adam and I had a long discussion over the second shot – it was so similar to the debate Greg and I had on the same fairway in 1989. We let our process play out, and Adam made his club selection: he wanted to hit 8-iron from 161 yards, which is what he'd hit in regulation.

I told him firmly – no.

'No, it's actually colder and more damp than when we played this hole half an hour ago. It's playing longer than you think.'

Where Greg had stuck to his guns over his 5-iron 24 years earlier, against my advice, Adam understood my argument and pulled out a 7-iron. While he didn't hit it perfectly – he held back a little – it landed close enough to the front of the green and he was able to chip it on to four feet.

This four-footer to stay alive in the playoff was no gimme, but all week Adam had been cleaning up from that range and I had no doubt he was going to do so again.

It was drizzling, the cloud ceiling was lowering, it was getting dark quickly and it was unlikely we would play another hole after the second playoff hole, the 10th, where Angel hit the best 2-iron tee shot I've seen in my life – he killed it – and then made the expected play: to the middle of the green leaving himself an uphill putt.

It was time for Adam to seize the moment. He was playing brilliantly but he was going to have do something special to beat Angel, who would fight all night if he had to.

If that had been the 64th hole of the tournament, we would have followed Angel's lead and hit a 7-iron into the middle of the green – you simply cannot challenge that back-pin placement because if you go over the back of the green you're out of the hole. You have to play safe to the middle of the green, get below the hole, and have an uphill look at birdie.

But this wasn't regulation. It was a sudden-death playoff against a fierce competitor – the time for percentage plays was over. Besides, it was gloomy, there was a chance this was going to be the last hole of the day, and it would have been hard to go home and sleep on the fact that you might be coming back for one hole the next day. It was time to end this. It was time for Adam to challenge himself and see what he was made of.

We agreed he had to get that second shot right back to the hole. If you were to ask Adam, he'd say the 6-iron he hit to a fraction above the

BROOMSTICK MAGIC

ADAM SCOTT USED TO COP A BIT OF FLAK FOR USING THE LONG PUTTER, which will be banned from 2016. Tiger hated the long putter and thought it was against the spirit of golf – but maybe he also hated it because he once had a practice swing with one and couldn't use it! It's a skill in itself to hold that broomstick steady and make a smooth swing. It's not a simple fix for a common problem, otherwise everyone would do it. It's hard to use. It's considerably heavier than a normal putter – you need a different stance, different set-up, different stroke. At the start of 2014, Adam thought he'd try a short putter again, as he knew he'd have to switch eventually when the ban came into effect. In his first tournament in three months, he finished fourth. But the next week, the greens were a bit bumpy and he missed a couple of short putts, and suddenly his confidence was dashed so it was back to the long putter.

hole was the best shot of his life. It took nerves of high-tensile steel to execute and land it where he did.

Angel knew it, too. He turned to Adam and gave him a thumbs up. For a competitor as bold as Angel to acknowledge how brave that play was says much about both men.

Suddenly, as I surveyed the green, Greg Norman was with us again.

I knew this putt. I had it written in my yardage book – I'd noted it when Greg had a similar putt when I worked for him in the late '80s. For a quarter of a century, I had carried this piece of information with me without having a need for it – until now. Until Adam needed it to win the Masters.

Whether he asked me or not I was going to tell him: this putt breaks more than it looks. I didn't have to offer my advice unsolicited. Adam asked, 'Steve, can you read this putt? I think it's a cup outside the hole.'

'Adam, that's not even close. It's at least two cups and a bit. Trust me, I know this putt. It breaks more than it looks.'

I knew it was on a great line as soon as he hit it.

And then it was in. Adam had won his first major. He'd become the first Australian to win the Masters – the joy was almost overwhelming. For myself, having been through all that heartbreak with Greg, as a caddy and as a friend, it was such a redemptive feeling. It was beyond my wildest dreams to be involved in the act of burying the multitude of Greg Norman ghosts once and for all. And it was perfect that it was Adam, an Australian, donning the green jacket.

From the 17th hole in regulation through to the second playoff hole, the discussions Steve and I had are the most critical discussions I've ever had on a golf course. The way we worked together that afternoon was the culmination of what we had set out to do 18 months earlier.

Steve has so many great attributes as a caddy but one of his best is that he's so in the moment – sometimes more than the player is. He really does feel like he's playing out there, and he feels and assesses the conditions and the shot the way a player does.

On the 18th in the playoff, the temperature and the heaviness of the air had changed in the half-hour since we'd been out there in regulation, and he was sensitive to that change and what it meant.

He has a great feel for how a shot should be played and he delivers that information with such conviction. Even though that shot on 18 came up a tad short, it was the right club and the right shot. I could have hit it a little bit harder. It's in those moments that Steve really shines. I can't imagine many other caddies who can live and breathe the moment like that.

On the second playoff hole, I was in a situation where what I did was dictated by how well Angel was playing. When Angel put his approach in close, I knew that hitting to 45 feet – which was the safe play – wasn't going to get the job done. It wasn't going to win the Masters.

Steve asked me, 'This is your moment – how much do you want it?' He made me feel that the six-iron was the right shot and that I could execute it. And it was the best shot I've hit in my life.

I don't actually call Steve in that much to read putts, but it was dark and a pressure situation. That's when you lean on Steve. He's been there so many times – and it was an incredible read. Not just the fact that he doubled how many cups outside the hole it was but also that he said it so firmly: 'Two!' I knew he wasn't guessing. It was 100 per cent belief – you live and die on that.

Adam asked me to join him for the champion's dinner in the clubhouse and was only slightly surprised when I declined. That's not my scene, to sit down to a formal dinner with all those fancy Masters members. Anyway, I was only wearing shorts and a T-shirt under the jumpsuit they make you wear and, although I'd quite enjoy sitting in a room with all those blokes while wearing my work clothes, I wasn't fussed about going.

I wandered back to the caddy room by myself and sat alone reflecting on what a special week it had been. And still that song kept going around in my head.

As I was driving back to the house, I felt this was the pinnacle of my career – that it was time to give it away. Then, almost immediately, Greg Norman was on the phone. It was so special to hear from him. He told me he knew exactly what I was saying to Adam on those crucial playoff shots. He said he could tell by my body language on 18 that I wanted Adam to hit one more club.

'And on the second playoff hole, I could read your lips. You said, "This putt breaks more than you think." Am I right?'

He knew me too well. Adam and I both had a lot to thank him for.

When I got back home, I was still thinking, 'I've had enough now.' I'd helped a great bloke win his first major, helped Australia break its Masters jinx, and I felt that was a great note to finish on. But when I discussed it with a few people, they all said the same thing: 'You can't leave Adam after he's just won the Masters!'

They were right. It wasn't the right thing to do by Adam.

CHAPTER 21
OUT OF THE ROUGH

Since our split, Tiger and I hadn't spoken to each other. I wondered if that might change when Adam, Tiger and Rory McIlroy – as the world's top-ranked players – were grouped together in the first two rounds of the US Open at Merion in 2013.

But there was no conversation at all, apart from a 'good luck' on the first tee, where the tension was almost unbearable. There was no ice-breaker – just more ice. I'd never seen two players look more apprehensive than Tiger and Adam that day. It was beyond awkward.

As usual, with his first-tee jitters, Tiger blocked it wildly to the right, but when Adam almost missed his tee shot completely – he hit it on the bottom of the club and it barely got off the ground – all I could think was, 'Shit, this is all my fault.'

A twist of fate put Adam and Tiger together again in the final round of the British Open at Muirfield a month later. This time, with only two players, it was harder for us to avoid each other. I could sense Tiger was still a little bit uneasy about being around me and decided I was going to be the one to open the door with a conciliatory conversation. Going down the 7th fairway I thought I'd draw him out by asking about his family.

'How's Sam? How's Charlie? How's your mum? How's the foundation going?'

Each question got batted back with a perfunctory answer, but I kept trying, and each time I was expecting him to turn around and ask, 'How's Jett doing? How's Kirsty?'

But . . . nothing.

I realised then that despite all we'd been through, he didn't give a shit about me or my family. I had been excommunicated. People he once held dear were now nobodies. He'd shut me and my family out of his life.

It was the first time in 36 years as a caddy that the end of a professional relationship had spelled the end of a personal relationship.

Other people I've worked with have remained friends to this day – and not just acquaintances, but close friends. Even with Greg Norman, while things ended tempestuously between us, we still have that brotherly bond.

But Tiger couldn't separate church and state. It was all or nothing and I was now, quite clearly, nothing.

Sure, I'd played my role in the demise of our working relationship with my stubborn determination to caddy for Adam at the AT&T National. We were both hard-headed over that.

While his sexual shenanigans had pulled at the edges of our personal relationship by breaking the bonds of trust we'd built over 12 years, there was no reason why we couldn't be civil to each other and share stories about our families – families who were once so close that we took holidays together.

We'd been great as a team and we'd been great friends. And now we were on opposite sides of an ice sheet. When Tiger had said 'we're done' that day in 2011, he meant it in every sense of the word. I had gone the way of all the others who'd been frozen out of Team Tiger.

I didn't think it needed to be this way and I was angry – again – at his selfishness, his inability to even ask a question about my family.

On the 18th, after he putted out, we shook hands and exchanged a few words. The TV commentators and writers all saw it as two old mates burying the hatchet. The TV commentators chirped in their very British way, 'Oh, isn't that nice. Lovely.'

At his press conference, Tiger was asked if that handshake was more than the usual courtesy at the end of the round. 'It was,' Tiger said. 'He was saying it was a good fight out there today.'

Nothing could be further from the truth. In those few moments, I told him what I thought of him. I told him how selfish he was and how it was time he stopped thinking about himself so much. If you look at photos or videos of that moment you can clearly see Tiger's reaction: his face looks like thunder.

I'm often asked whether I would go back and work for Tiger. On one side – the personal side – no, I don't want anything to do with him. But on the professional side, I'd relish the opportunity to sit down with him and see where he's at, because it's so sad to see where his game is now. Having spent so long with him and understanding how he operates and plays, I would love to try to figure out what's going on with his game and mind. It's hard to fathom, even putting aside the fact he'd had back surgery, how Tiger could play so badly in 2015 – especially in the majors where he missed the cut at the US Open, British Open and PGA Championship. You'd think someone who has been as successful as he has been, a player who was a supreme ball-striker in his prime, could have quickly worked out what was wrong with his game.

But as for trying to rekindle the friendship? It's like a nasty divorce and I don't think it can be done.

It would be a different story if he – or his team – had agreed to my one request to say something that cleared my name during the sex scandal. A simple line that said, 'Steve knew nothing about it.' The fact that he couldn't do that caused a lot of grief for my family and me. That one comment could have erased months of derogatory, nasty comments. That he couldn't do that for someone who had been loyal to him for more than decade, someone who he had been close to for so many years – well, there's something not right about that.

———

I knew it was time to quit caddying for good when I was sitting on a plane on the tarmac at Auckland airport, getting ready to fly back to the US for FedExCup playoff tournaments at the end of the 2014 season.

'What would be the consequences of pulling open the emergency exit?' I thought.

I'm not joking. I was so agitated and desperate to get off that plane, I would have quite happily pulled open the exit and scampered down the runway. What stopped me was not the fear of the consequences, but how pissed off all the other passengers would be if the flight got delayed because I did something stupid. I sat there and stewed.

My frustration spilled over into my work in a way I'd not experienced before. The minor details of a routine that hadn't got to me previously now bothered me a lot. In particular, I was increasingly upset with Adam, for little or no reason. If I said to him, 'You can't miss it there,' and he missed it, I would get annoyed. It wasn't right – it was no way to perform and I knew I had to finally get off this 36-year rollercoaster. The thrill had gone. And the travel, as much as anything, had finally worn me out.

People have often asked me why I bothered coming all the way back to New Zealand between tournaments and why we didn't set up camp in America. A lot of caddies live around Dallas for travel purposes – it's in the middle of the United States and a three-hour flight in any direction to get to a tournament. Whereas I would have a 30-hour commute to reach a tournament on the east coast of America.

The simple truth is that I love New Zealand more than any place in the world. Home was so special I could not bear to be away. The moment when the plane touches down on the tarmac I get butterflies. I love the country. I love New Zealand people. I love the way of life – it's incomparable. I've travelled the world as extensively as you can – in my career, I've been to almost every golf-playing country you can imagine and yet the thrill of coming home is still great. At the end of 2014, the magic of New Zealand and being with my family was too big a spell to break. I wanted to continue on a part-time basis but Adam had different ideas and we agreed to go our own ways.

I'm glad I stuck it out for that one extra year, though, because I got to see Adam ascend to the number-one ranking in the world. He did that in mid-May, winning the Colonial in a playoff over Jason Dufner to overtake Tiger Woods as the world number one when the updated rankings came out the following Monday.

Adam was the third number-one player I'd worked with, after Greg and Tiger, and he held that ranking for 11 weeks before handing it over to Rory McIlroy.

I felt I'd achieved everything I wanted to.

———

The telling moment for me in what was soon to be semi-retirement came as the build-up started for the 2015 Masters. Having been to Augusta for 28 consecutive years, was I really going to miss it? When I didn't have the inclination to watch even one minute of coverage on TV, I knew I had made the right decision to retire. The romance had gone. And I had other things to focus on in life, like Jett and Kirsty.

When Adam Scott rang in late May 2015, I thought nothing of it. We were chatting away one minute, catching up on life, and the next minute he's saying, 'There's something I need to ask you.' I immediately knew where this was heading.

I ummed and ahhed a bit about going back to work for him. He knew I wouldn't agree to a fulltime gig but wanted me for the remaining majors of 2015 – but mentally I had checked out. I'd removed myself from the game and didn't know if I'd be capable of getting back into the fray.

He rang back the next day and was persuasive. The bottom line was he needed help – he was looking for that shot of confidence he got when I first went to work for him. For my part, I wanted to find out if I could make a difference – if I could lift his game.

In the period from when I retired to when I got the SOS call from Adam, I'd also taken time to reflect on what a wonderful journey my career had been. And I realised that during my 36 years of caddying, time had flown by. It had all happened so quickly. When I was back home and retired I was surprised by how slowly time moved. I'd

MY TOP 10 WINS

1. **1980 NZPGA:** my first win as a caddy with New Zealand great Bob Charles.

2. **1983 AUSTRALIAN MASTERS:** my first win with Greg Norman.

3. **1999 PGA CHAMPIONSHIP:** my first major.

4. **2005 BRITISH OPEN:** at St Andrews – no better venue to win the Open.

5. **2000 US OPEN:** I never, ever thought you would see a 15-shot winning margin in the modern era.

6. **2001 MASTERS:** to complete the Tiger Slam.

7. **2013 MASTERS:** Adam Scott becomes first Aussie to win the Masters.

8. **2008 US OPEN:** Tiger's 'impossible' win.

9. **1985 MALAYSIAN OPEN:** Aussie battler Terry Gale played out of his skin.

10. **2014 COLONIAL INVITATIONAL:** Adam Scott wins and takes over the number-one ranking.

become used to a clock continuously ticking in the background – I'm leaving in a couple of days, a week, a month . . . the clock was always ticking – and suddenly time had slowed so much it was like being on a different planet.

The realisation that I'd perhaps failed to enjoy the ride jolted home, and the lure of going back to St Andrews was just too strong for me to ignore – to go back one more time to such an inspiring and historic place and enjoy that walk over the Swilcan Bridge . . . I wanted that experience again, even if just one last time.

The caddy Adam had been using, Mike Kerr, was a wonderful caddy, but he might have been too laid-back for Adam, who needs someone to kick him in the arse every now and then. Adam says he realised he needed an extra edge.

> I couldn't stand the thought of Steve, there on his couch wrapped up in his nana blanket in front of the fire!
>
> At the end of 2014, I knew Steve had been doing it for such a long time and wanted to cut back his schedule, but I'm in the prime of my career and had full commitment from everyone else in the team. I didn't want a guy who was going to be part-time.
>
> Once he left, it didn't take long for some frustration to build up. I decided it was time to change things and put the odds back in my favour. There was unfinished business and I felt the upside of having Steve there for the big events was so great that I would find a way to manage the other stuff.
>
> It's a big plus to have the intensity and focus Steve brings – he has the ability to bring out the best in me. I was pleased that Kirsty let him come back to work.

I knew Adam wasn't playing well so I arrived earlier than normal at the controversial Chambers Bay Golf Course near Seattle for the US Open. I identified quite quickly what had been going wrong. He was simply swinging too hard and hitting too hard.

We'd played only six holes in practice when I said to Brad, Adam's coach, 'What's going on? He's trying to kill it.' On the first hole he had 212 yards to the flag and pulled out a 6-iron, which he typically wouldn't hit that far. He was going full out on every shot – how that developed I don't know, but I didn't want to interfere with what his coach was telling him. After the first round, it was evident the key to the Chambers Bay course was playing a lot of three-quarter shots with shape – fades or holds – and it's hard to do that when you're swinging hard. So I thought if I could talk him into playing those types of shots it would slow down the swing a little bit. And that's exactly what happened. With each round he hit fewer bad shots.

The 64 he shot in the final round – and this was on a course where you could quite happily miss half your short putts because of the bumpy greens – was as good as a human can play. It was inexcusable how bad the greens were there, though. It's a spectacular course but some of the greens were pure fescue grass, others had poa in them and others were just dirt.

The thing that annoyed the players most was that Mike Davis from the US Golf Association kept saying the course was in good shape when it just wasn't. On top of that, it was a terrible venue for fans to watch at. There are some natural amphitheatres formed by mounds around the fairways but the grass was so dry and slippery that people couldn't navigate them.

When Adam plays his best, he can play as good as anyone – and no one drives it better. On that Sunday, if you'd put him on good greens, there's no telling how low his score could have been. I was proud to have played a part in lifting him back to that level.

———————

By contrast, Adam's British Open was incredibly disappointing. It was reminiscent of his final holes at Royal Lytham & St Anne's back in 2012, when he bogeyed the last four holes to lose by a shot to Ernie Els.

This time the implosion was greater. He came to the 14th hole on the last day in a tie for the lead with eventual winner Zach Johnson. A bogey there wasn't the end of the world, as the hole was playing very tough into the wind, but it's what happened on the 15th that sent him into a death spiral.

The putt he had there was so innocuous I wasn't even looking – I was getting ready to head to the next tee after Adam tidied up from about a foot. How he missed it I don't know – I'd counted it as in.

He still could have made the playoff with a 3-3 finish, but when he three-putted the 17th green for a bogey five, all the air went out of him and he was standing on the 18th at 12 under par – knowing that Zach was in the clubhouse at 15 under. He knew he couldn't win.

In that situation, it's not unusual for a player to make a bad swing – he's lost all focus and has nothing to play for – but Adam went and wiped it out of bounds. You could stand on that 18th tee for a month and not hit it out of bounds – it's the widest fairway in world golf. In fact, I don't know if anyone else has ever hit it out of bounds there. But when you've put so much effort into a tournament and you've gone from tied for the lead with a few holes to play to being out of it, that's what can happen.

That British Open was an important one for a young Kiwi, Ryan Fox, whose dad Grant is one of the most famous All Blacks in New Zealand's rich rugby history.

I'd helped Ryan with some of his planning for St Andrews, organising a practice round with Adam and giving him and his caddy some advice about how to tackle the course. I believe Ryan is a big talent – he's got the X-factor. I predict he can go a long way. Who knows – he might be the next New Zealander to hold up a major championship trophy.

———

It's humbling to have been involved in such a great game for your entire working career – a game you love so much. I realise how fortunate I've been to bear witness to some of the most remarkable achievements in a game that I adore and to have walked the very best golf courses in the world with the best golfers of my generation.

I'm very proud of what I've achieved. Along the way, there's been some negative stuff, sure, but there's only one thing I regret – that interview after Adam won at Bridgestone in 2011. I'm proud that he's the player I signed off with.

> It's obvious Steve believed in something from very early on. He also believes in himself, and that's why he's been so successful.
>
> With Tiger, he had a role to perform and he did a great job, but there's a lot more to Steve than most people would think from only seeing him with Tiger. He really does want to make a difference. He has a similar philosophy whether it's caddying, his charity work, his motor racing, coaching Jett's rugby – he wants to contribute and he wants to positively influence and that's a very humane characteristic.

When I look back at my career, I can see that sometimes I took it all too seriously. When I was with Tiger I was with someone who had the same mindset as me, so that when a tournament was over the focus went straight onto the next tournament and, as a result, when the success came we failed to actually enjoy it. The flipside is that that's my personality – if I wasn't like that in the first place, the success might not have come at all.

I look back, too, and see how important schooling is and acknowledge the value of education – I didn't do the right thing there, going away against my parents' wishes. I'm grateful that it turned out well for me, otherwise I'd have been in a very tough situation. If things hadn't worked out and I'd had to come back to New Zealand without an education behind me, there's no way I'd be in the position I am today.

But I had such a strong belief that anything was possible. I never looked at the negative side of things. It's a bit of a cliché to say 'follow your dream' or 'live your passion' but I preach that message to junior golfers. There's no reason, if you put the right pieces of the jigsaw together and work hard, you can't be one of the best players in the world. If you are passionate enough, dedicated and prepared to work incredibly hard, anything is possible. I honestly believe that.

Finally, I know I couldn't have achieved anything without the support of friends, family and my wife Kirsty.

My father is the first person I'm thankful for, because he got me into golf – he placed a lot of faith and trust in me as a junior and turned a blind eye to my non-attendance at school, which allowed me to pursue my dreams.

And I would never have been able to be a caddy without the support of Allan James. He was instrumental in helping me to get to where I did. I wouldn't have been able to set foot outside of New Zealand without the money I earned from working in Allan's butcher shop and caddying for him on so many weekends. He was my main source of income and a special person to me.

It's also a cliché to say 'behind every great man is a great woman', but there's so much truth to that in my case. Kirsty has backed me since we met in 2000. To have a partner in life who completely understands what I do and how I think, and yet is also prepared to play such a supportive role in my career, is more than I could have ever wished for. Kirsty is a loyal friend and great companion who has stuck with me through thick and thin.

Until I met Kirsty, I imagined my life on the road as a caddy would be as a single man – it didn't seem possible to live that life as well as having a home life and family. But, if anything, meeting Kirsty and having Jett allowed me to extend my career. Kirsty was especially instrumental in making sure I had such a thrilling experience with Tiger Woods. I met Kirsty at a time in my career when I was thinking of packing it in. I'd always seen the year 2000 as my final year on the circuit and, even though I'd started with Tiger, I still had reservations about how long I could keep doing it because of how incredibly stressful it was. When I met Kirsty, those thoughts disappeared – she gave me strength, convinced me to keep going, saying it was a once-in-a-lifetime experience, which is exactly what it turned out to be.

And now being father to Jett – and the absolute joy that brings – has brought me full circle in life. He is already at the age I was when I discovered caddying. As much as I love my job I don't want to miss those special moments of being a father – watching Jett play sport and the pride that gives me, being around to see him grow as a person, and yes, seeing him get an education.

When I set out as a kid with a heart full of determination and a head full of dreams, I had no idea it would lead me to a job with one of the greatest golfers to walk the planet. In fact, I had no idea where I was going full stop. All I did was set off on a journey with my eyes firmly fixed on the next shot, never looking back, and paced my life out one step – one perfectly measured yard – at a time.

ACKNOWLEDGEMENTS

STEVE

The journey from caddying as a kid at Paraparaumu Beach Golf Club to walking the fairways with some of the world's greatest players was made possible by some very special people.

Colin Wilson, Eric Fraser (Mighty Mouse) and Allan James were my regular loops on the weekends at PBGC. My father introduced me to Peter Thomson and, as they say, the rest is history.

My first travel companion, Irish, knew all there was to know about travelling the world and I'm forever grateful for his knowledge. Greg Norman took me under his wing and taught me everything about the professional game, giving me the confidence to pursue caddying as a career.

My wife Kirsty has been my rock in the later part of my career and has given me the ultimate gift in my son, Jett.

Thanks to all those who have supported me, and special thanks to Ian and Karen for your support and guidance. Thanks to Michael for somehow getting me to sit still long enough to tell my story – sitting still is not my normal.

And to all the players I've walked the fairways with, thanks for the memories.

MICHAEL

It was a pleasure and privilege to work with Steve. His openness was invaluable, and his immaculate record-keeping and detailed scrapbooks were a bonus in documenting large parts of a career that took place in a pre-internet era.

This book couldn't have happened without input from a number of key people, including Steve's wife Kirsty, his dad John, his mum Kay, Allan James, Peter Thomson, Fanny Sunesson, Mike Clayton, Ian Baker-Finch, Terry Gale, Greg Norman, Raymond Floyd, Hank Haney and Adam Scott.

Also providing vital background material were *The Big Miss* by Hank Haney, *Unplayable* by Robert Lusetich, *Amen* by Will Swanton and Brent Read, and *Are You Kidding Me?* by Rocco Mediate and John Feinstein.

GLOSSARY

albatross completing a hole in three shots under par, for example making a two on a par-5; also known as a double eagle.

Amen Corner the name given to a trio of holes at Augusta National (the venue for the Masters), comprising the 11th, 12th and 13th holes.

approach (shot) a shot into the green.

back nine the second nine holes of a golf course.

birdie completing a hole in one shot under par, for example making a four on a par-5.

blade (shot) a shot that hits the ball on its equator so it travels low and fast; also known as a thin shot.

bogey completing a hole in one shot over par, for example making a six on a par-5 (a double bogey is two shots over par; a triple bogey is three shots over par, and so on).

break the extent to which a putt will curve on its way to the hole.

carry the distance a ball has to travel through the air to avoid an obstacle, for example a commentator might say 'He had 200 yards to carry the bunker in the front of the green'.

chip (shot) a very short shot from just off the green.

chip and run a chip shot with no spin, causing the ball to land and keep rolling.

chunk (shot) *see* fat

cut the group of players that move forward after two rounds of a tournament, with the players below that score or position being eliminated. Usually the top 60 'make the cut' for weekend play, while those below that mark 'miss the cut'.

cut line the score at which the cut (see above) is made.

double bogey *see* bogey

double eagle *see* eagle; albatross

draw (shot) a shot that bends right to left (for a right-hander).

drive (shot) a shot made with a driver; the first shot on a hole.

driver the longest club, with the biggest head; designed to hit the ball the greatest distance.

drop a way of returning the ball to a playable position after it has gone into a water hazard or is deemed unplayable. A player can 'drop' the ball into a playable position at the cost of a penalty shot.

duck-hook (shot) a very sharp hook shot; usually with a low ball flight.

eagle completing a hole in two shots under par, for example making a three on a par-5 (a double eagle is three shots under par).

fade (shot) a shot that moves gently left to right (for a right-hander).

fairway the closely mown, defined area of the course between the tee and the green.

fat (shot) a shot in which the club hits the ground behind the ball before connecting with the ball; also known as a chunk shot.

flag *see* pin

four-ball a match-play format in which pairs of players compete and each member of the pair plays their own ball, with the lowest score winning the hole for the pair.

foursomes a match-play format in which pairs of players compete and each pair shares a ball, taking alternate shots to complete a hole.

front nine the first nine holes of a golf course.

green the tightly mown, clearly defined rolled surface surrounding the hole.

hazard an obstacle such as a bunker, creek (burn) or lake, designed to penalise a player for a bad stroke.

holing out getting the ball in the hole from off the green.

hook (shot) a shot that curves severely right to left (for a right-hander).

irons (1-iron through to 9-iron) a series of clubs with blade-like heads and increasing angles of loft, designed to hits shots of different distances and with different levels of backspin. A shot taken with a 9-iron travels higher in the air and covers a shorter distance than a shot taken with an 8-iron, etc. The 1- to 4-irons are known as long irons, 5- to 7- are mid-irons, and 8- and 9- are short irons.

lay-up (shot) a second shot on a par-5; also used to describe a shot in which a player deliberately plays short of the green to avoid a hazard such as a creek or bunker.

lie the position in which the ball is sitting, for example a ball in the rough can be said to have a 'bad lie'.

loop a round of 18 holes.

majors the four premier tournaments held every year: the Masters, the US Open, the Open Championship (British Open) and the PGA Championship.

match play a style of play in which players are matched in head-to-head contests (either in singles or pairs) and the result is measured by holes won as opposed to strokes taken.

out of bounds a ball that goes outside the border of the golf course, resulting in the player having to replay the shot and receiving a penalty stroke (for example if a tee shot goes out of bounds the next shot will count as the player's third).

par completing a hole in the designated number of shots, for example making a five on a par-5.

par-3 a hole designed to be completed in three shots: a tee shot and two putts.

par-4 a hole designed to be completed in four shots: a tee shot, an approach and two putts. A 'driveable' par-4 is a hole in which a player can reach the green in one shot.

par-5 a hole designed to be completed in five shots: a tee shot, a lay-up, an approach and two putts. Many par-5 holes can be 'reached' in two shots. A player who attacks a par-5 in such a fashion is described as 'going for it in two'.

pin a term used to describe the position on the green where the hole is located; may also be referred to as pin position or flag.

pitch (shot) a short aerial shot; generally less than 50 yards from the green.

plugged lie a ball position in which the ball settles into its own pitch mark, usually because the ground is soft.

Presidents Cup a match-play competition between the United States and an 'International' team (drawn from the rest of the world outside Europe), held every two years.

pull (shot) a shot that travels in a straight line but to the left of the target (for a right-hander).

pull-hook (shot) a shot that starts to the left of the target line then curves further left.

push (shot) a shot that travels directly right of the target line without curving (for a right-hander).

putt (shot) a shot along the ground with a putter.

putter a flat-faced club for rolling the ball along the surface of the green.

read   a study of the slopes and contours of a green in order to estimate how much a putt will break.

rough   an area of longer, thicker grass on the edge of the fairway, designed to make it harder for a player to make clean contact with the ball.

Ryder Cup   a match-play competition between the United States and Europe, held every two years.

shape   a term used to describe the line traced by a golf ball in flight, including how much it curves and how high or low it goes.

skins   a match-play format with prize money at stake on a per-hole basis, which can result in large jackpots if successive holes are halved (or shared).

skull (shot)   a shot in which a player hits the ball on its top half, causing it to stay low to the ground and travel only a short distance; also known as a top shot.

slice (shot)   a shot that curves severely left to right (for a right-hander).

stroke play   a style of play in which players compete to finish the tournament in the fewest strokes.

tee   the position from which players start a hole.

thin (shot) *see* **blade**

three-putt   taking three putts to get the ball in the hole once the green has been attained; regarded as a bad mistake for professionals.

threesomes   a stage in which players form groups of three in a stroke-play tournament (usually in the first two rounds of a four-round tournament).

top (shot) *see* **skull**

Tour a season-long series of events under the jurisdiction of a particular golfing body; hence PGA Tour, European Tour, Asian Tour, Japan Tour, Australasian Tour.

triple bogey *see* **bogey**

unplayable lie a ball position that is so bad (for example under a bush, behind a tree) that it forces the player to move the ball to a playable position at the cost of a penalty shot.

wedge (club) a club with a high degree of loft, designed to achieve pinpoint accuracy and maximum spin so that the ball stops quickly on the green. Examples include the pitching wedge, sand wedge and lob wedge. Wedges are also referred to in terms of their loft, with a measurement in degrees (for example 56-degree wedge) referencing the angle of the club face.

wedge (shot) a short shot (in the region of 50 to 100 yards) onto the green.

whiff (shot) a shot that completely misses the ball.

wood (3-wood, 5-wood) a club with a slightly smaller head than a driver and a more lofted face, designed to send the ball long distances from the fairway.

World Golf Championship a series of prestigious tournaments that sit outside the designated Tours.

yardage the distance from the ball's current position to the desired finishing point on the fairway or green.

yips uncontrolled, jerky movements that a player may experience when trying to putt.